*A Text Book Of*

# INTRODUCTION TO OPERATING SYSTEM

For

BCA Semester - III

As per New Revised Syllabus of Pune University

**GAJANAN DESHMUKH**
M.C.A.
Smt. Kashibai Navale, H.O.D. - BCA
College of Commerce
Pune

**INTRODUCTION TO OPERATING SYSTEM**

**ISBN 978-93-5164-077-6**

First Edition : June 2014

© : Author

The text of this publication, or any part thereof, should not be reproduced or transmitted in any form or stored in any computer storage system or device for distribution including photocopy, recording, taping or information retrieval system or reproduced on any disc, tape, perforated media or other information storage device etc., without the written permission of Author with whom the rights are reserved. Breach of this condition is liable for legal action.

Every effort has been made to avoid errors or omissions in this publication. In spite of this, errors may have crept in. Any mistake, error or discrepancy so noted and shall be brought to our notice shall be taken care of in the next edition. It is notified that neither the publisher nor the author or seller shall be responsible for any damage or loss of action to any one, of any kind, in any manner, therefrom.

**Published By :**
**NIRALI PRAKASHAN**
Abhyudaya Pragati, 1312, Shivaji Nagar,
Off J.M. Road, PUNE – 411005
Tel - (020) 25512336/37/39, Fax - (020) 25511379
Email : niralipune@pragationline.com

**Printed By :**
Repro Knowledgecast Limited,
Thane

## DISTRIBUTION CENTRES

### PUNE

*Nirali Prakashan*
119, Budhwar Peth, Jogeshwari Mandir Lane
Pune 411002, Maharashtra
Tel : (020) 2445 2044, 66022708, Fax : (020) 2445 1538
Email : bookorder@pragationline.com

*Nirali Prakashan*
S. No. 28/27, Dhyari,
Near Pari Company, Pune 411041
Tel : (020) 24690371
Email : dhyari@pragationline.com
bookorder@pragationline.com

### MUMBAI
*Nirali Prakashan*
385, S.V.P. Road, Rasdhara Co-op. Hsg. Society Ltd.,
Girgaum, Mumbai 400004, Maharashtra
Tel : (022) 2385 6339 / 2386 9976, Fax : (022) 2386 9976
Email : niralimumbai@pragationline.com

## DISTRIBUTION BRANCHES

**NAGPUR**
*Pratibha Book Distributors*
Above Maratha Mandir, Shop No. 3, First Floor,
Rani Jhanshi Square, Sitabuldi, Nagpur 440012,
Maharashtra, Tel : (0712) 254 7129

**JALGAON**
*Nirali Prakashan*
34, V. V. Golani Market, Navi Peth, Jalgaon 425001,
Maharashtra, Tel : (0257) 222 0395
Mob : 94234 91860

**BENGALURU**
*Pragati Book House*
House No. 1, Sanjeevappa Lane, Avenue Road Cross,
Opp. Rice Church, Bengaluru – 560002.
Tel : (080) 64513344, 64513355,
Mob : 9880582331, 9845021552
Email: bharatsavla@yahoo.com

**KOLHAPUR**
*Nirali Prakashan*
New Mahadvar Road,
Kedar Plaza, 1st Floor Opp. IDBI Bank
Kolhapur 416 012, Maharashtra. Mob : 9855046155

### CHENNAI
*Pragati Books*
9/1, Montieth Road, Behind Taas Mahal, Egmore,
Chennai 600008 Tamil Nadu, Tel : (044) 6518 3535,
Mob : 94440 01782 / 98450 21552 / 98805 82331, Email : bharatsavla@yahoo.com

## RETAIL OUTLETS

### PUNE

*Pragati Book Centre*
157, Budhwar Peth, Opp. Ratan Talkies,
Pune 411002, Maharashtra
Tel : (020) 2445 8887 / 6602 2707, Fax : (020) 2445 8887

*Pragati Book Centre*
676/B, Budhwar Peth, Opp. Jogeshwari Mandir,
Pune 411002, Maharashtra
Tel : (020) 6601 7784 / 6602 0855

*Pragati Book Centre*
Amber Chamber, 28/A, Budhwar Peth,
Appa Balwant Chowk, Pune : 411002, Maharashtra,
Tel : (020) 20240335 / 66281669
Email : pbcpune@pragationline.com

*PBC Book Sellers & Stationers*
152, Budhwar Peth, Pune 411002, Maharashtra
Tel : (020) 2445 2254 / 6609 2463

### MUMBAI
*Pragati Book Corner*
Indira Niwas, 111 - A, Bhavani Shankar Road, Dadar (W), Mumbai 400028, Maharashtra
Tel : (022) 2422 3526 / 6662 5254, Email : pbcmumbai@pragationline.com

www.pragationline.com  info@pragationline.com

# Preface ...

This textbook of "Introduction to Operating System" is created for the students of Second Year B.C.A. (Sem. – III) of the University of Pune.

The aim of this book is to provide readers with Fundamental Knowledge of Introduction to Operating System. This book covers all the basic concepts of Introduction to Operating System as per revised syllabus. We have done sincere efforts to explain this topics in as simple language as possible.

A special word of thanks to Shri. Dineshbhai Furia, Mr. Jignesh Furia for showing full faith in us to write this book. We also thank to Mahesh Swami, Mr. Akbar Shaikh and Vijay Shete of M/s Nirali Prakashan for their excellent co-operation.

Valuable suggestions communicated by the students and teachers are welcome.

**AUTHOR**

# Syllabus ...

**Unit 1: Introduction to Operating System** [02 Lectures]
    1.1  What is operating system
    1.2  Computer system architecture
    1.3  Services provided by OS
    1.4  Types of OS

**Unit 2: System Structure** [02 Lectures]
    2.1  User operating system Interface
    2.2  System Calls
    2.3  Process or job control
    2.4  Device Management
    2.5  File Management
    2.6  System Program
    2.7  Operating System Structure

**Unit 3: Process Management** [03 Lectures]
    3.1  What is Process
    3.2  Process State
    3.3  Process Control Block
    3.4  Context Switch
    3.5  Operation on Process
- Process Creation
- Process Termination

**Unit 4: CPU Scheduling** [08 Lectures]
    4.1  What is scheduling
    4.2  Scheduling Concepts
        4.2.1  CPU- I/O Burst Cycle
        4.2.2  CPU Scheduler
        4.2.3  Preemptive and Non-preemptive scheduling
        4.2.4  Dispatcher
    4.3  Scheduling criteria (Terminologies used in scheduling)
    4.4  Scheduling Algorithms
        4.4.1  FCFS
        4.4.2  SJF ( Preemptive & non-preemptive)
        4.4.3  Priority Scheduling (Preemptive & Nonpreemptive)
        4.4.4  Round Robin Scheduling
    4.5  Multilevel Queues
    4.6  Multilevel Feedback queues

**Unit 5: Process Synchronization** [06 Lectures]
    5.1  Introduction
    5.2  Critical section problem
    5.3  Semaphores
        5.3.1  Concept
        5.3.2  Implementation
        5.3.3  Deadlock & Starvation
        5.3.4  Binary Semaphores

- 5.4 Critical Sections
- 5.5 Classical Problems of synchronization
- 5.6 Bounded buffer problem
- 5.7 Readers & writers problem
- 5.8 Dining Philosophers problem

**Unit 6: Deadlock** [07 Lectures]
- 6.1 Introduction
- 6.2 Deadlock Characterization
- 6.3 Necessary Condition
- 6.4 Resource allocation graph
- 6.5 Deadlock Prevention
- 6.6 Deadlock Avoidance
  - Safe State
  - Resource allocation graph algorithm
  - Bankers algorithm
- 6.7 Deadlock Detection
- 6.8 Recovery from deadlock
  - Process Termination
  - Resource Preemption

**Unit 7: Memory Management** [08 Lectures]
- 7.1 Introduction to memory management
- 7.2 Address Binding
- 7.3 Dynamic Loading
- 7.4 Dynamic Linking
- 7.5 Overlays
- 7.6 Logical vs. physical addresses
- 7.7 Swapping
- 7.8 Contiguous memory allocation
  - 7.8.1 Single Partition Allocation
  - 7.8.2 Multiple Partition Allocation
  - 7.8.3 External and Internal Fragmentation
- 7.9 Paging
- 7.10 Segmentation
- 7.11 Segmentation with paging
- 7.12 Virtual memory
- 7.13 Demand paging
- 7.14 Page replacement algorithms
  - FIFO
  - MRU
  - LRU
  - LRU approximation using reference bit
  - MFU
  - LFU
  - Second Chance algorithm
  - Optimal replacement

## Unit 8: File System [07 Lectures]
8.1 Introduction & File concepts (file attributes, Operations on files)
8.2 Access methods
- Sequential access
- Direct access

8.3 File structure
- Allocation methods
- Contiguous allocation
- Linked Allocation
- Indexed Allocation

8.4 Free Space Management
- Bit Vector
- Linked List
- Grouping
- Counting

## Unit 9: I/O System [05 Lectures]
9.1 Introduction
9.2 I/O Hardware
9.3 Application of I/O Interface
9.4 Kernel I/O Subsystem
9.5 Disk Scheduling
- FCFS
- Shortest Seek time first
- SCAN
- C- SCAN
- C- Look

# Contents ...

| | |
|---|---|
| 1. Introduction to Operating System | 1.1 – 1.28 |
| 2. System Structure | 2.1 – 2.16 |
| 3. Process Management | 3.1 – 3.8 |
| 4. CPU Scheduling | 4.1 – 4.28 |
| 5. Process Synchronization | 5.1 – 5.20 |
| 6. Deadlock | 6.1 – 6.26 |
| 7. Memory Management | 7.1 – 7.42 |
| 8. File System | 8.1 – 8.22 |
| 9. I/O System | 9.1 – 9.28 |

## Publication Offices

**Pune Office**
1312, Shivaji Nagar, 'Abhyudaya Pragati'
Off. J. M. Road, Pune 411005
Tel: (+91-020) 2551 2336/7/9
Fax: (+91-020) 2551 1379
Email: niralipune@pragationline.com

**Mumbai Office**
385, S.V.P. Road, Rasdhara Co-op. Hsg. Society Ltd.
Girgaum, Mumbai 400004
Tel: (+91-022) 2385 6339 / 2386 9976
Fax: (+91-022) 2386 9976
Email: niralimumbai@pragationline.com

**Distribution**
119, Budhwar Peth,
Jogeshwari Mandir Lane, Pune 411 002
Tel: (+91-020) 2445 2044, 6602 2708
Fax: (+91-020) 2445 1538
Email: bookorder@pragationline.com

## Retail Outlets

**Mumbai**
**PRAGATI BOOK CORNER**
- Indira Niwas, 111 - A, Bhavani Shankar Road,
  Dadar (W) Mumbai 400 028
  Tel: (+91-022) 2422 3526  6662 5254
  Email: pbcmumbai@pragationline.com

**Pune**
**PRAGATI BOOK CENTRE**
- 157, Budhwar Peth, Pune 411 002
  Tel: (+91-020) 2445 8887
  Fax: (+91-020) 6602 2707

- 676/B, Budhwar Peth,
  Opp. Jogeshwari Mandir, Pune 411 002
  Tel: (+91-020) 6601 7784 / 6602 0855
  Email : pbcpune@pragationline.com

- 28/A, Budhwar Peth, Ambar Chamber,
  Appa Balwant Chowk, Pune 411 002
  Tel: (+91-020) 6628 1669 / 2024 0335

- 917/22, Sai Complex,
  F.C. Road, Opp. Hotel Roopali,
  Shivajinagar, Pune 411 004
  Tel: (+91-020) 2566 3372  6602 2728

- **PBC Book Sellers & Stationers**
  152, Budhwar Peth, Pune 411 002
  Tel: (+91-020) 2445 2254

## Distribution Branches

**NAGPUR :**
**Pratibha Book Distributors**
Lokratna Commercial Complex,
Shop No. 3, First Floor,
Rani Zanshi Square, Sitabuldi,
Nagpur 440 012, Maharashtra,
Tel: (+91-0712) 254 7129

**JALGAON :**
**Nirali Prakashan**
34, V. V. Golani Market, Navi Peth,
Jalgaon 425 001, Maharashtra,
Tel: (+91-0257) 222 0395

**KOLHAPUR :**
**Nirali Prakashan**
New Mahadvar Road,
Kedarling Plaza, 1st Floor,
Opp. IDBI Bank,
Kolhapur 416 012, Maharashtra.
Mob: 9855046155

**BANGALORE :**
**Pragati Book House**
House No.1, Sanjeevappa Lane,
Avenue Road Cross,
Off. Rice Church,
Bangalore 560 002, Karnataka
Tel : (+91-080) 6451 3344 / 6451 3355
Fax : (+91-080) 2332 4437
Mob : 98450 21552 / 98805 82331
Email:bharatsavla@yahoo.com

**CHENNAI :**
**Pragati Books**
9/1, Montieth Road, Behind Taas
Mahal, Egmore, Chennai 600 008,
Tamil Nadu,
Tel: (+91-044) 5518 3535
Mob: 94440 01782

Email: info@pragationline.com       Website: www.pragationline.com

# Chapter 1...

# Introduction to Operating System

## Contents ...
1.1 Introduction
    1.1.1 Need of Operating System
    1.1.2 What is Operating System?
    1.1.3 Objectives of Operating System
    1.1.4 Definition of Operating System
    1.1.5 Characteristics of Operating System
    1.1.6 Basic Functions of Operating System
    1.1.7 Desires of an Operating System
    1.1.8 Examples of Operating System
    1.1.9 Operating System Layers
1.2 Computer System Architecture
1.3 Services provided by Operating System
1.4 Types of Operating Systems
    1.4.1 Batch Operating System
    1.4.2 Multiprogramming
    1.4.3 Multiprocessing System
    1.4.4 Multitasking or Time Sharing
    1.4.5 Distributed Systems
    1.4.6 Real Time Systems
- Practice Questions
- University Questions and Answers

## 1.1 INTRODUCTION

- An **Operating System** is a software program or set of programs that mediate access between physical devices such as, a keyboard, mouse, monitor, disk drive or network connection and application programs such as, a word processor, World-Wide Web browser or electronic mail client.

- The operating system is a program that controls the execution of application programs and acts as an interface between applications and the computer hardware.
- Operating System is system software, whose main purpose is to make the computer easier to use. That is, the software provides an interface that is more user friendly than the underlying hardware.
- An operating system is a program designed to run other programs on a computer.
- A computer's operating system is most important program. It is considered the backbone of a computer, managing both software and hardware resources.
- Operating systems are responsible for everything from the control and allocation of memory to recognizing input from external devices and transmitting output to computer displays. They also manage files on computer hard drives and control peripherals, like printers and scanners.
- The operating system of a large computer system has even more work to do. Such operating systems monitor different programs and users, making sure everything runs smoothly, without interference, despite the fact that numerous devices and programs are used simultaneously.
- An operating system also has a vital role to play in security. Its job includes preventing unauthorized users from accessing the computer system.
- As a part of this process, the operating system manages the resources of the computer in an attempt to meet overall system goals such as efficiency and throughput. The details of this resource management can be quite complicated; however, the operating system usually hides such complexities from the user.
- An operating system (sometimes abbreviated as "OS") is the program that, after being initially loaded into the computer by a boot program, manages all the other programs in a computer.
- The other programs are called applications or application programs. The application programs make use of the operating system by making requests for services through a defined Application Program Interface (API).
- In addition, users can interact directly with the operating system through a user interface such as a command language or a Graphical User Interface (GUI).
- An operating system is an important part of almost every computer system.
- Fig. 1.1 shows components of operating systems.
- The computer system can be divided roughly into four components:
    1. Hardware
    2. Application programs
    3. Operational users
    4. End Users
    1. **Hardware:** The Central Processing Unit (CPU), memory and input/output devices constitute the basic hardware and provide the basic computing resources.

2. **Application programs:** Word processors, spreadsheets, compilers, web browsers etc. are example of application programs that define the way in which these resources are used to solve the computing problems of the users. The operating system controls and co-ordinates the use of the hardware among the various application programs for the various users.
3. **Operational Users:** Operational users are the users responsible for installation of the software, proper maintenance of software, making it available to the users, and housekeeping operations, taking regular backups, removing unnecessary files and directories, checking the disk space being used and space free.
4. **End Users:** End users are the actual users of the applications. Such users can perform limited tasks as defined by the application program they are using. Applications with user friendly environments and simplicity of operations are preferred in such cases.

- Some popular operating system's are listed below:
  1. **DOS:** Single-tasking, single-processing, single-user, unprotected with no built-in support for graphics or networking.
  2. **UNIX:** Multi-tasking, multi-processing, multi-user, protected, with built-in support for networking but not graphics.
  3. **Windows 3.x:** Single-tasking, single-processing, single-user, unprotected, with built-in support for graphics but not networking.
  4. **Windows 95/98:** Multi-tasking, multi-processing, single-user, unprotected, with built-in support for networking and graphics.
  5. **Windows NT:** Multi-tasking, multi-processing, single-user, protected, with built-in support for networking and graphics.
  6. **NetWare:** Multi-tasking, multi-processing, single-user, unprotected, with built-in support for networking but not graphics.

## 1.1.1 Need of Operating System

- The main feature of operating system is to execute multiple programs in interleaved fashion or different time cycle is called **multiple programming systems**.
- Some of the important reasons why we need an Operating System are as follows:
  o User interacts with the computer through operating system in order to accomplish his/her task since it is his primary interface with a computer.
  o It helps the user in understand the inner functions of a computer very closely.
  o Many concepts and techniques found in operating system have general applicability in other applications.
- An operating system is an essential component of a computer system. The primary objectives of an operating system are to make computer system convenient to use and utilizes computer hardware in an efficient manner.

- An operating system is a large collection of software which manages resources of the computer system, such as memory, processor, rite system and input/output devices.
- Operating system keeps track of the status of each resource and decides who will have a control over computer resources, for how long and when. The positioning of operating system in overall computer system is shown in Fig. 1.1.

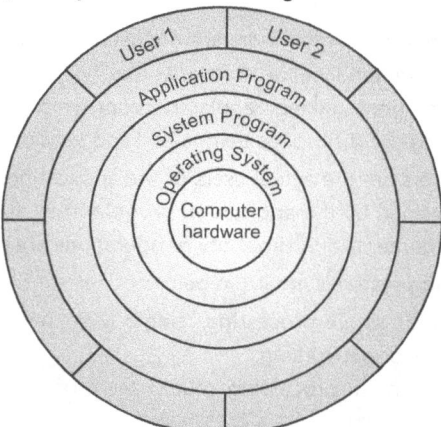

**Fig. 1.1: Component of Computer System**

- From the Fig. 1.1, it is clear that operating system directly controls computer hardware resources. Other programs rely on facilities provided by the operating system to gain access to computer system resources.
- There are two ways one can interact with operating system:
  o By means of Operating System Call in a program.
  o Directly by means of Operating System Commands.

### 1.1.2 What is Operating System?
- An operating system may be viewed as an organized collection of software extensions of hardware, consisting of control routines for operating a computer and for providing an environment for execution of programs.
- Other programs rely on facilities provided by the operating system to gain access to computer system resources, such as files and input/output devices.
- Programs usually invoke services of operating system by means of operating system calls. In addition users may interact with operating system directly by means of operating system commands. In either case, the operating system acts as interface between users and hardware of a computer system.

### 1.1.3 Objectives of Operating System
- An operating system is program that controls the execution of application programs and act as an interface between applications and the computer hardware.

- It can be thought of as having three objectives.
    - **Convenience:** An operating system makes a computer more convenient to use.
    - **Efficiency:** An operating system allows the computer system resources to be used in an efficient manner.
    - **Ability to evolve:** An operating system should be constructed in such a way as to permit the effective development testing, and introduction of new system functions without interfering with service.
- Let us examine these three aspects of operating system in detail.

### The Operating System as a User/Computer Interface

- The hardware and software used in providing applications to a user can be viewed in a layered or hierarchical fashion as shown in Fig. 1.2.
- The user of those applications, the end user, generally is not concerned with the details of the computer's hardware.
- An application can be expressed in a programming language and is developed by application programmer.
- To ease the task of application programmer, system programs are provided, some of these programs are **utilities**.
- The most important system program is the operating system.

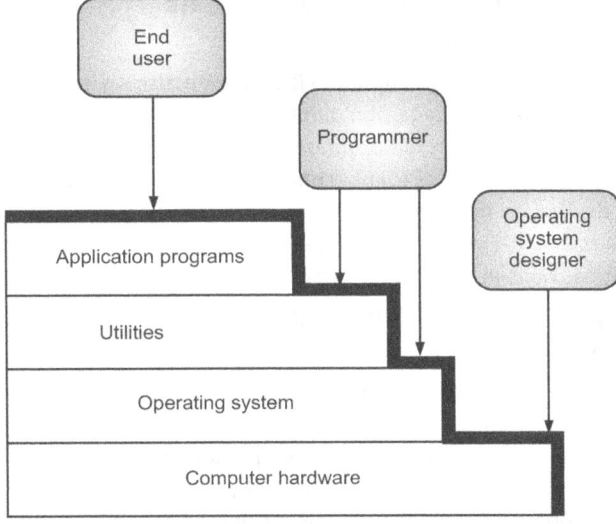

**Fig. 1.2: Layers and Views of a Computer System**

## The Operating System as Resource Manager

- A computer is a set of resources for the movement, storage and processing of data and for the control of these functions.
- The operating system is responsible for managing these resources. Therefore we can say an operating system as a **resource allocator.**

### 1.1.4 Definition of Operating System

- An Operating System is a computer program that manages the resources of a computer. It accepts keyboard or mouse inputs from users and displays the results of the actions and allows the user to run applications, or communicate with other computers via networked connections.

OR

- Operating system is a set of computer programs that manage the hardware and software resources of a computer system. We can add to that definition to say that an operating system rationally processes electronic devices in response to approved commands.

OR

- An Operating system is a collection of programs that control the application software that users run and provides a link between the hardware and software currently running on the computer. The operating system is also responsible for the management and control of all resources (memory, hard drives, monitor, etc.) that are shared amongst the different application programs that may be running simultaneously.

### 1.1.5 Characteristics of Operating Systems

- Some characteristics of an Operating System are:
    - Whether multiple programs can run on it simultaneously i.e. multi-tasking.
    - Whether it can take advantage of multiple processors i.e. multi-processing.
    - Whether multiple users can run programs on it simultaneously i.e. multi-user.
    - Whether it can reliably prevent application programs from directly accessing hardware devices i.e. protected.
    - Whether it has built-in support for graphics.
    - Whether it has built-in support for networks.

### 1.1.6 Basic Functions of Operating System

- Various operating system functions are listed below:
    1. **A task scheduler:** The task scheduler is able to allocate the execution of the CPU to a number of different tasks. Some of those tasks are the different applications that the user is running and some of them are operating system tasks. The task scheduler is the part of the operating system that lets you print a document from your word processor in one window while you are downloading a file in another window and recalculating a spreadsheet is a third window.

2. **A memory manager:** The memory manager controls the system's RAM and normally creates a larger virtual memory space using a file on the hard disk.
3. **A Disk manager:** The disk manager creates and maintains the directories and files on the disk. When you request a file, the disk manager brings it in from the disk.
4. **A network manager:** The network manager controls all the data moving between the computer and the network.
5. **Other I/O Services manager:** The operating system manages the keyboard, mouse, video, display, printers etc.
6. **Security manager:** The operating system maintains the security of the information in the computer's files and controls that can access the computer.

### 1.1.7 Desires of an Operating System
- Desires of an operating system are given below:
    1. **Usability:**
        (i) **Robustness:** OS accept all valid inputs without error, and gracefully handle all invalid inputs. OS would not be crashed in any circumstances, and could be recovered in the case that we suddenly remove hardware while they are running, or lost of power supplied.
        (ii) **Consistency:** For example, if "-" means options flags in one place, it means it in another. The key idea is conventions. We should base on the concept: The Principle of Least Astonishment. This helps us easy to understand and adapt with the new system.
        (iii) **Proportionality:** Simple, cheap and frequent things are easy. Also, expensive and disastrous things are hard.
        (iv) **Forgiving:** Errors can be recovered from. Reasonable error messages. Example from "rm"; UNIX vs. TOPS.
        (v) **Convenient:** Not necessary to repeat things, or do awkward procedures to accomplish things. Example copying a file took a batch job.
        (vi) **Powerful:** It has high level facilities.
    2. **Facilities:**
        (i) The system should supply sufficient for intended use
        (ii) The facilities is complete, do not leave out any part of a facility.
        (iii) Appropriate, e.g. do not use fixed-width field input from terminal
    3. **Cost:**
        (i) Want low cost and efficient services.
        (ii) Good algorithms. Make use of space/time tradeoffs, special hardware.
        (iii) Low overhead. Cost of doing nothing should be low. For example, idle time at a terminal.
        (iv) Low maintenance cost. System should not require constant attention.

4. **Adaptability:**
   (i) **Tailored to the environment:** Support necessary activities. Do not impose unnecessary restrictions. What are the things people do most make them easy?
   (ii) **Changeable over time:** Adapt as needs and resources change. For example, expanding memory and new devices, or new user population.
   (iii) **Extendible-Extensible:** Adding new facilities and features - which look like the old ones.

## 1.1.8 Examples of Operating System

- Before 1950 the programmers directly interact with hardware, there is no operating system at that time.
- If the programmer wish to execute on those days, the following serial steps are necessary:
  - Type the program on punched card.
  - Convert the punched card to card reader.
  - Submit to the computing machine, if there are any errors, the error condition was indicated by lights.
  - The programmer examines the registers and main memory to identify the cause of the error.
  - Take the output on the printers.
  - Then the programmer is ready for the next program.
- This mode of operating could be termed processing, this type of processing is difficult for users, it takes much time and next program should wait for the completion of previous one.
- The programs are submitted to the machine one after another, therefore this method is said to be serial processing.

1. **MS-DOS:**
- When IBM came out with their personal computer in the early 1980's, they also arranged for Microsoft to provide the MS-DOS operating system.
- MS-DOS was developed for very small personal computers and did not have many of the features expected of operating systems for larger computers. But the PC and its clones became much more successful than most people had imagined and MS-DOS has grown to be the most widely used operating system in the world.
- As the power and capabilities of the PC increased, features were added to MS-DOS to deal with the new hardware. Although MS-DOS is quite primitive by modern operating system standards, it is an open system, (due to the fact that there is no protection at all) and so it could be adapted and modified by add-on programs, MS-DOS has gone through six major versions over the years since the first PC was introduced.

- The MS-DOS system call interface is modeled after UNIX and has a similar set of system calls. One major difference is that it does not have the UNIX fork or exec system calls, but has a system call more like the create process.
- One add-on to MS-DOS is the Microsoft Windows windowing environment. Windows adds significant functionality to MS-DOS and could be considered an operating system on its own.

2. **UNIX:**
- The first version of UNIX was developed in 1969 by Ken Thompson of the research group of Bell laboratories to use for idle PDP-7.
- During the past 25 years the UNIX operating system has evolved into a powerful, flexible and versatile operating system.
- It serves as the operating system for all types of computers, including single-user personal computers, workstations, microcomputers, minicomputers and super computers as well as special purpose devices.
- The member of computer running by UNIX has grown explosively, with approximately 20 million computers now running by UNIX and more than 100 million people using these systems.
- This rapid growth is expected to continue. This success of UNIX is due to many factors, including its portability to a wide range of machines, its adaptability and simplicity, the wide range of tasks it can perform, its multi user and multi tasking nature, and its suitability for networking, etc.
- The main features of UNIX are:
    - Ability to support multiuser and multi tasking.
    - Portability
    - Excellent network environment.
    - Adaptability and simplicity
    - It provides better security
    - Flexible file system.

### Unix Architecture

- The architecture of UNIX can be divided into 4 layers: Hardware, Kernel, System call interface (shell), and application programs/libraries as shown in Fig. 1.3.

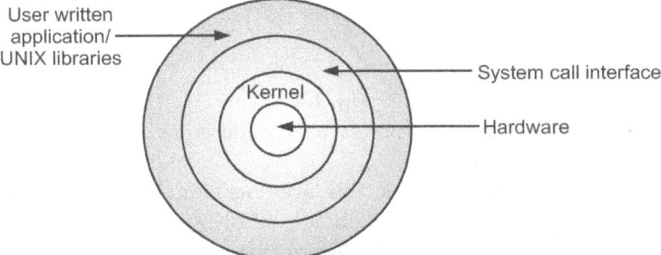

**Fig. 1.3: Architecture of UNIX**

(i) **The Kernel:** The Kernel is the part of the operating system; it interacts directly with the hardware of a computer, through device that is build into the Kernel. The main functions of Kernel are to manage computer memory to control access to the computer, to maintain the file system, to handle interrupts, to handle errors, to perform input and output services and to allocate the resources of the computers among users.

Programs interact with the Kernel through nearly 100 system calls. System calls tell the Kernel to carry out various tasks for the program, such as opening a file, writing to a file, obtaining information about a file, executing a program, terminating a process, changing the priority of a process and getting the time and data.

(ii) **The Shell:** Shell, it is the part of the operating system, it is a software program, and it acts as a mediator between Kernel and user. The shell reads the commands, what you typed at command lines, and interprets them and sends requests to execute a program. That is why Shell is also called command interpreter.

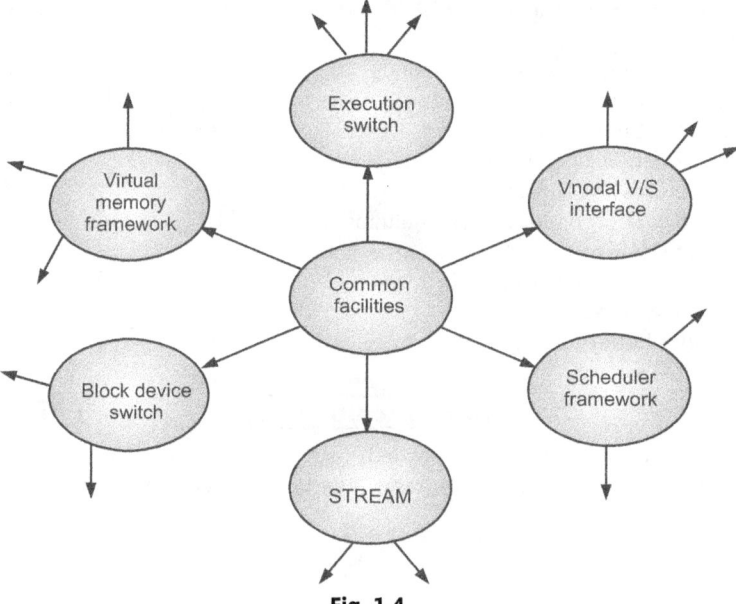

Fig. 1.4

(iii) **Hardware:** The hardware includes all the parts of a computer, include clocks, timers, devices, ports, etc.

(iv) **Unix Commands and Libraries:** This layer includes user written applications, using Shell programming language and libraries of UNIX.

(v) **Modern UNIX Systems:** A UNIX System that follows the designing principles and features of modern operating system, which is called modern UNIX System.

In the Fig. 1.4 the outer circle represents functions and an interface that may be implemented in a variety of ways.

(vi) **BSD: (Berkeley Software Distribution):** UNIX released by BSD has played a key role in the development of OS design theory.

Everything below the system call interface and above the physical hardware is the Kernel. The Kernel provides the file system. CPU scheduling memory management and other operating system functions through system calls.

(vii) **System V Release 4 (SVR4):** SVR4 developed jointly by AT&T and SUN MICRO Systems. It is the combination of features from SVR3, 4.3 BSD, and Microsoft XENIX system V. The new features of SVR4 are:
- Real time processing support,
- Process scheduling classes,
- Dynamically allocated data structures,
- Virtual memory management,
- Virtual file system, and
- Preemptive Kernel.

SVR4 can run on any 32-bit Microprocessors up to super computers and is one of the most important operating systems ever developed.

3. **LINUX:**
- Linux is UNIX based operating system originally developed as for Intel-Compatible PC's. It is now available for most types of hardware platforms, ranging from PDA's to main frames. Linux is "Modern Operating System", meaning it has such features as virtual memory, memory protection and preemptive multitasking.
- Linux is built and supported by a large international community of developers and users dedicated to free, open source software.
- This community sees Linux as an alternative to such proprietary systems are windows and Solaris, and a platform for alternatives to such proprietary applications as MS-Office, Internet Explorer and outlook.
- As a result of this community, there is a very large collection of free software available for Linux. There are Graphical Environments (GUI's), office applications, developer's tools, system utilities, business applications, document publishing tools, network client and server applications.
- The best part of this community is that all code is open. This means there is no barrier to entry for any given problem; there are generally several applications that solve the problem. These applications can also borrow the best parts from each other to become even better. An excellent example of this is Galeon.
- Galeon is a web browser which took Mozilla's web page rendering engine and integrated it with a GTK front end.

- Linux specifically refers to the Linux Kernel. However, the Kernel is useless without a set of tools and application to run on the Kernel Linux is most commonly distributed with this tool set and a collection of applications in what is called a "distribution".
- The most common are Redhat, Mandrake, Suse and Debian. Distributions differs in three basic ways the process for installing the distribution, the application available and the process for installing and managing these applications.
- Reasons to install Linux:
    (i) Configurability,
    (ii) Convenience,
    (iii) Stability,
    (iv) Community, and
    (v) Freedom.

    **(i) Configurability:** Linux distributions give the user full access to configure just about any aspect of their system. Option range from simple and straight forward (for instance changing the background image) to more esoteric (for instance, making the "Caps Lock" behave like "Control"). Almost any aspect of the user experience can be configured.

    Linux also allows automating just about any task. Advanced scripting and high-level programming are standard features. Most operations are accessible via these scripting options. Finally, Linux the ultimate in configurability: the source code, to the modified as you see fit.

    **(ii) Convenience:** While Linux takes some effort to get set up, once it is set up, it is surprisingly low-maintenance. package management can simply be a matter of running two commands in the shell. Linux also offers complete remote access. This allows the user to act exactly as if she is sitting at that computer's desk, potentially across town or on the other side of the world.

    **(iii) Stability:** Linux is based on the UNIX Kernel. It provides preemptive multitasking prevents any application from permanently stealing the CPU and locking of the machine. Protected memory prevents applications from interfering with the crashing one another.

    **(iv) Community:** Linux is part of the greater open - source community. This consists of thousands of developers and may more users world-wide who support open software. This user and developer base is also a support base.

    **(v) Freedom:** Linux is free. This means more than just cost nothing. This means that you are allowed to do whatever you want to with the software.

4. **Windows 95:**

   Microsoft launched an advanced Window in 1995 which was Windows 1995. It had 32-bit file system and could run programs that were written in MS-DOS.

5. **Windows 98:**

   An enhanced and highly developed version of Windows 95 was released in 1998 which is known as Windows 98.

6. **Windows NT:**

   Windows New Technology is powerful system with multitasking functionality. Windows NT was specially designed for computer networking and also called client/server operating system.

7. **Windows 2000:**

   Windows 2000 has four products each with specific functionality.
   - Windows 2000 professional
   - Windows 2000 Server
   - Windows 2000 Advanced server
   - Windows 2000 Data Center

8. **Windows XP:**

   Windows XP is more advance and high functionality window that is used in homes, offices and business places.

9. **Windows Vista:**

   Latest windows operating system introduced in 2006. Windows Vista required high level of hardware compatibility.

10. **Windows 7:**

    Windows 7 is the latest release of Microsoft Windows, a series of operating systems produced by Microsoft for use on personal computers, including home and business desktops, laptops, notebooks, tablet PCs, and media center PCs. Windows 7 was released to manufacturing on July 22, 2009, and reached general retail availability on October 22, 2009, less than three years after the release of its predecessor, Windows Vista. Windows 7's server counterpart, Windows Server 2008 R2, was released at the same time.

## 1.1.9 Operating System Layers

- The lowest layer consists of Physical devices such as integrated circuits, lines, cables, buses, the CPU, caches, hard-disks and so on.
- The layer above is primitive software that directly controls the physical devices and provides a cleaner interface to the next layer. This layer of software is called Microprogramming, which is used to fetch machine language instructions and is usually stored in the physical device ROM.

- Above the Microprogramming layer is the Machine language layer. Machine language is mainly used to move data around the computer machine itself. The machine language layer controls I/O devices.
- The operating system resides above the Machine language layer. A major function of an operating system is to hide the above complexities and to provide the user with a convenient set of instructions to work with.

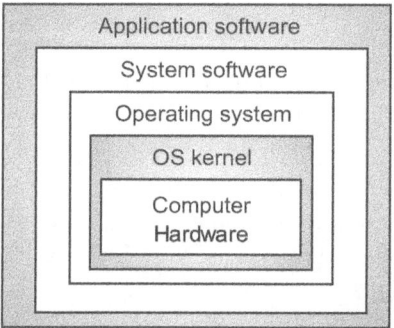

**Fig. 1.5: Layers of Operating System**

- Above the operating system are the rest of the system programs, such as the command interpreter (shell), compilers, and editors and so on. These programs are distinct from the operating system, even though a systems manufacturer usually provides them.
- The operating system is the portion of software that runs in kernel mode or supervisor mode.
- An operating system is protected from users tampering with it by the hardware. Compilers and interpreters run in user mode.
- For example, you can write your own Object Oriented Compiler for Eiffel code if you want to.
- The top layer of this hierarchy is the application program. These programs are written by users to solve problems, such as data processing, games and so on.

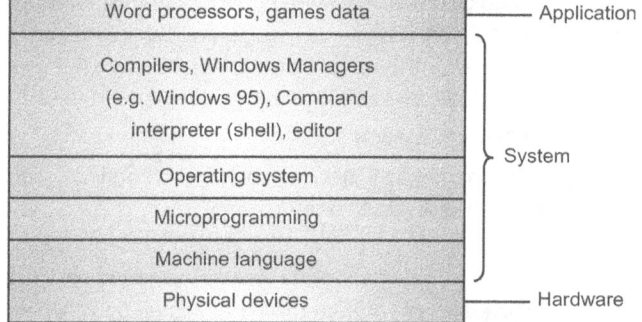

**Fig. 1.6: Operating System Structure**

## 1.2 COMPUTER SYSTEM ARCHITECTURE

In this section, we will discuss computer architecture. The computer system are categorized into single processor, dual processor, multiprocessor, parallel processor according to number of CPU used.

### 1.2.1 Single-Processor System
- Single-processor system contains only one CPU.
- The one CPU is capable of executing instruction set.
- Some device specific processors are used to reduce overhead of CPU.

  e.g. Disk-controller microprocessor receive a sequence of request from main CPU, creates its own disk queue and scheduling algorithm is implemented.

### 1.2.2 Multiprocessor System [April 2012, 2013]
- Mutliprocessor system is also called parallel system or tightly coupled system.
- The computer bus is shared by two or more processors. Also memory and peripheral devices can be shared.
- The Fig. 1.7 shows the multiprocessing architecture.

The multiprogramming system are of two types:

1. **Asymmetric multiprocessing:** Each processor is assigned a specific task. This is master-slave relationship. The master processor control the system and other processor follows the master processor instruction e.g. SunOS version 4.
2. **Symmetric multiprocessing (SMP):** Each processor performs all task within the operating system. All processors are peer, no master-slave relationship. All processors shares the physical memory.

Examples: Solaris, UNIX, Windows XP, Mac OS X, LINUX are SMP systems.

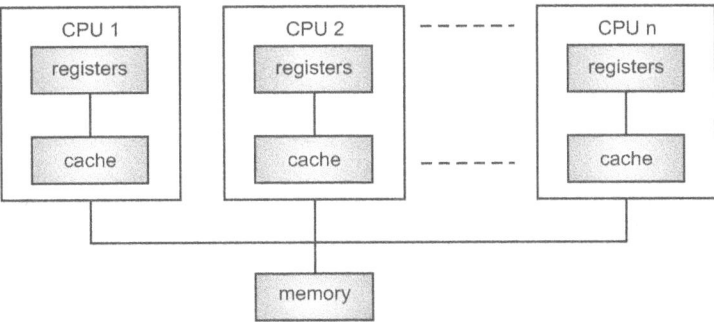

**Fig. 1.7: SMP architecture**

- The recent CPU design includes multiple computing cores on a single chip. This is suitable for server systems such as database server and web server.
- In dual-core system, two cores are present on the single chip, each core has its own register set and own local cache.

**Advantages of Multiprocessor System:**
1. **Increased throughput:** As the number of processor increases, the result or output is faster. The time required is less to compute the task.
2. **Economy of scale:** The cost of multiprocessor system is less than that of multiple single-processor system, because peripheral devices, memory, bus is shared. If the multiple user wants to share the same data, then instead of storing same data on each processor, it is stored only on one disk and that can be shared by all processors.
3. **Increased reliability:** In multiprocessor system, if any of the processor fails, the work of that processor is shared by remaining processor and system will not halt.

    e.g. if we have 5 processors and one fails, then remaining 4 processors can pick up a share of the work of the failed processor.

## 1.2.3 Clustered Systems [April 2007, 2012]

Clustered system keep multiple CPUs together like parallel systems. Clustered system use multiple CPU's like multiprocessor system, but they are composed of two or more individual systems or nodes joined together. The Fig. 1.8 shows the clustered system structure. This system is highly reliable to provide service to the user. The service will continue even if one or more systems in the cluster fail.

Clustering are of two types:
1. **Asymmetric clustering:** In this, one machine is in standby mode and other is running the applications. The standby machine is monitoring the task of others.
2. **Symmetric clustering:** In this, two or more hosts are running the applications and are monitoring each other. This clustering is more efficient.

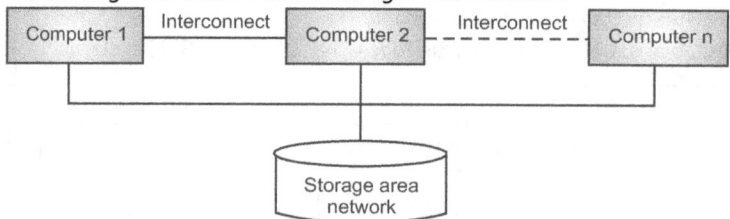

**Fig. 1.8: Clustered system structure**

- A cluster consisting of many computers are connected via a network (LAN or WAN).
- Such a system is used to run application concurrently on all computers in the cluster.
- Many computers can share the same database.
- Increasing performance and throughput.
- More reliable.
- Designed for solving high-performance computing tasks.
- Example, oracle parallel server is version of oracle's database which run on parallel clusters.

## 1.3 SERVICES PROVIDED BY OPERATING SYSTEM

- The services provided by the operating system differ from one another. The quality of the operating system depends upon the amount at services that the user can exploit with the system.
- Fig. 1.9 shows one view of the various operating-system services and show they interrelate.

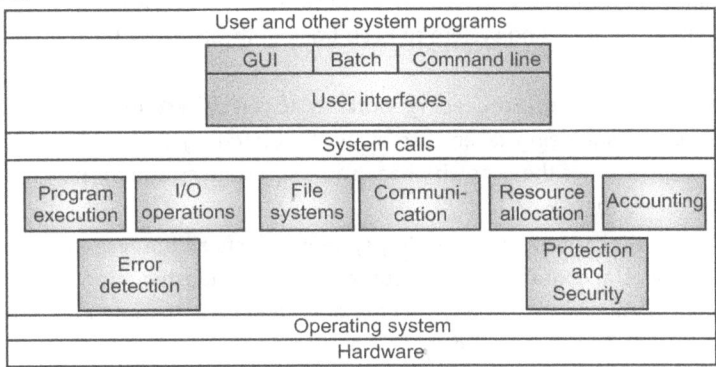

**Fig. 1.9: A view of Operating System Services**

- Following are the basic services which are provided by the operating system.
    1. **User interface:** Almost all operating systems have a User Interface (UI). This user interface can take several forms. One is a DTrace Command-Line Interface (CLI), which uses text commands and a method for entering them. Another is a batch interface, in which commands and directives to control those commands are entered into files, and those files are executed. Most commonly, a Graphical User Interface (GUI) is used. The GUI interface is a window system with a pointing device to direct I/O, choose from menus and make selections and a keyboard to enter text.
    2. **Program Execution:** The system must be able to load a program into memory and run the program. If due to some reason the program halts abruptly then an error is indicated by the operating system.
    3. **I/O Operations:** All the programs dealing with I/O operations relating to specific devices are to be dealt by the operating system. For example, if a user wants to print a page then operating system gives the command to I/O device for printing the particular pages.
    4. **File System Implementation:** The file system is of particular interest. Programs need to read and write files. Files can also be detected by their unique names.
    5. **Communications:** The communication which takes place between the concurrent processes can be divided into two parts. The first one takes place between the processes that are running on the same computer and the other type of processes are those that are being executed on different computer systems through a computer network.

6. **Protection:** In a multiuser environment, protection of valuable resources plays an important role. It ensures that all the access to system resource should be in a controlled manner. This is implemented by the help of security assigned at various levels.

7. **Error detection:** There are various types of errors that occur when the process is running. This error may be caused by CPU, memory hardware, I/O devices etc. It is the job of the operating system to keep track of these errors, raise appropriate errors at the user's screen.

8. **Accounting:** The record keeping work, as to which resource has been utilized by which process is being taken care at by the operating system. This record keeping also keeps track of the user who has used the resources and for how long so that he can be billed for that.

9. **Resource allocation:** The operating system collects all the resources in the network environment and grants these resources to be requested process. Many different types of resources are managed by the operating system; these are CPU cycles, Main memory, I/O devices, and File storage and so on.

## 1.4 TYPES OF OPERATING SYSTEM

### 1.4.1 Batch Operating System

- In olden days the computers were large systems run from a console. The common input devices were card readers and tape drives and output devices were line printers, tape drives and card punches.
- The computer system did not directly interact with the users instead the computer users used to prepare a format that consisted of the programs, the data and some control information about the nature of the job and submitted it to the computer operator.
- The job was usually in the form of punch cards. The process as a whole took a lot of time and was slow. To speed up the processing jobs with similar needs were batched together and were run through the computer as a group.
- Fig. 1.10 shows the memory layout for a simple batch system.

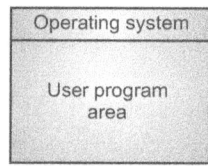

**Fig. 1.10: Memory Layout for a Simple Batch System**

- A batch operating system, thus normally Read a stream of separate jobs, each with its own control cards that predefine what the job does. When the job is complete, its output is usually printed.
- The important feature of a batch system is lack of interaction between the user and the job while that job is being executed. The job is prepared and submitted and at some later time, the output appears.
- In a batch processing system, a job is described by a sequence of control statements stored in a machine-readable form.
- The operating system can read and execute a series of such jobs without human intervention except for such functions as tape and disk mounting. The order in which the jobs are selected and executed can be scheduled using appropriate algorithms.
- A batch is a sequence of user jobs.
- Batch processing came into vogue at a time when punched cards were used to record user jobs.
- Processing of a job involved physical actions by the system operator, e.g. loading a deck of cards into the card reader, pressing switches on the computers console to initiate a job, etc., all of which wasted a lot of computer time. This wastage could be reduced by automating the processing of a batch of jobs.
- A computer operator forms a batch by arranging user jobs in a sequence and inserting special markers to indicate the start and end of the batch.
- After forming a batch, the operator submits it for processing. The primary function of the batch processing system is to implement the processing of a batch of jobs without requiring any intervention of the operator.
- The operating system achieves this by making an automatic transition from the execution of one job to that of the next job in the batch.
- Batch processing is implemented by locating a component of the batch processing operating system, called the batch monitor (or batch supervisor), permanently in one part of the computer's main memory.
- The remaining part of the memory is used to process a user job i.e. the current job in the batch.
- The batch monitor is responsible for:
  1. accepting command from the system operator,
  2. initiate the processing of a batch,
  3. sets up the processing of the first job,
  4. at end of the job, terminates process and initiate execution of the next job,
  5. At end of the batch, terminates batch and awaits initiation of the next batch by the operator.

- Fig. 1.11 depicts the schematic of a batch processing system.

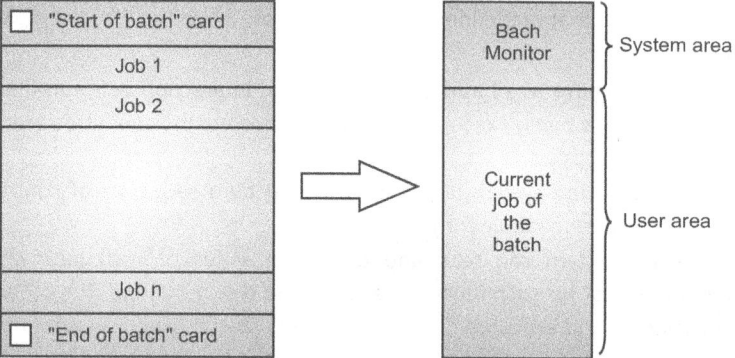

**Fig. 1.11: Schematic of a batch processing system**

- **Advantages** of Batch Operating System:
  1. Move much of the work of the operator to the computer.
  2. Increased performance since it was possible for job to start as soon as the previous job finished.
- **Disadvantages** of batch Operating System:
  1. Turn around time can be large from user standpoint.
  2. Difficult to debug program.
  3. Due to lack of protection scheme, one batch job can affect pending jobs.
  4. A job could corrupt the monitor, thus affecting pending jobs.
  5. A job could enter an infinite loop.

## Spooling

- In the batch operating system execution environment, the CPU is often idle. This idleness occurs because the speeds of the mechanical I/O devices are slower than those of electronic devices.
- As time passed, improvements are technology resulted in faster I/O devices and CPU speeds increased even faster, so the problem was not only unsolved but also increased.
- In the disk technology rather than the cards being read from the card reader directly into memory, and then the job being processed, cards are read directly from the card reader onto the disk.
- The location of the card images is recorded in a table kept by the operating system. When a job is executed, the operating system satisfied its request for card reader input by reading from the disk.

- Similarly, when the job requests the printer to output a line, that line is copied into a system buffer and is written to the disk. When the job is completed, the output is actually printed. This form of processing is called spooling as shown in Fig. 1.12.
- Spooling is used for data processing of remote sites. The CPU sends the data via communication paths to a remote printer. The remote processing is done at its own speed, with no CPU intervention.
- **Advantages** of spooling:
    1. Spooling overlaps the I/O of one job with the computation of other jobs.
    2. Spooling has a direct beneficial effect on the performance of the system.
    3. Spooling can keep both the CPU and the I/O devices working at much higher rates.
    4. Spooling operating uses a disk as a very large buffer.

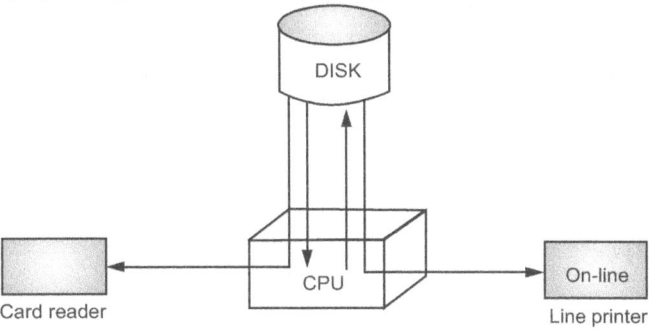

Fig. 1.12: Spooling

## 1.4.2 Multiprogramming

- Multiprogramming is a technique to execute number of programs simultaneously by a single processor.
- In multiprogramming number of processes reside is main memory at a time and the operating system picks and begins executing one of the jobs in the main memory.
- The Figs. 1.13 and 1.14 shows the layout of the multiprogramming system, which consists of 5 jobs.

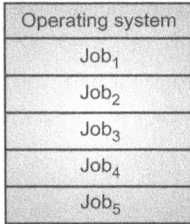

Fig. 1.13: Multiprogramming

- In non-multiprogramming system, the CPU can execute only one program at a time, if the running program waiting for any I/O device, the CPU sits idle, this will affect the performance of the CPU.
- But in case of multiprogramming environment any I/O wait by a process, will switch the CPU from that job to another job in the job pool eliminating the CPU idle time.
- This type of system permits several user jobs to be executed concurrently. The operating system takes care of switching the CPU among the various user jobs. It also provides a suitable run-time environment and other support functions, so the jobs do not interfere with each other.
- The goal of multiprogramming is to improve the system utilization by exploiting the concurrency between the CPU and the IO subsystem.
- The basic premise of multiprogramming is that while the IO subsystem is busy with an IO operation for a user job, the CPU can execute another user job.
- This requires the presence of multiple user jobs simultaneously in the computer's memory.

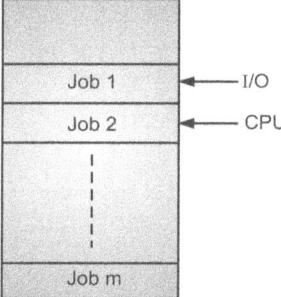

**Fig. 1.14: Schematic of Multiprogramming**

- Fig. 1.14 illustrates the schematic of a multiprogramming OS. The processor and IO channel are busy with different user jobs residing in the memory. Thus, they access different areas of memory.
- This ensures that their activities would not interfere with one another.
- One part of the main memory is occupied by the supervisor and it consists of a permanently resident part and a transient part which is loaded whenever required.
- The architectural (or hardware) features essential for multiprogramming are:
    o IO channels and the interrupt hardware,
    o Memory protection, and
    o Privileged mode of CPU operation.

- **Advantages** of multiprogramming are:
  1. Efficient memory utilization
  2. CPU never sits idle, so it increases the CPU performance
  3. Throughput of the CPU increases.
  4. In non-multiprogramming environment (mono programming) the user/ program has to wait for CPU much time. But waiting time is limited in multiprogramming.

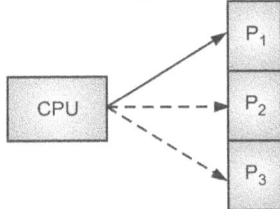

**Fig. 1.15: Multiprogramming – one CPU rapidly switched between processes**

## 1.4.3 Multiprocessing System

- This system is similar to multiprogramming system, except that there is more than one CPU available. In most multiprocessor systems, the processors share a common memory. Thus, the user can view the system as if it were a powerful single processor.
- Fig. 1.16 depicts the manner in which multiple processors may be used for multiprogramming. Usually, we visualize several separate processes as being in memory.
- In actuality, a process is often paged so that only part of it is in memory at one time; this allows the number of processes active in the system to be very large.

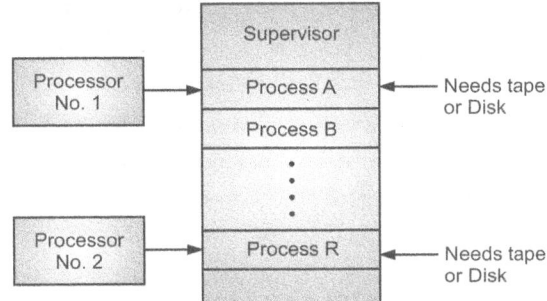

**Processor no. 1 working on process A**
**Processor no. 2 working on process R**
**Fig. 1.16: Multiprogramming with Multiprocessor**

- A processor is assigned to a task and operates on it until it is blocked. When a task is blocked, the processor selects another task and continues processing.
- After the blocking condition has been satisfied, a processor will eventually be assigned to the process; it need not be the same physical processor as before.

## 1.4.4 Multitasking or Time Sharing

- Time sharing or multitasking, is a logical extension of multiprogramming. Multiple jobs are executed by the CPU switching between them, but the switches occur so frequently that the users may interact with each program while running.
- Time sharing systems were developed to provide interactive use of a computer at reasonable cost.
- A time shared operating system uses CPU scheduling and multiprogramming to provide each user with a small portion of a time-shared computer. Each user has atleast one separate program in memory.
- A program that is loaded into memory and is being executed is commonly referred to as a process.
- A time shared operating system allows many uses to share the computer simultaneously. Since each action or command in, in a time-shared system tends to be short, only a little CPU time is needed for each user.
- Time sharing operating systems are even more complex than multi-programmed operating systems.
- As in multiprogramming several jobs must be kept simultaneously in memory, which require some form of memory management and protection.
- If a reasonable time can be obtained, jobs may have to be snapped in and out of main memory to the disk that now serves as a backing store for main memory.
- A common method for achieving this goal is virtual memory, which is a technique that allows the execution of a job that may not be completely in memory.
- A time sharing system provides an interactive or conversational access to a number of users. The operating system executes commands as they are entered, attempting to provide each user with a reasonably short response time to each command.
- Development of time sharing systems was motivated by the desire to provide fast response times to interactive users of a computer system.
- The response time is the time since the submission of a computational request by a user till its results are reported to the user.
- Emphasis on good response times, rather than good utilization efficiency or throughput, requires certain basic changes in the design of the operating system. These changes mainly concern the scheduling and memory management components of the time sharing supervisor.

## 1.4.5 Distributed Systems

- A distributed system is a collection of processors that do not share memory or a clock. Instead, each processor has its own local memory, and the processors communicate with each other through various communication lines.
- The processors in a distributed system vary in size and function.
- They may include small microprocessors, workstations, minicomputers and large general purpose computer systems.
- From the point of view of a specific processor in a distributed system, the rest of the processors and their respective resources are remote, whereas its own resources are local.
- The purpose of distributed system is to provide an efficient and convenient environment for this type of sharing of resources.
- A distributed system is shown in the Fig. 1.17.

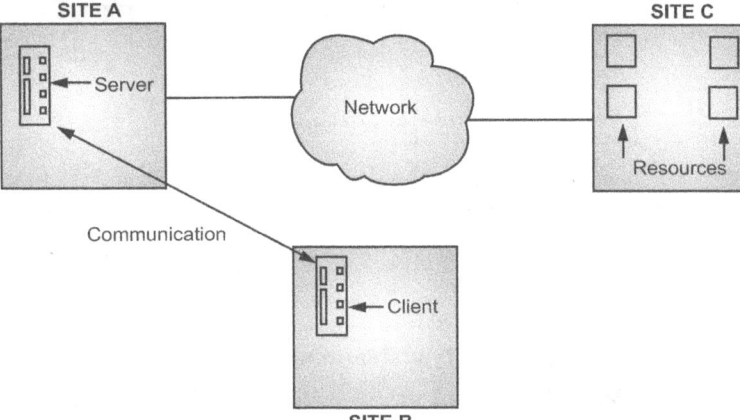

**Fig. 1.17: A Distributed System**

- Two general categories of network oriented operating systems are:
  1. Network operating systems, and
  2. Distributed operating systems.
  
  **1. Network operating systems:** A network operating system provides an environment in which users, who are aware of the multiplicity of machines, can access remote resources by either logging into the appropriate remote machine or transferring data from the remote machine to their own machines.
  
  **2. Distributed operating system:** In a distributed operating system, the users access remote resources in the same manner as they do local resources. Data and process migration from one site to another are under the control of the distributed operating system.

- A distributed operating system allows a more complex type of network organization. This kind of operating system manages hardware and software resources, so that a user views the entire network as a simple system.

- The user is unaware of which machine on the network is actually running a program or storing data.
- The major advantages of distributed systems are:
  - Resource sharing,
  - Reliability,
  - Computation speed-up,
  - Communication, and
  - Incremental growth.
- Fig. 1.18 depicts a distributed system.

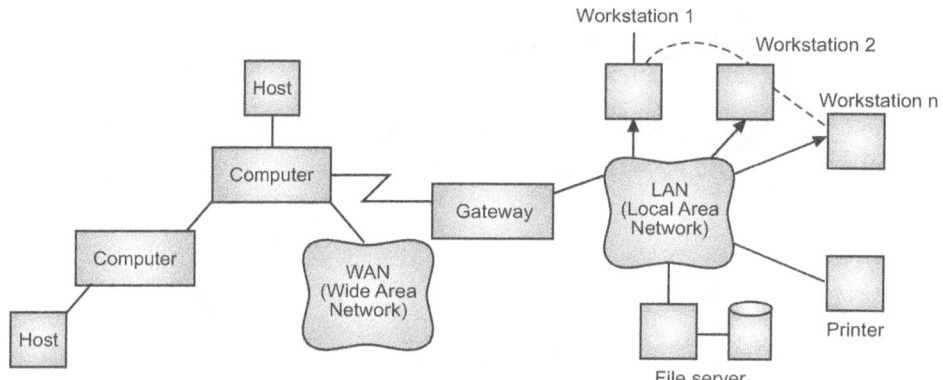

**Fig. 1.18: A Typical Distributed System**

## 1.4.6 Real Time Systems

- Real time systems are the special type of operating system.
- A real time system is used when there are rigid time requirements on the operation of a processor or flow of data, and thus if often used as a control device in a dedicated application.
- Sensors bring data to computer and the computer analyse the data and possibly adjust controls to modify the sensor inputs.
- Systems that control scientific experiments, medical imaging systems, industrial control systems and some display systems are real time systems.
- Also included are some automobile – engine fuel injection systems, home appliances controllers and weapon systems.
- Processing must be done within the defined constraints, or the system will fail. For instance, it would not do for a robot arm to be instructed to half after it had smashed into the car it was building.
- A real time system is considered to function correctly only if it returns the correct result within any time constraint.

- Real Time Systems are of two types:
    1. **Hard Real Time System:** Guarantees those critical tasks complete on time. This goal requires that all the delays in the system be bounded, from the retrieval of stored data to the time that it takes the operating system to finish any request made for it.
    2. **Soft Real Time System:** Less restrictive type, where a critical real time tasks get priority over other tasks and retain that priority until it completes.
- Soft real time is an achievable goal that is ammenable to mixing with other types of systems.
- A real-time system is designed to respond quickly to external signals such as those generated by data sensors.
- Real time systems are used on computers that monitor and control time-critical processes such as nuclear reactor operation or spacecraft flight.
- Hence, real-time application is an application which requires "timely" response from the computer system for the correctness of its functioning.
- A real-time operating system is one which helps to fulfill the worst-case response time requirements of an application.
- The real-time operating system provides the following facilities for this purpose:
    - Multitasking within an application,
    - Priority driven or deadline oriented scheduling, and
    - Programmer defined interrupts.

## Exercise

1. What is meant by operating system?
2. What are the basic functions of operating systems?
3. What is system call? How to implement it?
4. With suitable diagram describe structure of operating system.
5. Define operating system? Enlist various characteristics of operating system.
6. State various services of operating system.
7. Enlist various types of operating system.
8. Explain the following terms:
    (i) Process or Job control
    (ii) Real time systems, and
    (iii) File management.

9. What is meant by system program?
10. With suitable diagram describe batch operating system.
11. What is meant by multitasking and multiprogramming? Compare them.
12. What are the objectives of operating system?
13. Explain the term device management in detail.
14. With the help of diagram describe distributed system.
15. Differentiate between multiprogramming and multitasking operating systems.
16. Write short note on real-time systems.

# Chapter 2...

# System Structure

## Contents ...

2.1 User Operating System Interface
2.2 Concepts of System Calls
    2.2.1 What are System Calls?
    2.2.2 How to make a System Call?
2.3 Process or Job Control
2.4 Device Management
2.5 File Management
2.6 System Program
2.7 Operating System Structure
    2.7.1 Simple Structure
    2.7.2 Monolithic System
    2.7.3 Layered System
    Exercise

## 2.1 USER OPERATING SYSTEM INTERFACE

- Almost all operating systems have user interface (UI). This interface can take several Forms one is Command-Line User Interface, Batch Interface, Menu Driven User Interface and Graphical User Interface (GUI).
- The importance of user interfaces are:
  - To assist users interacting with a software
  - To control how a user enters data and instructions
  - To control how information is displayed

**Command-Line User Interface**

- The command-line user interface requires a user to type commands or press special keys on the keyboard to enter data and instructions that instruct the Operating system what to do. It has to be typed one line at a time.

- The Command-line user interface also requires memorization. The advantage of Command-line interface is, it helps the user to operate the computer quickly after Memorizing the keywords and syntax.

**Menu Driven User Interface**

- It avoids memorizing the commands. Also it is much easier than Command Line Interface. Here user is displayed with menus and submenus by clicking the appropriate option specific tasks carried out.

**Graphical User Interface**

- It is a software interface that user interacts with a pointing device, such as mouse. These are very user friendly because they are easy to interact with system and to execute instructions. For example, when you are using Internet you are looking at the GUI of web browser.

## 2.2 CONCEPTS OF SYSTEM CALLS

- They provide an interface between the process and the operating system.
- System calls allow user-level processes to request some services from the operating system which process itself is not allowed to do.
- System calls are programming interface to the services provided by the operating system.
- Typically, system calls written in a high level languages like C or C++.
- A system call is a request by the user to the operating system to do something on user's behalf. System call provides an interface between a running program and an operating system.
- In handling the trap, the operating system will enter in the kernel mode, where it has access to privileged instructions, and can perform the desired service on the behalf of user-level process. It is because of the critical nature of operations that the operating system itself does them every time they are needed.
- For example, for I/O a process involves a system call telling the operating system to read or write particular area and this request is satisfied by the operating system.

### 2.2.1 What are System Calls?

- System calls provide the interface between a process and the operating system.
- System calls are instructions that generate an interrupt that causes the operating system to gain control of the processor.
- The operating system then determines what kind of system call it is and performs the appropriate services for the system caller.

## 2.2.2 How to make a System Call?

- A system call is made using the system call machine language instruction. These calls are generally available as assembly language instructions and are usually listed in the manuals used by assembly - language programmers.
- Certain systems allow system calls to be made directly from a higher language program, in which case the calls normally resemble predefined function or subroutine calls. They may generate a call to a special run-time routine that makes the system call.
- Several languages such as C, C++ have been defined to replace assembly language for systems programming. These languages allow system calls to be made directly.
- For example, UNIX system calls may be invoked directly from a C or C++ program. System calls for Microsoft Windows Platforms are part of the Win 32 API, which is available for use by all the compilers written for Microsoft Windows.

**(i) File and I/O System Calls:**

| open | Get reading to read or write a file. |
|---|---|
| create | Create a new file and open it. |
| read | Read bytes from an open file. |
| write | Write bytes to an open file. |
| close | Indicate that you are done reading or writing a file. |

**(ii) Process Management System Calls:**

| create process | create a new process |
|---|---|
| exit | terminate the process making the system call |
| wait | wait for another process to exit |
| fork | create a duplicate of the process working the system call |
| execv | run a new program in the process making the system call |

**(iii) Interprocess Communication System calls:**

| createMessageQueue | create a queue to hold messages |
|---|---|
| SendMessage | send a message to a message queue |
| ReceiveMessage | receive a message from a message queue |

- **System calls can be roughly grouped into following major categories:**
    1. Process or Job Control.
    2. File Management.
    3. Device Management.
    4. Information Maintenance.

## 2.3 PROCESS OR JOB CONTROL

- A running program needs to be able to halt its execution either normally (end) or abnormally (abort).
- If the program discovers an error in its input and wants to terminate abnormally, it may also want to define an error level.
- A process or job executing one program may want to load and execute another program.
- This allows the control card interpreter to execute program as directly by the control cards of the user job.
- If we create a new job or process, we should be able to control its execution. We may also want to terminate a job or process that we created (terminate process).
- If we find that it is incorrect or no longer needed we may require waiting time to finish execution (wait time). Another set of system calls are helpful in debugging a program.
- **System calls related to process control are:**
    - (i) End, Abort.
    - (ii) Load, Execute.
    - (iii) Create process, Terminate process.
    - (iv) Ready process, Dispatch process.
    - (v) Suspend process, Resume process.
    - (vi) Get process attributes, Set process attributes.
    - (vii) Wait for Time.
    - (viii) Wait event, Signal event.
    - (ix) Change the priority of a process.

## 2.4 DEVICE MANAGEMENT

- Files can be thought of as abstract or virtual devices. Thus, many of the system calls for files are also needed for devices.
- If there are multiple users of the system however, the users must first request the device to ensure that they have an exclusive use of it.
- After the users are finished with the device, they must release it. These functions are similar to the open/close system calls for files.
- Once, the device has been requested the users can read, write and reposition the device just as with files.
- In fact the similarity between input/output devices and files is so great that many operating systems merge the two into a combined file/device structure. In this case input/output devices are identified by special file names.

**System calls related to device management are:**
- (i) Request a device, Release a device.
- (ii) Read, Write, Reposition.
- (iii) Get device attributes, Set device attributes.
- (iv) Logically attach or detach devices.

## 2.5 FILE MANAGEMENT

- Operating System provides several common system calls dealing with files.
- Users need to be able to create and delete files. Such system calls require the name of the file and perhaps some of its attributes. Once, the file is created, the users need to open it and use it.
- They may also need to read, write and reposition a file. Finally, they need to close the file, indicating that they are no longer using it.
- The users may need the same sets of operations for directories if there is a directory structure in the file system.
- In addition, for either files or directories, users need to be able to determine the values of various attributes and perhaps reset them if necessary.
- File attributes include the file name, a file type, protection codes, accounting information and so on. Two system calls get file attributes and set file attributes are required for this function.

**System calls for file manipulation are:**
    (i) Create a file, Delete a file.
    (ii) Open a file, Close a file.
    (iii) Create a directory.
    (iv) Read, Write, Reposition.
    (v) Get file attributes, Set file attributes.
    (vi) Create a link.
    (vii) Change the working directory.

**Information maintenance:**

- Many system calls exist simply for the purpose of transferring information between the user program and the operating system.
- For example, most systems have a system call to return the current time and date. Other system calls may return information about the system such as the number of current users, the version number of the operating system, the amount of free memory or disk space and so on.
- In addition the operating system keeps information about all of its jobs and processes and there are system calls to access this information.
- Generally, there are also calls to reset it, (get process attributes and set process attributes).

**System calls related to information maintenance are:**
    (i) Get Time or Date, Set Time or Date.
    (ii) Get system Data, Set system Data.
    (iii) Get process, File or Device attributes.
    (iv) Set process, File or Device attributes.

## Communication:

- There are two common models of interprocess communication one is the message-passing model and another is the shared-memory model.

    **(i) Message-passing model:** In this model the communicating processes exchange message with one another to transfer information. In this model the messages can be exchanged between the processes either directly or indirectly through a common mailbox. Before communication can take place, a connection must be opened and the name of the other communicator must be known, be it another process on the same system or a process on another computer connected by a communications network. Each and every computer in a network identifier, (IP address). Similarly, each and every process has a process name, and this process name is translated into an identifier by which the operating system can refer to the process. The get hosted and get processed system calls do this translation. The identifiers are then passed on the general purpose open and close calls provided by the file system or to specific open connection and close connection system calls, depending on the system's model of communication. The recipient process usually must give its permission for communication to take place with an accept connection call. Number of processes that will be receiving connections are special-purpose daemons, which are systems programs provided for that purpose. This process execute a wait for connection call and are awakened when a connection is made and the source of the communication, known as the client and the receiving daemon, known as a server, then exchange messages by using read message and write message system calls. The close connection call terminates the communication.

    **(ii) Share memory model:** In this model, processes used shared memory create and shared memory attach system calls to create and gain access to regions of memory owned by other processes. Normally, the operating system tries to prevent one process from accessing another process's memory. Share memory requires that more than two processes agree to remove this restriction. They can then exchange information by reading and writing data in the shared areas. The form of the data is determined by the processes and are not under the operating systems control. The process are also responsible for ensuring that they are not writing to the same location simultaneously.

**System calls related to communication are:**

   (i) create, delete communication connection.
   (ii) send, receive messages.
   (iii) transfer status information.

## System Call Implementation

- Basically, a number is associated with each system call. It is used to number the system calls.
- System call interface maintains a table indexed according to these numbers. The system call interface invokes intended system call is operating system kernel and return status of the system call and any return values.
- The caller needs to know nothing about how the system call is implemented. Just needs to obey API and understand what operating system will do as a result call.
- Most details of operating system interface hidden from programmer by API. It is managed by run-time support library.
- Some systems may allow system calls to be written in higher-level language program, in which the calls normally like predefined function or subroutine calls.
- They may be generated call to a special run-time routine that makes the system calls, or the system call may be generated directly in line.
- **Example:** Consider two files: input and output. The program is to read data from input file and copy into output file. To execute this program, the sequence of system calls occurs as follows:
    1. To obtain two file names from keyboard, system calls are required.
    2. Then system call is open input file and creates an output file.
    3. While opening, if file is not exist then program will print a message or terminate abnormally. This requires again system calls.
    4. If file exists, then for reading from the input file (a system call) and write to output file (another system call) calls are required.
    5. For closing both files, we required two system calls.
- Some operating system provides API which invokes the actual system calls on behalf of the application programmer. Most of the programming languages provides system call interface, which intercepts function calls in the API and invokes system calls within operating system.
- The relationship between an API, the system call interface and the operating system is shown in Fig. 2.1.

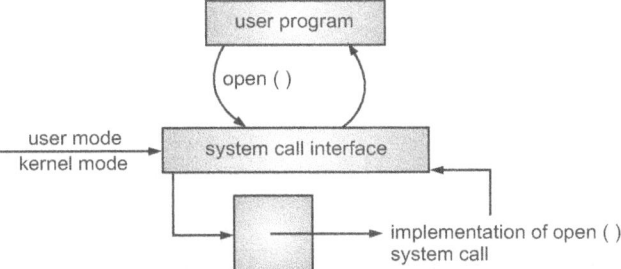

**Fig. 2.1: Invoking the system call**

- The parameter can be passed by using registers to implement system call. Sometimes parameters are stored in a block in memory and the address of block or table is passed as a parameter in register. UNUX uses such a mechanism.
- Implementation of system call vary on different systems. Generally, a unique number identifies the type of system call and a system call is made by calling the particular number.
- Sometimes there is a need of sending some additional information along with, when the call is made. That is called as, parameter or parameter list of the system call [e.g. to open file, we need to specify file name and mode in which to open the file along with system call fopen( )].
- Special register is kept aside for the purpose of sending parameters. If parameters are too many in number and are beyond the capacity of the register to hold, parameters are stored in a block or table in the memory and the base address of it is passed as parameter through the register.
- Most of the systems calls are available in assembly language. Some programming languages like C permit system calls through program. To really understand what operating system does, we must examine these calls closely.
- The system calls can categorised into five major categories: process and job control, file management, device management, information maintenance and communications. The system calls vary from operating system to operating system.
- **System calls in UNIX and WINDOW:**

| Types of System Calls | UNIX | Windows |
|---|---|---|
| Process control | fork()<br>wait()<br>exit() | CreateProcess()<br>WaitForSingleObject()<br>ExitProcess() |
| File manipulation | open()<br>read()<br>write()<br>close() | CreateFile()<br>ReadFile()<br>WriteFile()<br>CloseHandle() |
| Device manipulation | ioctl()<br>read()<br>write() | SetConsoleMode()<br>ReadConsole()<br>WriteConsole() |
| Information maintenance | getpid()<br>alarm()<br>sleep() | GetProcessId()<br>SetTimer()<br>Sleep() |
| Communication | pipe()<br>shmget()<br>mmap() | CreatePipe()<br>CrateFileMapping()<br>MapViewFile() |
| Protection and Security | chmod()<br>chown() | SetFileSecurity()<br>SetSecurityDescriptionGroup() |

- **Example:** Consider 'C' fragment running on UNIX and invokes system call open() for a file. Initially the program is loaded into memory and start the execution. The system uses fork() and exec() system calls. The configuration is shown in Fig. 2.2 (a).

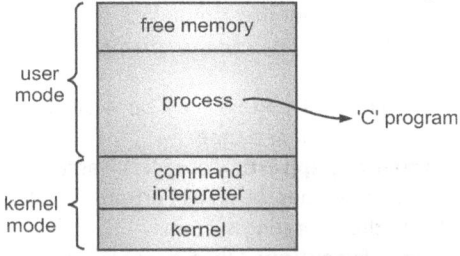

Fig. 2.2 (a): Running a program

- Let us assume 'C' program invoke a file opening statement. The Fig. 2.2 (b) shows how C library handles a open() calls.

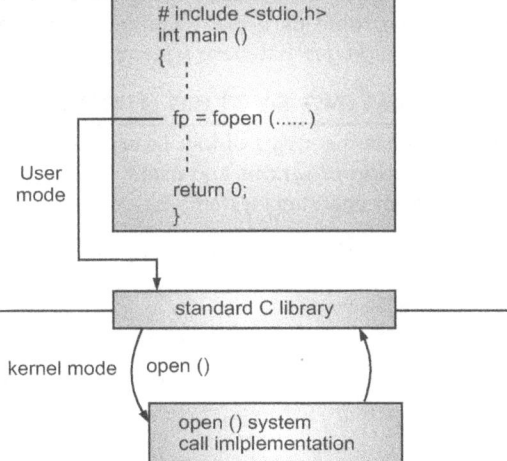

Fig. 2.2 (b): Handling a system call in 'C'

## 2.6 SYSTEM PROGRAM

- System programs provide basic functioning to users so that they do not need to write their own environment for program development (editors, compilers) and program execution (shells).
- In some sense, system programming is bundles of useful system calls.
- Modern systems consist of a collection of system programs.
- Most systems supply a large collection of system programs to solve commonly occurring problems and provide a more convenient and secure environment for program development and execution.

- System Programs can be divided into several categories:
    1. **File Manipulation:** These programs create, delete, copy, rename, print, dump, list and generally manipulate files and directories.
    2. **Status Information:** Some programs simply ask the operating system for the date, time, and amount of available memory or disk space, number of users or similar status information.
    3. **File Modification:** Several text editors may be available to create and modify the contents of files stored on a disk or a tape.
    4. **Programming Language Support:** Compilers, assemblers and interpreters for common programming languages. (such as Fortran, Cobol, Pascal, Basic, C and so on) are often provided with the operating system.
    5. **Program Loading and Execution:** Once a program is assembled or complied, it must be loaded into the memory to be executed. The operating system may provide absolute loaders, linkage editors and Debugging systems in order to achieve this.
    6. **Applications Programs:** In addition, most operating systems come with programs which are useful to solve some particularly common problems, such as compilers, text formatters, plotting packages, database systems and so on.

## 2.7 CONCEPT OF OPERATING SYSTEM STRUCTURE

- The structure of operating system consists of four layers, those are **hardware, operating system, System** and **application programs** and **users**.
- Fig. 2.3 shows the structures of operating system.

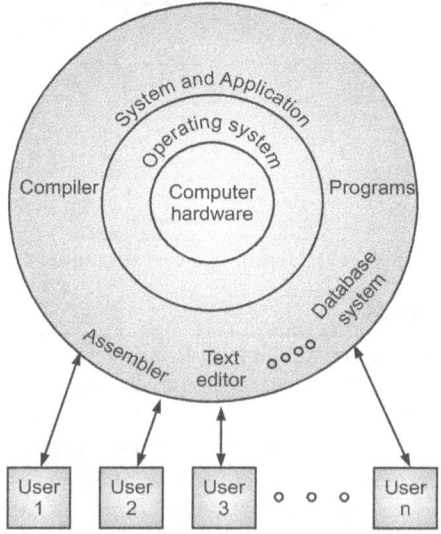

**Fig. 2.3: Structure of operating system**

- The hardware consists of Central Processing Unit (CPU), the main memory, I/O devices, secondary storage, etc.
- The operating system controls and co-ordinates the use of the hardware among the various application programs for the various users.
- The application programs such as word processors, spreadsheets, compilers and web browsers define the ways in which these resources are used to solve the Computing Problems of the users.
- There may be many different users as people, machines, other computers trying to solve different problems. Accordingly there may be many different application programs.
- There are various types of operating system structures, some of them are given in this section.

### 2.7.1 Simple Structure

- Many commercial systems are not well defined structures. Such operating systems started as small, simple and limited systems. For example, MS-DOS: it was not divided into modules carefully.

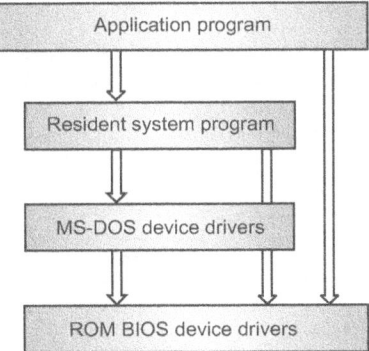

**Fig. 2.4: MS-DOS layer structure**

- UNIX is another system that was initially limited by hardware functionality. It consists of two parts one is kernel and second is system programs.
- The kernel provides the file systems, CPU scheduling, memory management and other operating system functions through System calls.
- System calls define the API to UNIX; the set of system programs commonly available defines the user interface. The programmer and user interfaces define the context that the kernel must support.
- The operating system has a much greater control over the computer and over the applications that make use of that computer. Implementers have more freedom to make changes to the inner workings of the system and in the creation of modular operating systems.

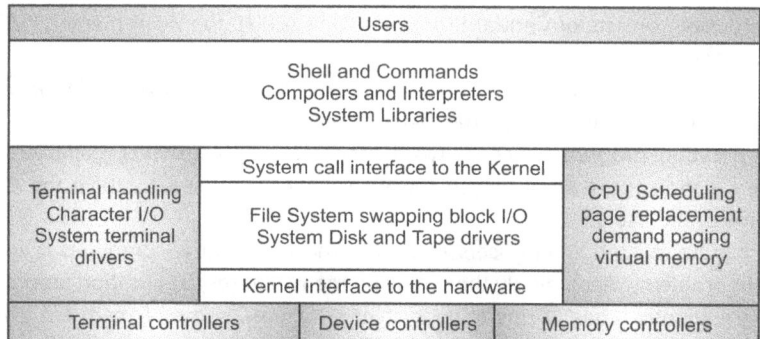

**Fig. 2.5: UNIX system structure**

## 2.7.2 Monolithic System

- The operating systems are written as a collection of procedures, each of which can call any of the other ones whenever it needs to. When this technique is used, each procedure in the system has a well defined interface in terms of parameters and results, and one is free to call any other one, if the latter provides some useful computation that the former needs.
- To construct the actual object program of the operating system when this approach is used, one compiles all individual procedures, or files containing the procedures and the binds them all together into a single object file using the system linker.
- In terms of information hiding, there is essentially none- every procedure is visible to every other one, (as opposed to a structure containing modules or packages, in which much of the information is local to a module and only officially designated entry points can be called from outside the module).

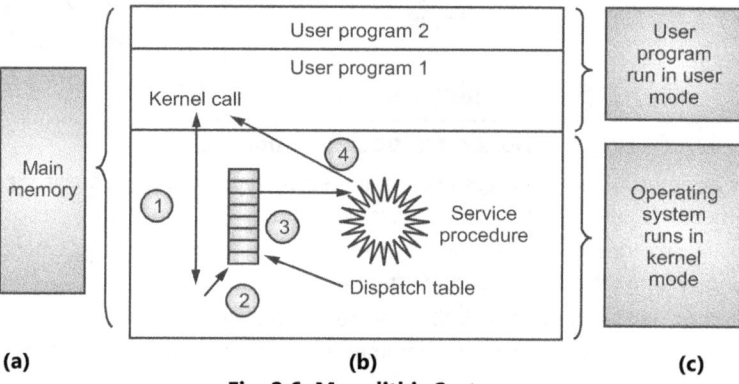

**Fig. 2.6: Monolithic System**

- Even in monolithic systems, however it is possible to have at least a little structure. The services (System Calls) provided by the operating system are requested by putting the parameters in well defined places, such as in registers or on the stack and then executing a special trap instruction known as a **kernel call** or **supervisor call**.

- This instruction switches the machine from user mode to kernel mode, and transfers control to the operating system shown in Fig. 2.6.
- Most CPU's have two operating modes.
  1. Kernel mode (priviledged mode) in which all instructions.
  2. User mode.
- Most CPU's have two modes: kernel mode for operating system in which all instructions are allowed, and user mode for user programs, in which I/O and certain other instructions are not allowed.
- The operating system then examines the parameters of the call to determine which system call is to be carried out shown in Fig. 2.6.
- Next the operating system then examines indexes into a table that contains in slot k a pointer to the procedure that carries out system call k. This operation shown in Fig. 2.6, identifies the service procedure, which is then called.
- Finally, the system call is executed and control is transferred back to the user program.
  1. A main program that invokes the requested service procedure.
  2. A set of service procedures that carry out the system calls.
  3. A set of utility procedures that help the service procedures.
- In this mode, for each System Call there is one service procedure that takes care of it. The utility procedures do things that are needed by several service procedures, such as fetching data from user programs.
- This division of the procedure into three layers is shown in Fig. 2.7.

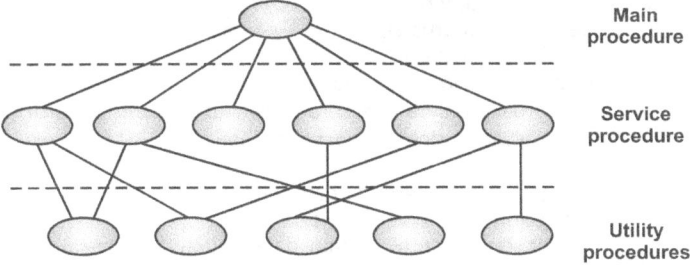

Fig. 2.7: Simple structuring model for a monolithic system

### 2.7.3 Layered Systems

- The modularization of a system can be done in many ways. One method is the layered approach, in which the operating system is broken up into a number of layers (or levels), each built on top of lower layers.
- The bottom layer (0) is the hardware and highest (layer N) is the user interface.
- A generalized approach is to organize the operating system as a hierarchy of layers, each one constructed upon the one below it.

- The system had 6 layers as below.

| Layer | Function |
|---|---|
| 5 | The operator. |
| 4 | User program. |
| 3 | Input / Output management. |
| 2 | Operator process communication. |
| 1 | Memory and Drum management. |
| 0 | Processor allocation and Multiprogramming. |

- Layer 0 deals with allocation of the processor, switching between processes when interrupts occurred or timers expired.
- Above **layer 0**, the system consists of sequential processes, each of which could be programmed without having to worry about the fact that multiple processes are running on a single processor. Layer 0 provides the basic multiprogramming of the CPU.
- **Layer 1** does the memory management. It allocates space for processes in main memory and on a 512 K word drum used for holding parts of processes (pages) for which there was no room in main memory.
- Above **layer 1**, processes did not have to worry about whether they are in memory or on the drum; the layer 1 software takes care of making sure that pages are brought into memory whenever they are needed.
- **Layer 2** handles communication between each process and the operator console.
- Above this layer each process effectively had its own operator console. Layers 3 takes care of managing the I/O devices and buffering the information streams to and from them.
- Above **layer 3** each process can deal with abstract I/O devices with nice properties instead or real devices with many peculiarities.
- **Layer 4** is where the user programs are found. They do not have to worry about process memory, console or I/O management.
- The system operator process is located in **layer 5**.
- The layering scheme is really only a design aid, because all the parts of the system are ultimately linked together into a single object program.

**Advantages:**
1. The main advantages of the layered approach is modularity.
2. Easy for debugging and system verification.
3. Each layer hides the existence of certain data structures, operations and hardware from higher level layers.

**Disadvantages:**
1. Careful definition of the layers.
2. Less efficient than other types.

## 2.7.4 Micro Kernels

- As the kernels became larger, they were difficult to manage.
- In the mid 1980's, researchers at Carnegie Mellon University developed an operating system called Mach that modularizes the kernel using the microkernel approach.
- This method structures the operating system by removing all nonessential components from the kernel and implementing them as system and user level programs. The result is a smaller kernel.

- Micro kernels typically provide minimal process and memory management, in addition to a communication facility.
- The main function of the microkernel is to provide a communication facility between the client program and the various services that are also running in user space. Communication is provided by message passing.
- The benefits of the microkernel approach include the ease of extending the operating system. All new services are added to user space and consequently do not require modification of the kernel.
- Microkernel also provides more security and reliability. Several contemporary operating systems have used the microkernel approach. Tru64 UNIX provides a UNIX interface to the user, but it is implemented with a Mach Kernel. The Apple MacOS X Server operating system is based on the Mach kernel. QNX a real time operating system, is also based upon the microkernel design.
- Because of small size of kernel, it is easy to port operating system from one hardware to other.
- Fig. 2.8 shows architecture of micro-kernel.

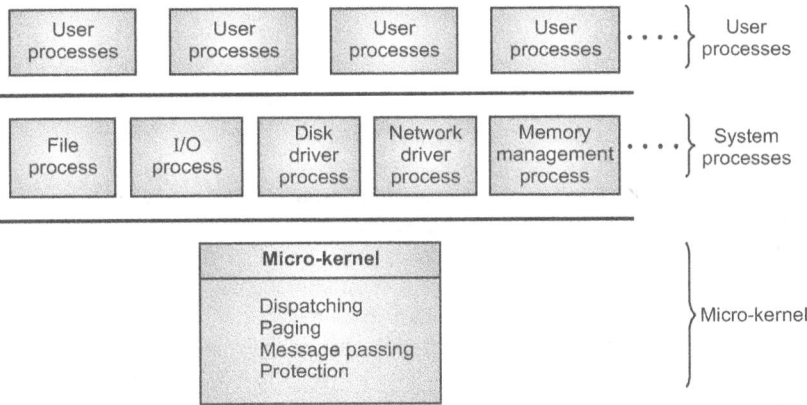

**Fig. 2.8: Micro-kernel**

**Advantages:**
1. To provide communication facility between the client program and various services running in user mode, communication is achieved by message passing.
2. Extending of operating system is easier, since all new services are added to user space and kernel modification is not required.
3. Portability: Because of small size of kernel, it is easy to port operating system from one hardware to other.
4. More secure and reliable.

**Disadvantages:**
1. Suffer from performance decreases due to increased system function overhead.

## Exercise

1. Define operating system.
2. What is operating system? What are its types?
3. Enlist various components of operating system.
4. What are the three main purposes of an operating system?
5. Enlist various services of operating system.
6. Enlist various functions of operating system.
7. Explain the following terms:
   (a) Time sharing systems, and
   (b) Batch systems.
8. Explain the evolution of operating system.
9. Explain the multiprogrammed batch systems with an example.
10. Is there any difference between multiprogramming and multitasking? If so explain.
11. What is the difference between a hard real time system and a soft real time system?
12. Write a short note on virtual machine.
13. Explain the following terms:
    (a) User view
    (b) Logical view.
14. What is meant by system calls? How to make It?
15. With suitable diagram explain virtual machine.
16. State advantages and disadvantages of operating systems.
17. With neat diagram describe structure of operating system.
18. With the help of diagram describe spooling.
19. Describe distributed operating system diagrammatically.
20. Distinguish between batch and multiprogramming.
21. Enlist various advantages, disadvantages, uses of following operating systems:
    (a) Batch system.
    (b) Multitasking system.
    (c) Parallel system.
    (d) Time-sharing system.
22. What is system program? What are its types? Explain in detail.
23. Write any two system calls of device manipulation.
24. Explain the layered structure of operating system?
25. State the advantages and disadvantages of layered operating system.
26. Compare layered operating system with microkernels operating system.
27. Write a note on microkernels.
28. State the advantages of microkernels.
29. Write benefits of virtual machine.
30. Write a note on virtual machine.

■■■

# Chapter 3...

# Process Management

## Contents ...
3.1 What is Process?
3.2 Process States
3.3 Process Control Block (PCB)
3.4 Context Switch
3.5 Operations on Processes
    3.5.1 Process Creation
    3.5.2 Process Termination
    Exercise

## 3.1 WHAT IS PROCESS?

- A process is a program in execution. As the program executes the process changes state.
- The state of a process is defined by its current activity.
- Process execution is an alternating sequence of CPU and I/O bursts, beginning and ending with a CPU burst. Thus, each process may be in one of the following states: **New, Active, Waiting** or **Halted**.

### The Process Model

- In process model the operating system is organized into a number of sequential processes, or just processes for short.
- A process is just an executing program, including the current values of the program counter, register and variables.
- Conceptually, each process had its own virtual CPU.
- In reality, of course, the real CPU switches back and forth from process to process; thus it is much a collection of processes running in parallel.
- This rapid switching back and forth is called multiprogramming.
- In Fig. 3.1 (a), a computer multiprogramming four programs in the memory. In Fig. 3.1 (b) we can see how this has been abstracted into four processes, each with its own flow of control (i.e. its own program counter), and each one running independent of the other ones. In third Fig. 3.1 (c), we can see that viewed over a long enough time interval, all the processes have made progress, but at any given instant only one process is actually running.

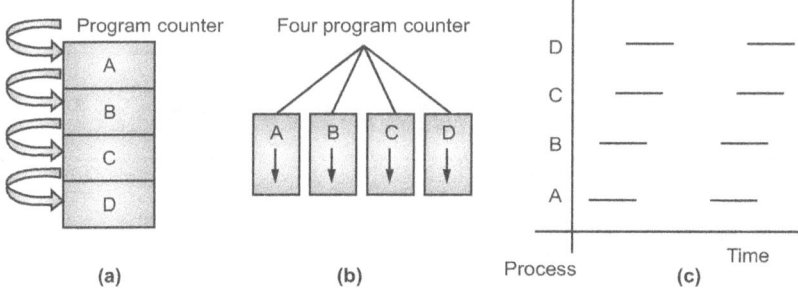

**Fig. 3.1: The process model**

- With the CPU switching back and forth among the processes, the rate at which a process performs its computation will not be uniform, and probably not even reproducible if the same processes are run again.
- Thus, processes are an activity of some kind. It has a program, input, output and a state a single processor may be shared among several processes, with some scheduling algorithm being used to determine when to stop work on one process and service a different one.

## 3.2 PROCESS STATES

- A process is a program in execution which includes the current activity and this state is depicted by the program counter and the contents of the processor's register.
- There is a process stack for storage of temporary data.
- There may be a situation when two processes may be associated with the same program but they are considered for two separate execution processes.
- A user can have several programs running and all these programs may be of a similar nature but they must have different processes.
- As a process executes, it changes state. The state of a process is defined in part by the current activity of that process.
- We have two types of process state models.
    1. **Two State Model:** This represents a simple model by observing that a process is either being executed by a processor or not. It can be n two states running or not running. When the operating system creates a new process, it enters that into the system in the NOT RUNNING state as shown in Fig. 3.2.

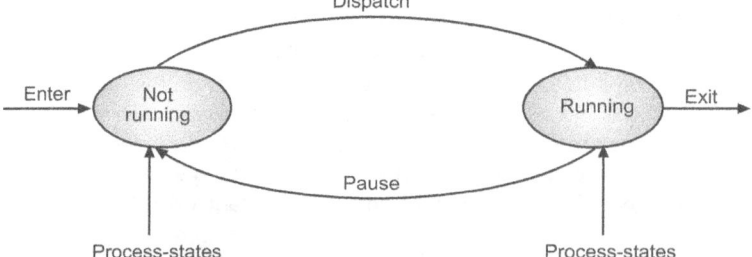

**Fig. 3.2: State Transition diagram of Two-State Process Model**

The process is waiting for an opportunity to operate, at times the currently running process will be interrupted and the dispatcher of the operating system will select a new process to run, one of the processes is now in the **running** state. Processes that are not running must be kept in some queue waiting their turn to be executed.

2. **Five state model :** In this, there are five stages and each process may be in one of the following states :
   (a) **New**        : The process is being created.
   (b) **Running**    : The process is being executed.
   (c) **Waiting**    : The process is waiting for some event to occur such as an I/O completion.
   (d) **Ready**      : The process is waiting to be assigned to a processor.
   (e) **Terminated** : The process has finished execution.

- These names are arbitrary and they vary from operating systems to operating systems. The important thing is only one process can be running in any processor at any time. Many processes may be ready and waiting state.
- The state diagram corresponding to these states is shown in Fig. 3.3.

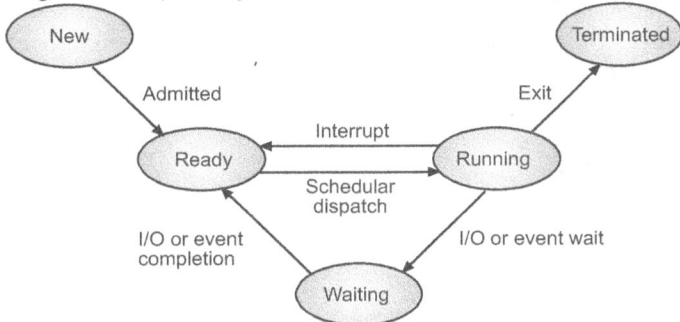

**Fig. 3.3: Diagram of process state**

- **New → Ready:** The operating system creates a process and prepares the process to be executed, and then the operating system moves the process into "Ready" queue.
- **Ready → running:** When it is time to select a process to run, the operating system selects one of the jobs from the ready queue and moves the process from ready state to running state.
- **Running → Terminated:** When the execution of a process has completed, then the operating system terminates that process from running state. Sometime, operating system terminates the process some other reasons also include time limit exceeded, memory unavailable violation, protection error, I/O failure, data misuse and so on.
- **Running → Ready:** When the time slot of the processor expired or if processor received any interrupt signal, then the operating system shifted running process to ready state. For example, $P_1$ is executed by processor; in the mean time process $P_2$ generates an

interrupt signal to the processor. Then, the processor compares the priorities of process $P_1$ and $P_2$, if $P_1 > P_2$ then the processor continues the process $P_1$ otherwise, the processor switched to process $P_2$, and the process $P_1$ moved to ready state.

- **Running → Waiting:** A process is put into waiting state, if the process need an event to occur or an I/O device requires. The operating system does not provide the I/O or event immediately then the process moved to waiting state by the operating system.
- **Waiting → Ready:** A process in the blocked state is moved to ready state when the event for which it has been waiting to occur. For example, a process is in running state need an I/O device, then the process moved to block or waiting state. When the I/O device provided by the operating system, the process moved to ready state from waiting or blocked state.

## 3.3 PROCESS CONTROL BLOCK (PCB)

- Each process is represented in the operating system by a **Process Control Block** (PCB) also called as **task control block**.
- The operating system groups all information that it needs about a particular process into a data structure called a **PCB** or **process descriptor**.
- When a process is created, the operating system creates a corresponding PCB and releases whenever, the process terminates.
- The information stored in a PCB includes :
  o Process name (ID).
  o Priority.

A PCB is shown in Fig. 3.4. It contains many pieces of information associated with a specific process.

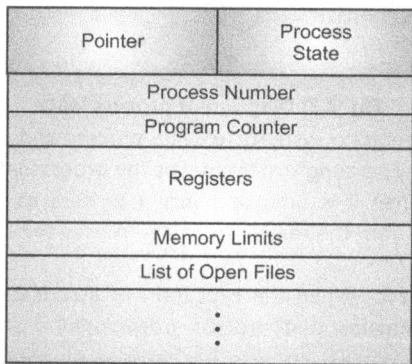

**Fig. 3.4: Process Control Block (PCB)**

  o **Process state:** The state may be new, ready, running, and waiting, halted and so on.
  o **Program counter:** The counter indicates the address of the next instruction to be executed for this process.

- o **CPU registers:** The registers vary in number and type, depending on the computer architecture. They include accumulators, index registers, stack pointers and general purpose registers, plus any condition - code information.
- o **CPU – Scheduling Information:** The information includes a process priority, pointers to scheduling queues, and any other scheduling parameters.
- o **Memory – Management Information:** This information may include such information as the value of the base and limit registers, the page tables or the segment tables, depending on the memory system used by the operating system.
- o **Accounting information :** This information includes the amount of CPU and real time used, time limits, account number, job or process numbers and so on.
- o **I/O Status information:** The information includes the list of I/O devices allocated to this process, a list of open files and so on.

## Threads

- The process model discussed so far has implied that a process is a program that performs a single thread of execution of execution.
- For example, when a process is running a word-processor program, a single thread of instructions is being executed.
- This single thread of control allows the process to perform only one task at one time for this reason the user cannot simultaneously type in characters and run the spell checker within the same process, for example.
- Number of modern operating systems have extended the process concept to allow a process to have multiple threads of execution and thus to perform more than one task at a time.
- On a system that supports threads, the PCB is expanded to include information for each thread. Other changes throughout the system are also needed to support threads.

## 3.4 CONTEXT SWITCH

- Switching the CPU to another process requires saving the state of the old process and loading the saved state for the new process. This task is known as a context switch.
- The context of a process is represented in the PCB of a process; it includes the value of the CPU registers, the process state and memory – management information.
- When a context switch occurs, the Kernel saves the context of the old process in its PCB and the loads the saved context of the new process scheduled to run.
- Context-switch time is pure overhead, because the system does no useful work while switching. Its speed varies from machine to machine, depending on the memory speed, the number of registers that must be copied, and the existence of special instructions.
- Context-switch times are highly dependent on hardware support. For instance, some processors provide multiple sets of registers.
- A context switch simply includes changing the pointers to the current register set. Of course, if active processes exceed register sets, the system resorts to copying the register data to and from memory.
- Also, the more complex the operating system, the more work must be done during a context switch.

## 3.5 OPERATIONS ON PROCESSES

- The processes in the system can execute concurrently and they must be created and deleted dynamically.
- Operations on processes are process creation and termination.

### 3.5.1 Process Creation

- When a new process is to be added to those currently being managed, the operating system builds the data structures that are used to manage the process, and allocates address space in main memory to the process. This is the creation of a new process.
- In a batch environment, a process is created in response to the submission of a job. In an interactive environment, a process is created when a new user attempts to log on. In both cases, the operating system is responsible for the creation of the new process.
- Operating system created all processes in a way that was transparent to the user or application program, and this still commonly found with many contemporary operating systems. When the operating system creates a process at the explicit request of another process, the action is referred to as process spawning.
- When one process spawns another, the former is referred to as the parent process, and the spawned process is referred to as the child process. The parent may have to partition its resources among its children, or it may be able to share some resources among several of its children.
- A sub-process may be able to obtain its resources directly from the operating system. When a process creates a new process, two possibilities exist in terms of execution :
    - The parent continues to execute concurrently with its children.
    - The parent waits until some or all of its children have terminated.
- A process creates a child process in UNIX through the system call fork.
- fork system call creates a child process and sets up its execution environment, then it allocates an entry in the process table i.e. a PCB for the newly created process and marks its state as ready.
- Fork also returns the id of the child process to its creator also called the parent process.
- The child process shares the address space and file pointers of the parent process, hence data and files can be directly shared.
- A child process can in turn create its own child processes, thus leading to the creation of a process tree.
- The UNIX operating system keeps track of the parent-child relationships throughout the lives of the parent and child processes.
- The child process in UNIX environment called its context is a copy of the parent's environment. Hence, the child executes the same code as the parent. At creation, the program counter of the child process is set at the instruction at which the fork call returns.
- The only difference between the parent and the child processes is that in the parent process fork returns with the process id of the child process, while in the child process it returns with a '0'.

## 3.5.2 Process Termination

- A computer system must provide a means for a process to indicate its completion.
- A batch job should include a halt instruction or an explicit operating system service call for termination.
- When processes terminate, it returns data to its parent process.
- Resources like memory, files and I/O are de-allocated by the operating system.
- If a process terminates either normally or abnormally, then all its children must also be terminated.
- Any process $p_i$ can terminate itself through the exit system call,

    ```
    exit (status_code);
    ```
    Where the value of status_code is saved in the kernel for access by the parent of $p_i$. If the parent is waiting for the termination of $p_i$, a signal is sent to it. The child processes of $p_i$ are made the children of a kernel process.

- Waiting for process termination : A process $p_i$ can wait for the completion of a child process through the system call,

    ```
    wait(add(abc));
    ```
    Where abc is a variable. When a child of $p_i$ terminates the wait call returns after storing the termination status of the terminated child process into abc. The wait call returns with a '–1' if $p_i$ has no children.

```
main ()
{
   int saved_status;
   for (i = 0; i < 3; i++)
   {
      if fork()== 0
      {
         /* code for child processes */
         exit ();
      }
   }
   while(wait(&saved_status) != -1)
         /* All child processes terminated? */
}
```

## Exercise

1. What is meant by process?
2. Explain the term process concept in detail.
3. With suitable diagram describe process model.
4. What is context switch?
5. With the help of diagram describe process states.
6. How to create a new process?
7. How to terminate a process?
8. Describe PCB in details.
9. What is Thread?

# Chapter 4...

# CPU Scheduling

## Contents ...
4.1 Introduction
4.2 Scheduling Concepts
4.3 CPU – I/O Burst Cycle
    4.3.1 CPU Scheduler
    4.3.2 Preemptive Scheduling
    4.3.3 Non-preemptive Scheduling
    4.3.4 Dispatcher
4.4 Scheduling Criteria
4.5 Scheduling Algorithms
    4.5.1 First-Come First-Served Scheduling (FCFS)
    4.5.2 Shortest-Job-First Scheduling (SJF)
    4.5.3 Priority Scheduling
    4.5.4 Round Robin (RR) Scheduling
    4.5.5 Multilevel Queue Scheduling
    4.5.6 Multilevel Feedback Queue Scheduling
    Exercise

## 4.1 INTRODUCTION

- CPU scheduling is the basis of multiprogrammed operating system.
- The idea of multiprogramming is relatively simply, if a process (job) is waiting for an I/O request, then the CPU switches from that job to another job, so the CPU is always busy in multi-programming.
- But in a simple computer system, the CPU sit idle until the I/O request granted.
- By switching the CPU among processes, the operating system can make the computer more productive.
- Scheduling is a fundamental operating system function, almost all the computer resources are scheduled before use.
- The CPU is also one of the primary resources. So CPU is also schedule before use.
- The CPU scheduling algorithm determines how the CPU will be allocated to the process.

- CPU scheduling algorithms are two types one is non-preemptive and second one is preemptive scheduling algorithms.
- In the non-preemptive scheduling once the CPU is assigned to a process, the processor do not **release Switch** until the completion of that process.
- The CPU is assigned to some other job only after the previous job has been finished. But in the preemptive scheduling the CPU can release the processes even in the middle of the execution.
- For example, when the CPU executing the process $P_1$ receives a request signal from process $P_2$ in the middle of the execution, then the operating system compares the priorities of $P_1$ and $P_2$.
- If the priority of $P_1$ is higher than $P_2$, then the CPU continues the execution of process $P_1$. Otherwise the CPU preempts the process $P_1$ and assigns to process $P_2$ [priority ($P_1 < P_2$)].
- CPU scheduling is the basis of multiprogrammed operating system. By switching the CPU among different processes, operating system can improve your degree of resource utilization.
- In this chapter we can study different scheduling policies and how to select particular algorithm, which is best suited for our system.

## 4.2 SCHEDULING CONCEPTS

- The main goal of multiprogrammed system is to maximize the CPU utilization. For uniprocessor system there will never be more then one running process, all other processes are in state of waiting.
- In multiprogramming environment several processes are kept in memory at one time.
- When one process is in the state of wait, Operating system switches the CPU from this process to another one. This pattern continues among all.
- Scheduling is the one of the most important function of operating system so almost all computers resources are scheduled before use.
- So CPU is one of the primary computer resources for this reason its scheduling is central to operating system design.

## 4.3 CPU-I/O BRUST CYCLE

- CPU-I/O burst cycle contains:
  - **CPU Burst:** A period of uninterrupted CPU activity.
  - **I/O Burst:** A period of uninterrupted Input output activity.
- Process execution consists of a cycle of CPU execution and I/O wait. Processes alternate back and forth between these two states. Process starts with CPU burst followed by I/O burst and so on.
- An I/O bound program would typically have many short CPU bursts where as CPU bound program consist of few long CPU bursts.

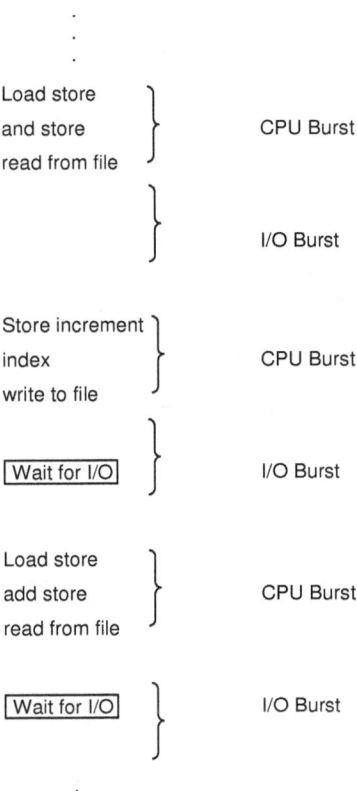

**Fig. 4.1: Alternating Sequence of CPU and I/O Bursts**

### 4.3.1 CPU Scheduler
- The operating system must select one of the processes in the ready queue to be executed. This is carried out by short term scheduler.
- A ready queue may be FIFO, priority queue, tree, linked list.
- Operating system selects from among the processes in memory that are ready to execute, and allocates the CPU to one of them.

### 4.3.2 Preemptive Scheduling
- In this, we will look at several methods of preemptive scheduling of the processor.
- We will assume a system where processes enter the processor scheduling system and remain there sometimes executing and sometimes waiting to execute until they have finished execution.

- By "finished execution", we do not mean that the process terminates rather we mean that the process becomes blocked waiting for an event waiting for a message or an I/O operation to complete.
- At that point, the process can no longer use the processor and so it is considered to be finished as shown in Fig. 4.2.

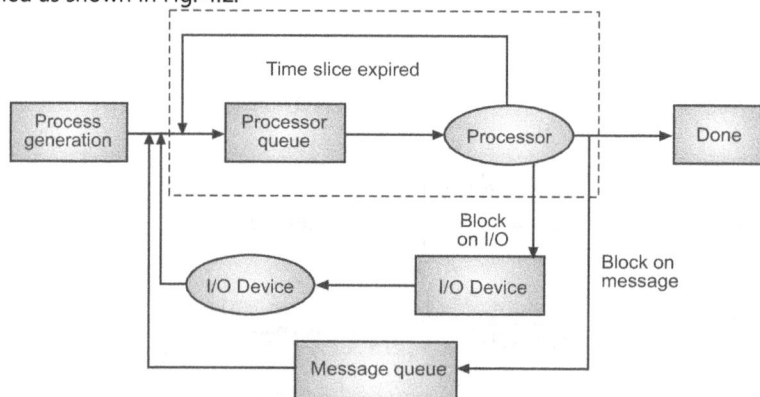

**Fig. 4.2: The Flow of Processes in an Operating System**

- The currently running process may be interrupted and moved to the ready state by the operating system. This is known as pre-empting. The decision to preempt may be performed.
    - When a new process arrives.
    - When an interrupt occurs that places a blocked process in the ready state or
    - Periodically base on a clock interrupt.
- A process will enter and leave the processor scheduling system many times during its entire execution, may be hundreds of thousands of times. Still, each one is a separate transaction as far as the processor scheduling system is concerned.
- The processor scheduling algorithm might look at the history of the process, that is, what happened on previous trips through the processor scheduling system. For example, the scheduler might want to estimate how much processor time the process will consume on this trip though the scheduling system.
- One rough estimate would be the same amount of time it used last trip. A better estimate might be weighted average of the last 10 trips.

### 4.3.3 Non-preemptive Scheduling
- In non-preemptive scheduling, once the CPU has been allocated to a process, the process keeps the CPU until it releases the CPU either by terminating or by switching to the working state.
- This method uses some hardware platforms. Microsoft Windows and Apple Macintosh Operating System use this type of scheduling method. Non-preemptive scheduling in attractive due to its simplicity.

- In scheduling non-pre-emptive, once a process is in the running state, it continues to execute until it terminates or blocks itself to wait for I/O or by requesting some operating system services.
- In short we can define the preemptive and non-preemptive scheduling as follows:
    1. **Preemptive scheduling:** CPU allocated to a process may be switched if another process is scheduled which is of higher priority.
    2. **Non-preemptive scheduling:** Once the CPU has been allocated to a process, it keeps the CPU until process terminates or by switching to the wait state.

### 4.3.4 Dispatcher

- A Dispatcher is a module; it connects the CPU to the process selected by the short-term scheduler.
- The main function of the dispatcher is switching, it means switching the CPU from one process to another process.
- The function of the dispatcher is 'jumping to the proper location in the user program and ready to start execution'.
- The dispatcher should be fast, because it is invoked during each and every process switch.
- The time it takes by the dispatcher to stop one process and start another running is known as the 'dispatch latency'.
- The degree of multiprogramming is depending on the dispatch latency. If the dispatch latency is increasing then the degree of multiprogramming decreases.
- **Dispatch latency:** Time it takes for the dispatcher to stop one process and start another running process.

### Types of Processor Scheduling

- The aim of processor scheduling is to assign processes to be executed by the processor, in a way that meets system objectives, such as response time, throughput and processor efficiency.
- In many systems, this scheduling activity is broken down into three separate functions: long, medium and short-term scheduling. The names suggest the relative time scales with which these functions are performed.
- Fig. 4.3 relates the scheduling functions to the process state transition diagram.

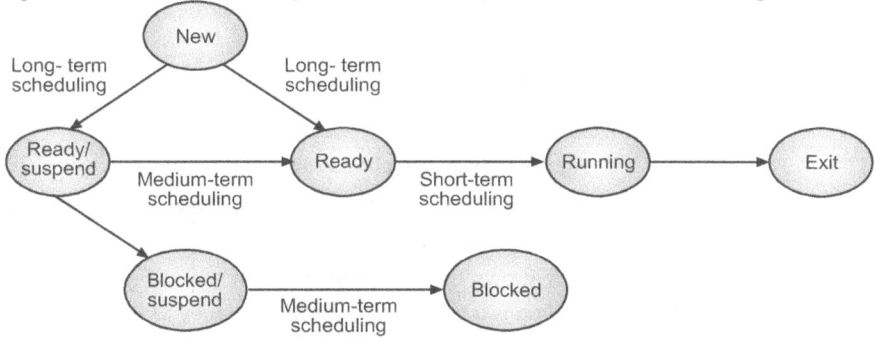

**Fig. 4.3: Scheduling and Process State Transitions**

- Long-term scheduling is performed when a new a new process is created. This is a decision to add a new process to the set of processes that are currently active.
- Medium-term scheduling is a part of the swapping function. This is a decision to add a process to those that are at least partially in main memory and therefore available for execution.
- Short-term scheduling is the actual decision of which ready process to execute next.

| Long-term scheduling | The decision to add to the pool of processes to be executed. |
|---|---|
| Medium-term scheduling | The decision to add to the number of processes that are partially or fully in main memory. |
| Short-term scheduling | The decision as to which available process will be executed by the processor. |

- Fig. 4.4 shows the state transition diagram to suggest the nesting of scheduling functions.

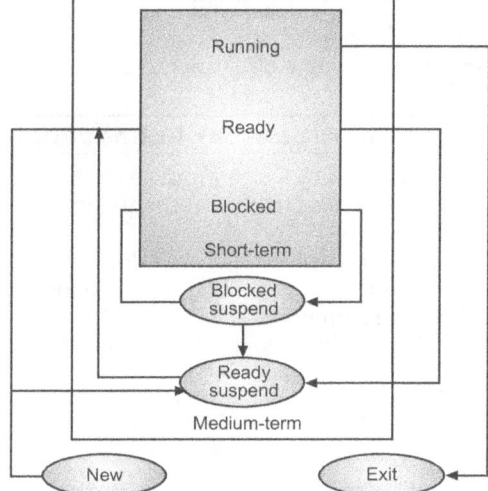

**Fig. 4.4: Levels of Scheduling**

- Scheduling affects the performance of the system because it determines which process will wait and which will progress.
- This is shown in Fig. 4.5, which shows the queue involved in the state transitions of a process. Fundamentally, scheduling is a matter of managing queues to minimize queuing delay and to optimize performance in a queuing environment.

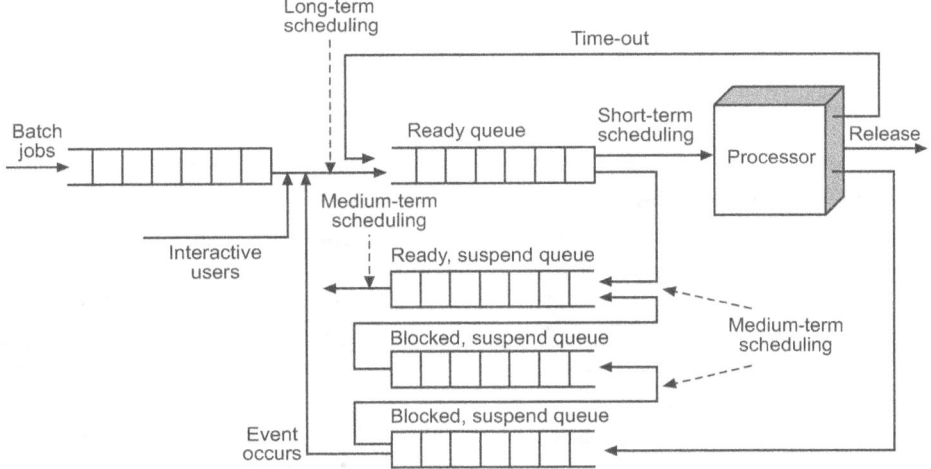

**Fig. 4.5: Queuing Diagram for Scheduling**

1. **Long-term Scheduling:**
- The long-term scheduler determines which programmers are admitted to the system for processing. Thus, it controls the degree of multiprogramming.
- Once, admitted a job or user program becomes a process and is added to the queue for the short-term scheduler. In some systems, a newly related process begins in a swapped-out condition, in which case it is added to the queue for the medium-term scheduler.
- In a batch system or for the batch portion of a general purpose operating system, newly submitted jobs are routed to disk and held in a batch queue.
- The long-term scheduler creates processes from the queue when it can. There are two decisions involved here.
- First, the scheduler must decide that the operating system can take on one or more additional processes.
- Second, the scheduler must decide which job or jobs to accept and turn into processes.
- The decision as to when to create a new process is generally driven by the desired degree of multiprogramming.
- The more processes that are created, the smaller is the percentage of time that each process can be executed, (i.e. more processes are competing for the same amount of processor time).
- Thus, the long-term scheduler may limit the degree of multiprogramming to provide satisfactory service to the current set of processes.
- Each time a job terminates, the scheduler may take the decision to add one or more new jobs. Additionally, if the fraction of time that the processor is idle exceeds as certain threshold, the long-term scheduler may be invoked.

- The decision as to which job to admit next can be on a simple first-come-first served basis. The criteria used may include priority, expected execution time, and I/O requirements.
- For example, if the information is available, the scheduler may attempt to keep a mix of processor-bound and I/O bound processes. Also, the decision may be made depending on which I/O resources are to be required in an attempt to balance I/O usage.

2. **Medium-Term Scheduling:**
- If a process request an I/O in the middle of the execution, then the process is removed from the main memory and loaded into waiting queue.
- When the I/O operation is completed, then the job is moved from waiting queue to ready queue.
- These two operations are performed by medium-term scheduler.

3. **Short-term Scheduling:**
- The long-term scheduler executes relatively infrequently and makes the decision of whether or not to take on new processes, and which one to take.
- The medium-term scheduler is executed some what more frequently to make a swapping decision.
- The short-term scheduler, also known as the dispatcher, executes most frequently and makes the fine-grained decision of which processes to execute next.
- The short-term scheduler is invoked whenever an event occurs that may lead to the suspension of the current process or that may provide an opportunity to preempt a currently running process in favor of another.
- For examples,
    - Clock interrupts,
    - Signals,
    - Operating system calls, and
    - I/O interrupts.
  
  Are such events.

## 4.4 SCHEDULING CRITERIA

- There are many different CPU - Scheduling algorithms are available and different CPU scheduling algorithms have different properties and may favour one class of processes over another.
- To choose a particular algorithm for a particular situation, we must consider the properties of the various algorithms.
- For comparing CPU - scheduling algorithms many criteria have been suggested. The characteristics used for comparison can make a substantial difference in the determination of the best algorithm.

- The following scheduling criteria are listed below:
  1. **CPU utilization:** Our main aim is to keep the CPU as busy as possible. The utilization of CPU may range from 0 to 100 percent. In real time lightly loaded systems the range is from 40 per cent to 90 per cent for heavily loaded systems.
  2. **Throughout:** If the CPU is busy executing processes, then work is being done. One measure of work is the number of processes completed per time unit, called throughput. For long processes, this rate may be one process per hour, for short transactions, throughput might be Ten processes per second.
  3. **Turnaround time:** For a process, the important criterion is how long it takes to execute that process. The interval from the time of submission of a process to the time of completion is the turn around time. It is the sum of the periods spends waiting to get into memory, waiting in the ready queue, executing on the CPU and doing I/O.
  4. **Waiting time:** The CPU scheduling algorithm does not affect the amount of time during which a process executes or does I/O. The CPU - scheduling algorithm affects only the amount of time during which a process spends waiting in the ready queue. Waiting time is the addition of the periods spends waiting in the ready queue.
  5. **Response time:** Response time is the time from the submission of a request until the first response is produced or we can say that it is the amount of time it takes to start responding, but not the time that it takes the output that response. To guarantee that all users get good service, we may want to minimize the maximum response time.

## 4.5 SCHEDULING ALGORITHMS

- CPU scheduling algorithms deals with the problem of deciding which of the processes in the ready queue is to allocate the resource that is the CPU.
- There are many different algorithms, here we will discuss the below mentioned algorithms only.

### 4.5.1 First-Come, First-Serve Scheduling (FCFS)

- The simplest among all is the FCFS scheduling algorithm.
- The process that requests the CPU first, is allocated CPU first.
- It can be implemented with FIFO queue.
- When a process enters in a ready queue, get allocated with CPU.
- When CPU is free it is allocated at the head of the queue.
- The running process is then removed from the queue. The average waiting time under FCFS policy, however, is often quite long.

**Ex. 1:** Calculate Average Turn Around Time and Average Waiting Time for all set of processes using FCFS:

| Process | Burst Time | Arrival Time | Waiting Time | Turn Around Time |
|---------|------------|--------------|--------------|------------------|
| $P_1$ | 5 | 1 | | |
| $P_2$ | 6 | 0 | | |
| $P_3$ | 2 | 2 | | |
| $P_4$ | 4 | 0 | | |

**Sol.:** Waiting time= Start Time – Arrival Time

The Gantt chart for the schedule is:

| $P_1$ | $P_2$ | $P_3$ |
|---|---|---|

0     24    27    30

Waiting time for $P_1$ = 0; $P_2$ = 24; $P_3$ = 27

Average waiting time: $(0 + 24 + 27)/3 = 17$

So we can say that the waiting period of process $P_1$ is 0 milliseconds and for Process $P_2$ is 24 milliseconds and for process $P_3$ is 27 milliseconds.

Suppose, now that the processes arrive in the order

$P_2, P_3, P_1$

The Gantt chart for the schedule is:

| $P_2$ | $P_3$ | $P_1$ |
|---|---|---|

0     3     6           30

Waiting time for $P_1$ = 6; $P_2$ = 0; $P_3$ = 3

Average waiting time: $(6 + 0 + 3)/3 = 3$

- Here, we have the waiting period for process $P_1$ is 6 and for process $P_2$ waiting period is 0 and for process $P_3$ the waiting period is 3.
- Then the average waiting period/time is 3, therefore, we can say that the waiting Time is much better than the previous case.
- Now consider the performance of FCFS scheduling in dynamic situation. Assume that we have one CPU bound process and many I/O bound processes.
- As processes flow around the system, we may have the following scenario, the CPU bound process will get the CPU and it will hold it.
- During that time all other process will finish their I/O and now they are ready to move into the ready queue, and waiting for the CPU. As the processes are waiting in the ready queue mean while the I/O devices are sitting idle.

# Introduction to Operating System  4.11  CPU Scheduling

- The CPU bound process finishes its CPU burst and moves to an I/O device for I/O related work. Now all the I/O bound processes, which have very short CPU burst get execute quickly and moves back to the I/O queues.
- At this point the CPU sits idle. The CPU-bound process will then move back to the ready queue and be allocated the CPU. Again, all the I/O processes end up waiting in the ready queue until the CPU bound process is done.

**Ex. 2:** Consider the following set of processes all arriving at time 0 and the burst time of each process is given below:

| Process | Burst Time (Milli seconds) |
|---|---|
| $P_1$ | 5 |
| $P_2$ | 24 |
| $P_3$ | 16 |
| $P_4$ | 10 |
| $P_5$ | 3 |

The processes arrive in the order given below as $P_1, P_2, P_3, P_4$ and $P_5$.

The Gantt chart for the above scenario would be as shown below:

| $P_1$ | $P_2$ | $P_3$ | $P_4$ | $P_5$ |
|---|---|---|---|---|
| 0   5 | 29 | 45 | 55 | 58 |

Calculate:
(i) Average Waiting Time
(ii) Average Response Time
(iii) Average Turn Around time.

**Sol.:**

**(i) Average Waiting Time:**

Waiting Time = Starting Time – Arrival Time

| Process | Starting Time | Arrival Time | Waiting Time |
|---|---|---|---|
| $P_1$ | 0 | 0 | 0 |
| $P_2$ | 5 | 0 | 5 |
| $P_3$ | 29 | 0 | 29 |
| $P_4$ | 45 | 0 | 45 |
| $P_5$ | 55 | 0 | 55 |

$$\therefore \text{ Average waiting time } = \frac{0 + 5 + 29 + 45 + 55}{5}$$

$$= 26.8 \text{ milliseconds}$$

### (ii) Average Response Time:

Response Time = First Response − Arrival Time

| Process | Starting Time | Arrival Time | Waiting Time |
|---------|---------------|--------------|--------------|
| $P_1$ | 0 | 0 | 0 |
| $P_2$ | 5 | 0 | 5 |
| $P_3$ | 29 | 0 | 29 |
| $P_4$ | 45 | 0 | 45 |
| $P_5$ | 55 | 0 | 55 |

$$\therefore \text{Average Response Time} = \frac{0 + 5 + 29 + 45 + 55}{5}$$

= 26.8 milliseconds

### (iii) Average Turn Around Time:

Turn around Time = Finished time − Arrival Time

| Process | Starting Time | Arrival Time | Waiting Time |
|---------|---------------|--------------|--------------|
| $P_1$ | 5 | 0 | 5 |
| $P_2$ | 29 | 0 | 29 |
| $P_3$ | 45 | 0 | 45 |
| $P_4$ | 55 | 0 | 55 |
| $P_5$ | 58 | 0 | 58 |

$$\therefore \text{Average Turn around Time} = \frac{5 + 29 + 45 + 55 + 58}{5}$$

= 38.4 milliseconds

Since, it is non-preemptive scheduling algorithms the average response time and average waiting time is same in both the cases.

**Note:** Non-preemptive means once the CPU is allocated to one process it keeps it as long as it needs and release only when it finishes its jobs either by terminating or by requesting an I/O.

**Ex. 3:** In Ex. 2 the arrival time for all the processes was 0. But if we change the arrival time of the processes then the whole calculation changes as shown below.

| Process | CPU burst Time | Arrival Time |
|---------|----------------|--------------|
| $P_1$ | 3 | 0 |
| $P_2$ | 6 | 2 |
| $P_3$ | 4 | 4 |
| $P_4$ | 5 | 6 |
| $P_5$ | 2 | 8 |

# Introduction to Operating System     4.13     CPU Scheduling

Order of Arrival of processes is $P_1, P_2, P_3, P_4$ and $P_5$.

$P_1$ arrived a Time 0 milliseconds
$P_2$ arrived after 2 milliseconds
$P_3$ arrived after 4 milliseconds
$P_4$ arrived after 6 milliseconds
$P_5$ arrived after 8 milliseconds.

The Gantt chart of the above problem is shown below:

| P$_1$ | P$_2$ | P$_3$ | P$_4$ | P$_5$ |
|---|---|---|---|---|
| 0    3 |    9 |    13 |    18 |    20 |

Calculate:
(i) Average Relative Delay
(ii) Average Response Time
(iii) Average Turn Around Time.

**Sol.:**

**(i) Average Relative Delay:**

$$\text{Relative delay} = \frac{\text{Turn around time}}{\text{Burst Time}}$$

| Process | Turn Around Time | Burst Time | Relative delay |
|---|---|---|---|
| $P_1$ | 3 | 3 | 1 |
| $P_2$ | 7 | 6 | 1.16 |
| $P_3$ | 9 | 4 | 2.25 |
| $P_4$ | 12 | 5 | 2.4 |
| $P_5$ | 12 | 2 | 6 |

$$\text{Average relative delay} = \frac{1 + 1.16 + 2.25 + 2.4 + 6}{5}$$

$$= \frac{12.81}{5} = 2.56 \text{ milliseconds}$$

**(ii) Average Turn around Time:**

Turn Around Time = Finish Time − Arrival Time

| Process | Finish Time | Arrival Time | Turn Around Time |
|---|---|---|---|
| $P_1$ | 3 | 0 | 3 |
| $P_2$ | 9 | 2 | 7 |
| $P_3$ | 13 | 4 | 9 |
| $P_4$ | 18 | 6 | 12 |
| $P_5$ | 20 | 8 | 12 |

$$\therefore \text{Average Turn Around Time} = \frac{3 + 7 + 9 + 12 + 12}{5}$$

$$= 8.6 \text{ millisecond}$$

### (iii) Average Response Time:

Response Time = First Response Time − Arrival Time

| Process | Finish Time | Arrival Time | Response Time |
|---------|-------------|--------------|---------------|
| $P_1$ | 0 | 0 | 0 |
| $P_2$ | 3 | 2 | 1 |
| $P_3$ | 9 | 4 | 5 |
| $P_4$ | 13 | 6 | 7 |
| $P_5$ | 18 | 8 | 10 |

$$\therefore \text{Average Response time} = \frac{0 + 1 + 5 + 7 + 10}{5}$$

= 4.6 millisecond

### Advantages

1. Easy to implement.
2. It is very simple.

### Disadvantages

1. Problematic with some time sharing systems.
2. Average waiting time is very high with respect to others.
3. Because of this performance is affected or degraded.

**Note:** To summarize FCFS algorithm
- FCFS scheduling algorithm is non-preemptive.
- For time-sharing system we cannot implement FCFS, because process will hold the CPU until it finishes or changes a state to wait state.
- Average waiting time for FCFS algorithm is not minimal, and it also varies substantially if the process CPU burst time vary greatly.

## 4.5.2 Shortest–Job–First Scheduling (SJF)

- Different method of CPU scheduling is the Shortest-Job-First (SJF).
- It allocates the CPU to a process having smallest next CPU burst. When the CPU is available, it is assigned to the process that has the smallest next CPU burst.
- If the two processes having same CPU burst then they will be scheduled according to FCFS algorithm. For example consider the following set of processes.

| Process | Burst-time (milliseconds) |
|---------|---------------------------|
| $P_1$ | 6 |
| $P_2$ | 8 |
| $P_3$ | 7 |
| $P_4$ | 3 |

- The Gantt chart for the above problem is

| P$_4$ | P$_1$ | P$_3$ | P$_2$ |
|---|---|---|---|
| 0 | 3 | 9 | 16 | 24 |

Waiting Time for Process P1 = 3 milliseconds
Waiting Time for Process P2 = 16 milliseconds
Waiting Time for Process P3 = 9 milliseconds
Waiting Time for Process P4 = 0 milliseconds

∴ Average Waiting Time is $\frac{(3 + 16 + 9 + 4)}{4}$ = 8 milliseconds

- The SJF scheduling algorithm is probably optimal, it gives minimal average waiting time for a given set of processes.
- By moving short process before a long one, the waiting time of short process decreases. Consequently average waiting time reduces.
- The real difficulty with SJF knows the length of next CPU request so it can not be implemented at the level of short term scheduling. Instead it can be used for long term scheduling where user estimates the process time limit.
- At short term scheduling there is no way to find out the length of next CPU burst. One approach is to approximate SJF scheduling. We can predict the next CPU burst from previous value.
- The next CPU burst is generally predicted as an exponential average of the measured lengths of previous CPU burst.
- Let $t_n$ be the length of the $n^{th}$ CPU burst, and let $T_{n+1}$ be our predicted value for the next CPU burst. Then for $\alpha$, $0 <= \alpha <= 1$,

$$\boxed{T_{n+1} = \alpha t_n + (1 - \alpha) T_n}$$

- This gives exponential average. Here,
    - $t_n$ : Most recent information
    - $T_n$ : Stores the past history
    - $\alpha$ : Relative weight of recent and past history
  
  If $\alpha = 0$, Then $T_{n+1} = T_n$ (Current $T_n$ and recent having same values)
  
  If $\alpha = 1$, Then $T_{n+1} = t_n$ (Most recent CPU burst matters)

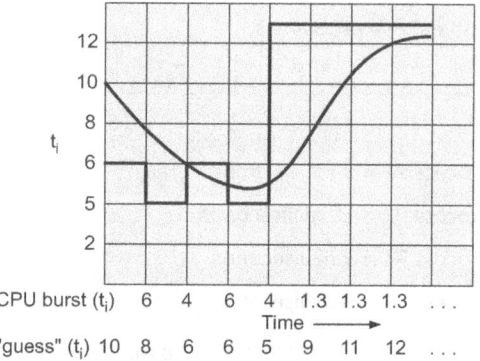

CPU burst ($t_i$)   6   4   6   4   1.3  1.3  1.3  ...
                              Time ———▶
"guess" ($t_i$)  10   8   6   6   5   9   11   12  ...

**Fig. 4.6: Prediction of the length of the next CPU Burst**

- Two types of SJF algorithm are:
    1. Preemptive, and
    2. Non-preemptive.
- The choice arises when a new process arrives at the ready queue while a previous process is executing.
- The new process may have a shorter next CPU burst than what is left at the currently executing process.
- A preemptive SJF algorithm will preempt the currently executing process, whereas as a non-preemptive SJF algorithm will allow the currently running process to finish its CPU burst.
- Preemptive SJF scheduling is sometimes called shortest-remaining time first scheduling.
- For example consider the processes below:

| Process | Arrival Time | Burst-time (milliseconds) |
|---------|--------------|---------------------------|
| $P_1$   | 0            | 8                         |
| $P_2$   | 1            | 4                         |
| $P_3$   | 2            | 9                         |
| $P_4$   | 3            | 5                         |

- The Gantt chart for the above problem is shown below:

| $P_1$ | $P_2$ | $P_4$ | $P_1$ | $P_3$ |
|-------|-------|-------|-------|-------|
| 0   1 | 5     | 10    | 17    | 26    |

- Process $P_1$ arrives at Time 0.
- Process $P_2$ arrives at Time 1. The remaining time for process $P_1$ is 7 milliseconds is larger than the time required by process $P_2$ i.e. 4 milliseconds, so process $P_1$ is preempted and process $P_2$ is scheduled. The average waiting time for this is:

Formula for Waiting time in preemptive SJF Scheduling:
Waiting time = start time − arrival time +new start time − old finish time.

$$\frac{((10-1)+(1-1)+(17-2)+(5-3))}{4} = \frac{(9+0+15+2)}{4}$$

$$= \frac{26}{4}$$

$$= 6.5 \text{ milliseconds}$$

- A non-preemptive SJF scheduling would have average waiting time at 7.75 milliseconds. The calculation is left for the students to solve.

**Ex. 1: Non-Preemptive SJF.**

| Process | Arrival Time | Burst Time |
|---------|--------------|------------|
| $P_1$ | 0.0 | 7 |
| $P_2$ | 2.0 | 4 |
| $P_3$ | 4.0 | 1 |
| $P_4$ | 5.0 | 4 |

**Sol.:**

- SJF (Non-Preemptive)

| $P_1$ | $P_3$ | $P_2$ | $P_4$ |

0   7   8   12   16

$$\therefore \text{ Average waiting time } = \frac{0+6+3+7}{4} = \frac{16}{4} = 4$$

**Ex. 2: Preemptive SJF.**

| Process | Arrival Time | Burst Time |
|---------|--------------|------------|
| $P_1$ | 0.0 | 7 |
| $P_2$ | 2.0 | 4 |
| $P_3$ | 4.0 | 1 |
| $P_4$ | 5.0 | 4 |

**Sol.:**

- SJF (Preemptive)

| $P_1$ | $P_2$ | $P_3$ | $P_2$ | $P_4$ | $P_1$ |

0   2   4   5   7   11   16

$$\therefore \text{ Average waiting time } = \frac{9+1+0+2}{4} = \frac{12}{4} = 3$$

**Ex. 3:** Consider the process and CPU burst time in milliseconds.

| Process | CPU Burst-time (milliseconds) |
|---------|-------------------------------|
| $P_1$   | 5                             |
| $P_2$   | 24                            |
| $P_3$   | 16                            |
| $P_4$   | 10                            |
| $P_5$   | 3                             |

The Gantt chart for the above problem is shown below:

| $P_5$ | $P_1$ | $P_4$ | $P_3$ | $P_2$ |
|-------|-------|-------|-------|-------|
| 0     3 | 8 | 18 | 34 | 58 |

By observing the above example, we see that $P_5$ has the shortest CPU burst time. So we allocate $P_5$ the CPU first. After finishing $P_5$ the next shortest job is searched which is $P_1$ and CPU is given to $P_1$ the same process continuous till all the processes are finished. Now we calculate the average waiting time, Average turn around time and Average response time.

**(i) Average Waiting Time:**

Waiting time = Starting time − Arrival time

| Process | Starting Time | Arrival Time | Waiting Time |
|---------|---------------|--------------|--------------|
| $P_1$   | 3             | 0            | 3            |
| $P_2$   | 34            | 0            | 34           |
| $P_3$   | 18            | 0            | 18           |
| $P_4$   | 8             | 0            | 8            |
| $P_5$   | 0             | 0            | 0            |

∴ Average waiting time = 3 + 34 + 18 + 8 + 0

$$= \frac{63}{5} = 12.6 \text{ milliseconds}$$

**(ii) Average Turn Around Time:**

Turn around time = Finish time − Arrival time

| Process | Finish Time | Arrival Time | Turn Around Time |
|---------|-------------|--------------|------------------|
| $P_1$   | 8           | 0            | 8                |
| $P_2$   | 58          | 0            | 58               |
| $P_3$   | 34          | 0            | 34               |
| $P_4$   | 18          | 0            | 18               |
| $P_5$   | 3           | 0            | 3                |

$$\therefore \quad \text{Average turn around time} = \frac{8 + 58 + 34 + 18 + 3}{5}$$

$$= \frac{121}{5} = 24.2 \text{ milliseconds}$$

**(iii) Average Response Time:**

Response time = First Response Time – Arrival time

| Process | First Response Time | Arrival Time | Response Time |
|---|---|---|---|
| $P_1$ | 3 | 0 | 3 |
| $P_2$ | 34 | 0 | 34 |
| $P_3$ | 18 | 0 | 18 |
| $P_4$ | 8 | 0 | 8 |
| $P_5$ | 0 | 0 | 0 |

$$\therefore \quad \text{Average Response time} = \frac{3 + 34 + 18 + 8 + 0}{5}$$

$$= \frac{63}{5} = 12.6 \text{ milliseconds}$$

### Advantage

1. It's having the least Average waiting time, Average turn around time and Average Response time.

### Disadvantages

1. It is difficult to know the length of the next CPU burst time.
2. As it is optimal algorithm it cannot be implemented in short-term CPU scheduling.
3. "Aging is another problem where big jobs are waiting for long-time in the CPU.
4. Starvation of process having long burst time may cause because processor is selecting the process having smallest burst time.

## 4.5.3 Priority Scheduling

- SJF algorithm is a special case of Priority scheduling algorithm.
- Priority is assigned to each process and CPU is allocated to the process with highest priority. Equal priority process is scheduled with FCFS algorithm.
- Priorities are the numbers ranging from 0 to 7 or 0 to 4095 given to each processes. Some systems use low numbers to represent low priority and other use low numbers for high priority. Here we use low numbers to represent high priority.
- Protocol is set whether 0 is the highest or lowest priority.
    1. **Starvation:** A major problem with priority scheduling is indefinite blocking or starvation. The high priority process indefinitely blocks a low priority process in a

heavily loaded system. As per algorithm high priority processes can prevent the low priority process for allocating CPU and thus such a process will never get a chance to allocate a CPU.

2. **Aging:** A solution to this problem is to gradually increase the priority of a process that wait in the system for a long time called as Aging.

**Note: Priority Scheduling (summarize):**
- A priority number (integer) is associated with each process.
- The CPU is allocated to the process with the highest priority (smallest integer = highest priority).
- Preemptive
- Non-preemptive
- SJF is a priority scheduling where priority is the predicted next CPU burst time.
- Problem = Starvation-low priority processes may never execute.
- Solution = Aging-as time progresses increase or decrease the priority of the process.

- Priorities are of two types:
  1. **Internal priorities:** Internally defined priorities use some measurable quantity to compute the priority of a process.
  2. **External priorities:** External priorities are set by criteria that are external to the operating system, such as the importance of the process.
- Priority scheduling are of two types:
  1. preemptive, and
  2. non-preemptive.
- When a process arrives at the ready queue, its priority is compared with the priority of the currently running process.
- A preemptive priority - scheduling algorithm will preempt the CPU if the priority of the newly arrived process is higher than the priority of the currently running process.
- A non-preemptive priority - scheduling algorithm will simply put the new process at the head of the ready queue.

**Ex. 1:** Consider the following set of processes. All processes arrived time 0 and in the order $P_1$, $P_2$, $P_3$, $P_4$, $P_5$ having CPU burst time in milliseconds.

**Sol.:**

| Process | Burst Time (in milliseconds) | Priority |
|---------|------------------------------|----------|
| $P_1$   | 10                           | 3        |
| $P_2$   | 1                            | 1        |
| $P_3$   | 2                            | 3        |
| $P_4$   | 1                            | 4        |
| $P_5$   | 5                            | 2        |

The Gantt Chart is:

| P$_2$ | P$_5$ | P$_1$ | P$_3$ | P$_4$ |
|---|---|---|---|---|
| 0 | 1 | 6 | 16 | 18 | 19 |

$$\text{Average waiting time} = \frac{6+0+16+18+1}{5} = 8.2 \text{ milliseconds}$$

**Ex. 2:** Consider the following set of processes:

| Process | CPU Burst Time (in milliseconds) | Priority |
|---|---|---|
| P$_1$ | 6 | 2 |
| P$_2$ | 12 | 4 |
| P$_3$ | 1 | 5 |
| P$_4$ | 3 | 1 |
| P$_5$ | 4 | 3 |

By observing the above example we can say that process P$_4$ has highest priority. Therefore, we allocate CPU to process P$_4$ first. The next priority is given to process P$_1$ and CPU is allocated to process P$_1$, next priority is given to process P$_5$, so the CPU is allocated to P$_5$ and this process continuous until all the process are completed.

The Gantt chart for the above example is shown below:

| P$_4$ | P$_1$ | P$_5$ | P$_2$ | P$_3$ |
|---|---|---|---|---|
| 0 | 3 | 9 | 13 | 25 | 26 |

**(i) The Average waiting time:**

| Process | Waiting time |
|---|---|
| P$_1$ | 3 |
| P$_2$ | 13 |
| P$_3$ | 25 |
| P$_4$ | 0 |
| P$_5$ | 9 |

$$\text{Average waiting time} = \frac{3 + 13 + 25 + 0 + 9}{5}$$

$$= \frac{50}{5}$$

$$= 10 \text{ milliseconds}$$

**(ii) The average turn around time:**

| Process | Turn around time |
|---------|------------------|
| $P_1$   | 9                |
| $P_2$   | 25               |
| $P_3$   | 26               |
| $P_4$   | 3                |
| $P_5$   | 13               |

$$\therefore \text{Average turn around time} = \frac{9 + 25 + 26 + 3 + 13}{5}$$

$$= \frac{76}{5}$$

$$= 15.2 \text{ milliseconds}$$

### 4.5.4 Round Robin (RR) Scheduling

- Round Robin (RR) Scheduling is designed for time-sharing system.
- Round Robin (RR) Scheduling is also called as FCFS scheduling along with preemption to switch between processes.
- In this scheduling algorithm we will define a time slice or time quantum generally from 10 to 100 ms. Ready queue is treated as circular queue and processes are entered in ready queue as they are coming in the system.
- CPU scheduler goes around this circular queue and CPU is allocated to each process for a fixed time slice.
- To implement RR algorithm, we keep the ready queue as a FIFO.
- New processes are added to the tail of the ready queue.
- The CPU scheduler picks from the ready queue, sets a timer to interrupt after 1 time quantum which will interrupt the operating system.
- A context switch will be executed, process will be put at a tail of ready queue.
- Example of RR with Time Quantum = 20

| Process | Burst Time |
|---------|------------|
| $P_1$   | 53         |
| $P_2$   | 17         |
| $P_3$   | 68         |
| $P_4$   | 24         |

The Gantt Chart is:

| $P_1$ | $P_2$ | $P_3$ | $P_4$ | $P_1$ | $P_3$ | $P_4$ | $P_1$ | $P_3$ | $P_3$ |
|-------|-------|-------|-------|-------|-------|-------|-------|-------|-------|
| 0   20 | 37 | 57 | 77 | 97 | 117 | 121 | 134 | 154 | 162 |

- Typically, higher average turnaround than SJF, but better response.
- In RR scheduling algorithm, no process is allocated to the CPU for more then one time quantum in a row. If a process CPU burst exceeds 1 time quantum, that process is preempted and is put back in ready queue. RR scheduling algorithm is preemptive.
- If there are n processes in ready queue and the time quantum is q, then each process gets 1/n of the CPU time in chunks of at most q time units.
- Each process must wait no longer then (n-1)*q time units until its next time quantum.
- For example, If there are 5 processes, with a time quantum of 20 ms, then each process will get up to 20 ms every 100 ms.
- The performance of RR algorithm depends heavily on then size of the time quantum.
- At one extreme, if the time quantum is very large (Infinite), RR policy is the same as the FCFS policy.
- If the time quantum is very small (say 1 Ms), RR approach is called processor sharing, and appears (in theory) to the users as though each on n processes has its own processor running 1/n in the speed of the real processor. This approach was used in the Control Data Corporation (CDC).
- In software, however, we need also to consider the effect of context switching on the performance of RR scheduling.
- Let's assume that we have only one process of 10 time units. If the quantum 12 time units, the process finishes in less then 1 time quantum with no overhead.
- If the quantum is 6 time units, however the process required 2 quanta, resulting in a context switch. If the time quantum is 1 time unit, 9 context switches will occurred, slowing the execution of the process accordingly, (Fig. 4.7)

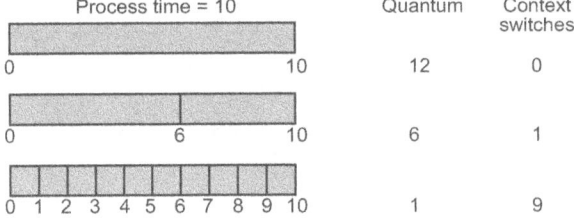

**Fig. 4.7: Time Quantum and Context Switch Time**

- Thus, we want the time quantum to be large with respect to the context switch time. If the context switch time is approximately 10 % of the time quantum, then about 10 % of the CPU time will be spent in the context switch.
- Turn around time also depends on the size of time quantum. As we can see from Fig. 4.8, the average turn around time of a set of processes does not necessarily improve as the time quantum size increases.
- In general, the average turn around time can be improved if most processes finish their next CPU burst in a single time quantum.
- For example, given three processes of 10 time units each and a quantum of 1 time unit, the average turn around time is 29. If the time quantum is 10, however, the average turn around time drops to 20.

- If context-switch time is added in, the average turn around time increases for a smaller time quantum, since more context switches will be required.

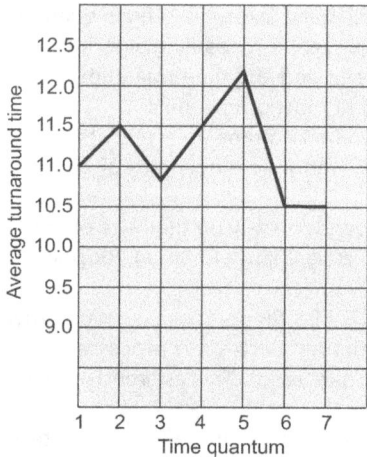

| Process | Time |
|---------|------|
| $P_1$ | 6 |
| $P_2$ | 3 |
| $P_3$ | 1 |
| $P_4$ | 7 |

**Fig. 4.8: Turnaround time varies with the Time Quantum**

- On the other hand, if the time quantum is too large, RR scheduling degenerates to FCFS policy. A rule of thumb is that 80% of CPU bursts should be shorter than the time quantum.
- Average waiting time is (0 + 20 + 37 + 57 + 57 + 40 + 40)
  - Each process gets a small unit of CPU time *(time quantum)*, usually 10-100 milliseconds. After this time has elapsed, the process is preempted and added to the end of the ready queue.
  - If there are *n* processes in the ready queue and the time quantum is q, then each process gets 1/*n* of the CPU time in chunks of at most *q* time units at once. No process waits more than (n-1)*q* time units.
  - Performance
    * Œq large .FIFO
    * Œq small .*q* must be large with respect to context switch, otherwise overhead is too high.

**Ex. 1:** Consider the following set of process that arrives at time 0, with the length of the CPU burst time given in milliseconds.

| Process | Burst Time |
|---------|------------|
| $P_1$ | 24 |
| $P_2$ | 3 |
| $P_3$ | 3 |

**Sol.:** If we use a time quantum of 4 milliseconds, then process $P_1$ gets the first 4 milliseconds. Since, it requires another 20 milliseconds, it is preempted after the first time quantum and the CPU is given to the next process in the queue process $P_2$. Since, process $P_2$ does not need 4 milliseconds, it quits before its time quantum expires. The CPU is then given to the next process, process $P_3$. Once, each process has received 1 time quantum, the CPU is returned to process $P_1$ for an additional time quantum. The resulting RR schedule is:

| $P_1$ | $P_2$ | $P_3$ | $P_1$ | $P_1$ | $P_1$ | $P_1$ | $P_1$ |
|---|---|---|---|---|---|---|---|
| 0    4 |    7 |   10 |   14 |   18 |   22 |   26 |   30 |

Round robin scheduling is always Preemptive Scheduling.
Waiting time = Start time – arrival time + new start time – old finish time.

∴ the average waiting time is $\frac{17}{3}$ = 5.66 milliseconds.

In RR scheduling algorithm, no process is allocated to the CPU for more than 1 time quantum in a row. If a process CPU burst time exceeds 1 time quantum, that process is preempted and is input back in the ready queue. The RR scheduling algorithm is preemptive.

**Ex. 2:** Consider the following set of processes

| Process | CPU Burst Time (in milliseconds) |
|---|---|
| $P_1$ | 30 |
| $P_2$ | 6 |
| $P_3$ | 8 |

Given the quantum is of 5 milliseconds.

**Sol.:** Initially process $P_1$ is given 5 milliseconds. When time quantum of $P_1$ expired, the CPU switches from process $P_1$ to $P_2$. When the time quantum of P2 expired, the process switches to process $P_3$. When time quantum of $P_3$ expired, the CPU switch to $P_1$ as $P_1$ was in the ready queue.

The below Gantt chart shows this:

| $P_1$ | $P_2$ | $P_3$ | $P_1$ | $P_2$ | $P_3$ | $P_1$ | $P_1$ | $P_1$ | $P_1$ |
|---|---|---|---|---|---|---|---|---|---|
| 0 | 5 | 10 | 15 | 20 | 21 | 24 | 29 | 34 | 39   44 |

**(i) Average waiting time:**
Waiting time = Start time – arrival time + new start time – old finish time.

For $P_1$ = 0 + (15 – 5) + (24 – 20) = 14
10 + 4 = 14
$P_2$ = 5 + (20 – 10) = 15
$P_3$ = 10 + (21 – 15) = 16
∴ Average waiting time =
= 45/3 = 15 milliseconds

## (ii) Average turn around time:

Turn around time for $P_1$ = 44
Turn around time for $P_2$ = 21
Turn around time for $P_3$ = 24

$$\therefore \text{ The average turn around time} = \frac{44 + 21 + 24}{3}$$

$$= \frac{89}{3}$$

$$= 29.66 \text{ milliseconds}$$

## (iii) Average response time:

Response time for $P_1$ = 0
Response time for $P_2$ = 5
Response time for $P_3$ = 10

$$\text{The average response time} = \frac{0 + 5 + 10}{3}$$

$$= \frac{15}{3}$$

$$= 5 \text{ millisecond}$$

- The performance of round robin depends on the size of time quantum chosen.

### 4.5.5 Multilevel Queue Scheduling

- These scheduling algorithms are created for areas in which we classify process into different groups.
- For example a common division can be made between foreground (or interactive) processes and background (or batch) processes.
- Priority of foreground processes may be higher than background processes.
- The multilevel queue - scheduling algorithm partitions the ready queue into several separate queues as shown in Fig. 4.9.

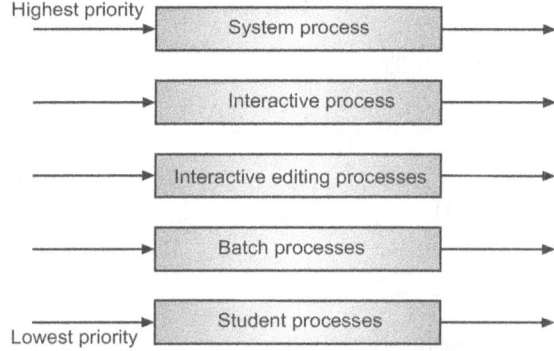

**Fig. 4.9: Multilevel Queue Scheduling**

- The processes are assigned to one queue depending on some property of the process.
- The property may be memory size, process priority or may be process type. Each queue is associated with its own scheduling algorithm.
- For example, separate queues might be used for foreground and background processes. The foreground queue might be scheduled by an RR algorithm and the background queue is scheduled by an FCFS algorithm.

### 4.5.6 Multilevel Feedback Queue Scheduling
- Multilevel feedback queue allows a process to move between queues. The idea is to separate process with different CPU - Burst characteristics.
- If a process uses too much CPU times, it will be moved to a lower priority queue. This leaves I/O bound and interactive processes in the higher priority queues.
- If a process waits for long time in a lower priority queue, then it is moved to a higher priority queue.
- This form of aging prevents starvation.
- **Example:** Consider a multilevel feedback queue scheduler with three queues and number them from 0 to 2 as shown in Fig. 4.10.

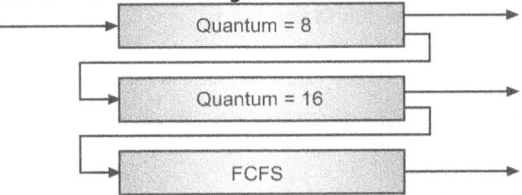

**Fig. 4.10: Multilevel Feedback Queues**

- The first task the scheduler does is that it executes all processes in queue 0. Only when queue 0 is empty then only it will go to queue 1 and then executes the process there in queue 1.
- Similarly, when queue 0 and queue 1 are empty then only it will process the processes in queue 2. But when a process is getting executed in queue 2 and at that time if a process arrives for queue 1 then it will preempt a process in queue 2. Similarly, when a process arrives for queue 0 will in turn preempt a process in queue 1.
- A process entering the ready queue is put in queue 0.
- A process is queue 0 is given a time quantum of 8 milliseconds.
- If it does not finish within this time, it is moved to the tail of queue 1.
- If queue 0 is empty, the process at the head of queue 1 is given a quantum of 16 milliseconds. If it does not complete, it is preempted and is put into queue 2.
- Processes in queue 2 are run on an FCFS basis only when queues 0 and 1 are empty.
- The below are the parameters for a multilevel feedback queue scheduler:
  o The number of queues.
  o The scheduling algorithm for each queue.
  o The method used to determine when to upgrade a process to a higher-priority queue.
  o The method used to determine when to demote a process to a lower priority queue.
  o The method used to determine which queue a process will enter when that process needs service.

## Exercise

1. What is meant by CPU scheduling?
2. What is CPU scheduler?
3. Describe the following scheduling schemes:
   (i) Preemptive scheduling, (ii) Non-primitive scheduling.
4. Explain scheduling criteria in detail.
5. With the help of example describe following scheduling algorithms:
   (i) FCFS (ii) RR (iii) SJF
6. With the help of diagram explain multilevel queue scheduling.
7. Describe the term priority scheduling with example.
8. What is the difference between preemptive and non-preemptive scheduling?
9. With the help of diagram describe CPU-I/O burst cycle.
10. Explain the term dispatcher in detail.
11. With suitable diagram describe multilevel feedback queue scheduling.
12. Compare RR and SJF scheduling algorithm.
13. Differentiate SJF and FCFS.
14. Calculate Average Turn Around Time and Average Waiting Time for all set of processes using SJF.

    | Process | Burst Time | Arrival Time |
    |---------|------------|--------------|
    | P1      | 4          | 1            |
    | P2      | 3          | 0            |
    | P3      | 2          | 2            |
    | P4      | 4          | 3            |
    | P5      | 1          | 2            |

15. Consider the following set of processes:

    | Process CPU | Burst Time (in milliseconds) |
    |-------------|------------------------------|
    | P1          | 30                           |
    | P2          | 6                            |
    | P3          | 8                            |

    Calculate the Average Waiting Time and Average Turnaround Time by using Round Robin CPU Scheduling Algorithm. (The time quantum is of 5 milliseconds).

16. Calculate Average Turn Around Time and Average Waiting Time for all set of processes using SJF.

    | Process | Burst Time | Arrival Time |
    |---------|------------|--------------|
    | P1      | 4          | 1            |
    | P2      | 3          | 0            |
    | P3      | 2          | 2            |
    | P4      | 4          | 3            |
    | P5      | 1          | 2            |

■■■

# Chapter 5...

# Process Synchronization

## Contents ...

5.1 Introduction
5.2 Critical Section Problem
5.3 Semaphores
    5.3.1 Concept
    5.3.2 Implementation
    5.3.3 Binary Semaphore
5.4 Deadlock and Starvation
5.5 Classical Problems of Synchronization
    5.5.1 Bounded Buffer Problem
    5.5.2 Readers and Writers Problem
    5.5.3 Dining Philosophers Problem
5.6 Critical Sections
    Exercise

## 5.1 INTRODUCTION

- The basic technique used to implement synchronization is to block a process until an appropriate condition is fulfilled.
- There are two kinds of synchronization one is control synchronization and another is data access synchronization.
    1. **Control synchronization:** In this synchronization the processes may wish to co-ordinate their activities with respect to one another such that a process performs an action only when some other processes reach specific points in their execution.
    2. **Data access synchronization:** In this synchronization race conditions should not arise when concurrent processes access shared data. It is used to ensure this by implementing mutual exclusion over accesses to shared data.
- In this chapter we discuss process synchronization techniques.

## 5.2 CRITICAL SECTION PROBLEM

- Consider a system consisting of n processes $\{P_0, P_1 ... P_{n-1}\}$. Each process has a segment of code, called a **Critical Section** in which the process may be changing common variables, updating a table, writing a file and so on.
- In a sense, updating of a shared variable may be regarded as a critical section. The critical section is a sequence of instructions with a clearly marked beginning and end. It usually safeguards of updating of one or more shared variables.
- When a process enters a critical section, it must complete all instructions there in before any other process is allowed to enter the same critical section. Only the process executing the critical section is allowed to access the shared variable.
- Thus, is often referred to as **mutual exclusion,** in which a single process temporarily excludes all other from using a shared resource in order to ensure the system's integrity.
- To be acceptable as a general tool, a solution to mutual exclusion problem should:
  1. Ensure mutual exclusion between processes accessing the protected shared resources.
  2. Make no assumption about relative speeds and priorities of contending processes.
  3. Guarantee that crashing of process outside of its critical section does not affect the ability of other contending processes to access the shared resource.
  4. When more than one process wishes to enter critical section, grant entrance to one of them in finite time.

```
            do
            {
                entry section
                critical section
                exit section
                remainder section
            } while(1);
```
**Fig. 5.1: General Structure of a Typical Process $P_i$**

1. **Software Approach:**
- Software approaches can be implemented for concurrent processes that execute on a single processor or a multiprocessor machine with shared main memory.
- The algorithms are explained for mutual exclusion for two processes.

2. **Processes:**
- When no process is executing in its critical section and some processes wish to enter their critical sections, then only those processes that are not executing in their remainder sections can participate in deciding which will enter its critical section next, and this selection cannot be postponed indefinitely.

## 3. Bounded waiting:

- There exists a bound on the number of times that other processes are allowed to enter their critical sections after a process has made a request to enter its critical section and before that request is granted.

### (i) First Algorithm:

Any attempt at mutual exclusion must rely on some fundamental exclusion mechanism in the hardware. The most common of these is the constraint that only one access to a memory location can be made at a time. Using this constraint, we reserve a global memory location labeled turn. A process ($P_0$ or $P_1$) wishing to execute its critical section first examines the contents of turn. If the value of turn is equal to the number of the process, then the process may proceed to its critical section. Otherwise, it is forced to wait. Our waiting process repeatedly reads the value of turn until it is allowed to enter its critical section. This procedure is known as **busy waiting** because the **thwarted** process can do nothing productive until it gets permission to enter its critical section. After a process has gained access to its critical section and after it has completed that section, it must update the value of turn to that of the other process. In formal terms there is a shared global variable.

```
int turn=0;
/* PROCESS 0 */
while(turn !=0)
    /* do nothing */;
/* critical section */;
    turn=1;
    /* PROCESS 1 */
while(turn !=1)
    /* do nothing */;
/* critical section */;
    turn=0;
```

**Fig. 5.2: First Algorithm**

- **Disadvantages:**
  - This solution guarantees the mutual exclusion property but has two drawbacks. First, processes must strictly alternate in their use of their critical section; thus the pace of execution is dictated by the slower of the two processes.
  - A much more serious problem is that if one process fails, the other process is permanently blocked. This is true whether a process fails in its critical section or outside of it.
- For example, assume process 0 is running. It finishes the critical section but crashes before it set turn = 1. Meanwhile process 1 wants to enter in critical section. But since value of variable turn is still zero. (Since, process 0 has crashed and unable to set turn = 1) process 1 will also go in loop.

### (ii) Second Algorithm:

The problem with the first algorithm is that it stores the name of the process that may enter its critical section, when in fact we need state information about both processes. In effect, each process should have its own key to the critical section so that if one fails, the other can still access its critical section. To meet this requirement a boolean vector flag is defined with flag [0] corresponding to $P_0$ and flag [1] corresponding to $P_1$. Each process may examine the others flag but may not alter it. When a process wishes to enter its critical section it periodically checks the other's flag until if that flag has the value false, indicating that the other process is not in its critical section. The process immediately sets its own flag to true and proceeds to its critical section. When it leaves its critical section, it sets its flag to false.

The shared global variable now is:
```
boolean flag [2] = {false, false}
```
Now, if one process fails outside the critical section, including the flag-setting code, then the other process is not blocked. In fact, the other process can enter its critical section as often as it likes, because the flag of the other process is always false. However, if a process fails inside its critical section or after setting its flag to true just before entering its critical section, then the other process is permanently blocked.

This solution is, if anything, wrong than the previous the first algorithm because it does not even guarantee mutual exclusion. Consider the following sequences:
- P0 executes the while statement and finds flag [1] set to false.
- P1 executes the while statement and finds flag [0] set to false.
- P0 sets flag [0] to true and enter its critical section.
- P1 sets flag [1] to true and enter its critical section.

Because both processes are now in their critical sections, the second algorithm is incorrect. The problem is that the proposed solution is not independent of relative process execution speeds.

```
/* Process 0 */
   :
   :
while(flag[1])
  /*do nothing */;
  flag[0] = true;
  /* critical section */
  flag[0] = false;
/* Process 1 */
   :
   :
while(flag[0])
  /*do nothing */
  flag[1] = true;
  /* critical section */
  flag[1] = false
```

**Fig. 5.3: Second Algorithm**

### (iii) Third Algorithm:

Because a process can change its state after the other process has checked it but before the other process can enter its critical section, the second algorithm failed. Perhaps we can fix this problem with a simple interchange of two statements, as shown in Fig. 5.4.

As before, if one process fails inside its critical section, including the flag setting code controlling the critical section, then the other process is blocked, and if a process fails outside the critical section, then the other process is not blocked.

Next, let us check that mutual exclusion is guaranteed. Using the point of view of process P0. Once P0 has set flag [0] to true, P1 cannot enter its critical section until after P0 has entered and left its critical section. It could be that P1 is already in its critical section when P0 sets its flag. In that case, P0 will be blocked by the while statement until P1 has left its critical section. The same reasoning applies from the point of view of P1.

This guarantees mutual exclusion but creates yet another problem. If both processes set their flags to true before either has executed the while statement, then each will think that the other has entered its critical section, causing deadlock.

```
P0 sets flag [0] to true
P1 sets flag [1] to true
P0 checks flag [1]
P1 checks flag [0]
P0 sets flag [0] to false
P1 sets flag [1] to false
P0 sets flag [0] to true
P1 sets flag [1] to true
```

This sequence could be extended indefinitely and neither process could enter its critical section.

```
/* Process 0*/
:
:
flag[0] = true;
while(flag [1])
/* do nothing */;
/* critical section */
flag[0] = false;
/* Process 1*/
:
:
flag[1] = true;
while(flag [0])
/* do nothing */;
/* critical section */
flag[1] = false;
```

**Fig. 5.4: Third Algorithms**

- The three failed attempts indicates that the mutual exclusion is not trivial one. The Dutch mathematician **Dekker** is believed to have been the first to solve the problem. Dekker's solution in its original form works for only two processes and cannot be easily extended beyond that number. **Dijkstra's** proposal of a mechanism for mutual exclusion among an arbitrary number of processed called **Semaphore,** has gained wide acceptance and found its way into number of experimental and commercial operating systems.

## 5.3 SEMAPHORES

### 5.3.1 Concept

- A semaphore is a shared integer variable with non-negative values which can only be subjected to following two operations.
    1. Initialization, and
    2. Invisible operations.
- The first major advance in dealing with the problems of concurrent processes came in 1965 with **Dijkstra's** solution. Dijkstra's proposal for mutual exclusion among an arbitrary number of processes is called **Semaphore.**
- A semaphore mechanism basically consists of two primitive operations SIGNAL and WAIT, (originally defined as P and V by Dijkstra), which operate on a special type of semaphore variables s.
- The semaphore variable can assume integer values, and except possibly for initialization may be accessed and manipulated only by means of the SIGNAL and WAIT operations.
- The two primitives take one argument each the semaphore variable and may be defined as follows.
    1. **Wait(s):** Decrements the value of its argument semaphore, s, as soon as it would become non-negative. Completion of WAIT operation, once the decision is made to decrement its argument semaphore, must be indivisible.
    2. **Signal(s)**: Increments the value of its argument semaphore, s, as an indivisible operation. The logic of busy wait versions of the WAIT and SIGNAL operations is given in Fig. 5.5.

```
                struct semaphore
                    { int count;
                      queue Type queue;
                    };
                void wait(semaphore s)
                { s.count--;
                    if(s.count<0)
                    {
                    place a process P in s.queue;
                      block this process.
                    }
                }
                void signal(semaphore s)
                  {
                    s.count++;
                    if(s.count<=0)
                    {
                      remove a process P from s.queue;
                      place process P on ready list;
                    }
                  }
```

**Fig. 5.5: A Busy – wait Implementation of WAIT and SIGNAL**

## 5.3.2 Implementation

- A semaphore is a protected variable whose value can be accessed and altered only by the operations P and V and initialization operation called 'Semaphoiinitislize'.
- Binary Semaphores can assume only the value 0 or the value 1 counting semaphores also called general semaphores can assume only nonnegative values.
- The P (or wait or sleep or down) operation on semaphores S, written as P(S) or wait (S), operates as follows:

    P(S): IF S > 0
    THEN S:= S - 1
    ELSE (wait on S)

- The V (or signal or wakeup or up) operation on semaphore S, written as V(S) or signal (S), operates as follows:

    V(S): IF (one or more process are waiting on S)
    THEN (let one of these processes proceed)
    ELSE S:= S +1

- Operations P and V are done as single, indivisible, atomic action. It is guaranteed that once a semaphore operations has stared, no other process can access the semaphore until operation has completed. Mutual exclusion on the semaphore, S, is enforced within P(S) and V(S).
- If several processes attempt a P(S) simultaneously, only process will be allowed to proceed. The other processes will be kept waiting, but the implementation of P and V guarantees that processes will not suffer indefinite postponement.
- Semaphores solve the lost-wakeup problem.
- Producer-Consumer Problem Using Semaphores
- The Solution to producer-consumer problem uses three semaphores, namely, full, empty and mutex.
- The semaphore 'full' is used for counting the number of slots in the buffer that are full. The 'empty' for counting the number of slots that are empty and semaphore 'mutex' to make sure that the producer and consumer do not access modifiable shared section of the buffer simultaneously.

**Initialization**

Set full buffer slots to 0.

i.e., semaphore Full = 0.

Set empty buffer slots to N.

i.e., semaphore empty = N.

For control access to critical section set mutex to 1.

i.e., semaphore mutex = 1.

 Producer ( )
 WHILE (true)
 produce-Item ( );
 P (empty);
 P (mutex);
 enter-Item ( )
 V (mutex)
 V (full);
 Consumer ( )
 WHILE (true)
 P (full)
 P (mutex);
 remove-Item ( );
 V (mutex);
 V (empty);
  consume-Item (Item)

### 5.3.3 Binary Semaphore

- A more restricted version is called **Binary semaphore.** It may only take on the values 1 and 0. It can be implemented as shown in Fig. 5.6.
- For both semaphores a queue is used to hold processes waiting on semaphore. The process that has been blocked the longest is released from the queue first. A semaphore whose definition includes this policy is called a **Strong Semaphore.**
- A semaphore that does not specify the order in which processes are removed from the queue is a **Weak Semaphore.**

```
Struct binary-semaphore
    {
    enum (zero, one) value;
    queueType queue;
    };
void waitB (binary-semaphore s)
    {
    if(s.value==1)
      s.value=0;
    else
        {
            place this process in s.queue;
        block this process;
        }
    }
void signalB (binary semaphore s)
{if (s.queue is_empty( ) )
    s.value = 1;
    else
        {
        remove a process P from s.queue;
        place process P on ready list;
        }
    }
```

**Fig. 5.6: Binary Semaphore**

- To illustrate use of semaphores consider Fig. 5.7.
- A binary semaphore MUTEX is used to protect the shared resource by enforcing its use in mutually exclusive manner. Each process ensures the integrity of its critical section by opening it with WAIT and closing it with SIGNAL operations.
- To illustrate the behaviour and functioning of semaphores, a possible scenario of run-time behaviour of the three processes is shown in Table 5.1.
- Initially MUTEX is initialized to 1 to indicate availability of shared resources at time M1. At time M2, all processes are active and ready to enter their respective critical sections, so they executes a WAIT statement and semaphore variable is decremented to 0, indicating that a process has been granted permission to enter critical section. Line M3 tells P1 is the winner.
- The WAIT activated on P1's behalf, after having read value of MUTEX as 1, must immediately seize the semaphore variable and prevent other, concurrent WAITS from reading it until decrementing of MUTEX to 0 is completed. After this P1 enters critical section and uses the shared resource during the subsequent time M3.
- P1 relinquishes the resources, leaves critical section and announces the fact by executing SIGNAL operation. The two waiting processes P2 and P3, have an equal chance of obtaining next permission. Assume P2 gets permission and it enters in critical section.
- At time M7 process P2 releases the resource and semaphore variable is equal to 1. At this time P1 and P3 attempt to access resource.
- As per our example P1 wins and P3 continue to wait for next opportunity.

```
program smutex;
var mutex: semaphore; {binary}
  void P1( )
{
  while(true)
    {
    wait(mutex);
    critical section;
    signal (mutex);
  other - processing;
    { while {
{P1}

  void P2 ( )
   {
   while (true)
     {
```

```
   wait (mutex);
   critical section;
   signal (mutex);
   other processing;
   { while }
   { P2 }
   void P3( )
   {
   while(true)
   {
    wait(mutex);
    critical section;
    signal(mutex);
    other processing;
   { while }
   { P3 }

   void smutex( )
   {
   mutex=1;
   initiate P1, P2, P3
   }
```

Fig. 5.7: Mutual Exclusion with Semaphore

**Table 5.1: A scenario of execution**

| Time | Process Status / Activity | | | Mutex 1 = FREE 0 = BUSY | Processes: In critical section; attempting to enter |
|------|---|---|---|---|---|
| | P1 | P2 | P3 | | |
| M1 | - | - | - | 1 | - ; - |
| M2 | Wait (mutex) | Wait (mutex) | Wait (mutex) | 0 | ; P1, P2, P3 |
| M3 | Critical section | Waiting | Waiting | 0 | P1; P2, P3 |
| M4 | Signal (mutex) | Waiting | Waiting | 1 | - ; P2, P3 |
| M5 | Other P1 process | Critical Section | Waiting | 0 | P2; P3 |
| M6 | Wait (mutex) | Critical Section | Waiting | 0 | P2; P3, P1 |
| M7 | Waiting | Signal (mutex) | Waiting | 1 | -; P3, P1 |
| M8 | Critical Section | Other process | Waiting | 0 | P1; P3. |

## 5.4 DEADLOCKS AND STARVATION

- The implementation of a semaphore with a waiting queue may result in a situation where more than two processes are waiting indefinitely for an event that can be caused only by one of the waiting processes.
- The event in question is the execution of a signal() operation.
- When such a state is reached, these processes are said to be deadlocked.
- To illustrate this approach, we consider a system consisting of two processes, $P_0$ and $P_1$, each accessing two semaphores, S and Q, set to the value 1:

| $P_0$ | $P_1$ |
|---|---|
| wait(S); | wait(Q); |
| wait(Q); | wait(S); |
| . | . |
| . | . |
| . | . |
| signal(S); | signal(Q); |
| signal(Q); | signal(S); |

- Suppose that $P_0$ executes wait(S) and then $P_1$ executes wait(Q).
- When $P_0$ executes wait(Q), it must wait until $P_1$ executes signal(Q). Similarly, when $P_1$ executes wait(S), it must wait until $P_0$ executes signal(S).
- Since, these signal() operations cannot be executed, $P_0$ and $P_1$ are deadlocked.
- We say that a set of processes is in a deadlock state when every process in the set is waiting for an event that can be caused only by another process in the set.
- The events with which we are mainly concerned here are resource acquisition and release.
- Another problem related to deadlocks is indefinite blocking, or starvation, a situation in which processes wait indefinitely within the semaphore. Indefinite blocking may occur if we remove processes from the list associated with a semaphore in LIFO (Last-In, First-Out) order.

## 5.5 CLASSICAL PROBLEM OF SYNCHRONIZATION

### 5.5.1 Bounded Buffer Problem

- Bounded buffer problem is commonly used to illustrate the power of synchronization primitives.
- In general, the producer/consumer problem may be stated as follows:
  - Given a set of co-operating processes, some of which 'produce' data item (producers) to be consumed by others (consumers), with possible disparity between production and consumption rates.
  - Devise a synchronization protocol that allows both producers and consumers to operate concurrently as their respective service rates in such a way that produced items are consumed in the exact order in which they are produced (FIFO).

## (i) Producer and Consumer with an unbounded buffer:

Here, we assume that buffer is of unbounded capacity. After the system is initialized, a producer must be the first process to run in order to provide the first item. From that point on, a consumer process may run whenever there is more than one item in the buffer produced but not yet consumed. Given the unbounded buffer, producers may run at any time without restrictions. We also assume that all items produced and subsequently consumed have identical, but unspecified structure. The buffer may be implemented as an array, a linked list, or any other collection of data items. The first solution is as given in Fig. 5.8.

Since, producer and consumer both accesses same buffer, buffer manipulation procedure must be placed within a critical section protected by a semaphore.

```
/* Program producer - consumer */
int n;
binary semaphore mutex = 1;
general_semaphore produced = 0;
void producer( )
  {
    while(true)
    {
    produce( );
    wait(mutex);
    place_in_buffer;
    signal (mutex);
    signal (produced);
    }
  }
void consumer( )
  {
    while(true)
    {
    wait(produce);
    wait(mutex);
    take_from_buffer;
    signal(mutex);
    consume;
    }
  }
void main( )
  {
      initiate producer, consumer;
  }
```

**Fig. 5.8: Producer/Consumer Bounded Buffer**

Consequently, a number of producers and consumers may execute concurrently. The initial value of produced is set to 0. When an item is produced, it is placed in the buffer, and the fact is signaled by means of the general semaphore PRODUCED. The nature of the problem implies that the consumer can never get ahead of the producer; since consumer is waiting on PRODUCED semaphore. When item is produced then only consumer can enter in critical section by applying wait on mutex semaphore.

Adding two semaphores must be handled with care because two semaphores may interact in a undesirable manner. Consider for e.g. Reversing the order of WAIT operations in consumer process. As a consequence, waiting on PRODUCED semaphore is moved into critical section controlled by MUTEX. This in turn, may deadlock the system from very start. For instance assume that where a producer is busy preparing in first item, a consumer process becomes scheduled. MUTEX is initially FREE and consumer enters in critical section. It has no item to consume and it is forced to wait on PRODUCED semaphore. However no producer can ever succeed in placing its item in buffer since MUTEX is busy. Consequently consumer remains in critical section forever and system is deadlocked. This tells that although semaphores are powerful tool, their use by no means automatically solve all timing problems.

**(ii) Producers and Consumers with a bounded buffer:**

The unbounded – buffer assumption simplifies analysis of producer – consumer problem by allowing unrestricted execution of producers. However this assumption unrealistic since, computer system, which have finite memory capacity.

The main difference imposed by bounded buffer is that both consumer and producer may be halted under certain circumstances. At any particular time the shared global buffer may be empty, partially filled or full. A producer process may run in either of two former cases, but all producers must be kept waiting when buffer is full similarly when buffer is empty consumer must wait.

Let i count be the number of items produced but not yet consumed so,

```
icount = produced - consumed.
```

If we have finite capacity then,

```
0 < icount < capacity.
```

Since, producer may run only when there are some empty slots in buffer it can be said,

```
mayproduce: icount < capacity.
```

Consumers can execute only when there is atleast one item produced but not yet consumed i.e.

```
mayconsume: icount>0.
```

In practice, buffers are usually implemented in circular fashion, using linked list. Two indices in and out, point to next slot available for a produced item and to the place where the next item is to be consumed from respectively.

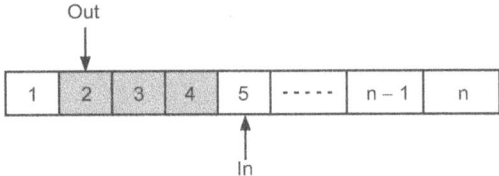

**Fig. 5.9: Producer/Consumer Buffer**

Fig. 5.10 shows a solution to bounded buffer producer/consumer problem. General semaphores MAYPRODUCE and MAYCONSUME represent two conditions introduced earlier to control execution of producer and consumer. Two binary semaphores PMUTEX and CMUTEX protect buffer and index manipulations of producers and consumers.

```
buffer → array [1 - capacity];
Semaphore mayproduce, mayconsumer, /* general */
binary semaphore Pmutex, cmutex;
void producer( )
{
item pitem;
 while(true)
    {
        wait(mayproduce);
        pitem=produce;
    wait(pmutex);
    buffer[in] = pitem;
    In=(in mod capacity) +1;
    Signal(pmutex);
    Signal(mayconsume);
    }
}
void consumer( )
{
    item citem;
    {
    while(true)
    {
    wait(mayconsume);
    wait(cmutex);
    citem = buffer [out];
    out=(out mod capacity) +1;
    signal(cmutex);
    signal(mayproduce);
    consume (item);
    }
    }
void paraent process( )
    {
```

```
                        in = 1;
                        out = 1;
                        signal(pmutex);
                        signal(cmutex);
                        mayconsume = 0;
                        for(i=1 to capacity)
                        {signal(mayproduce);
    }
    }
```

**Fig. 5.10: Producer / Consumer Bounded Buffer**

Initially mayproduce is set to capacity to indicate producer can produce that many item. Whenever consumer completes its cycle, it implies a slot by removing the consumed item from buffer and signals the fact via the mayproduce. The mayconsume semaphore indicates availability of produced items, and it functions much the same way as in unbounded buffer.

### 5.5.2 Readers and Writers Problems

- Readers and writers is another classical problem in concurrent programming. It basically resolves around a number of processes using a shared global data structure.
- The processes are categorized depending on their usage of the resource, as either readers or writers.
- A reader never modifies the shared data structure, whereas a writer may both read it and write into it. A number of readers may use the shared data structure concurrently because no matter how they are interleaved, they cannot possibly compromise its consistency.
- Writers, on the other hand, must be granted exclusive access to data.
- The problem may be stated as follows:
  o Given a universe of readers that read a common data structure and a universe of writers that modify the same common data structure.
  o Device a synchronization protocol among the readers and writers that ensure consistency of common data while maintaining as high a degree of concurrency as possible.
- One approach to solve readers/writers problem is as shown in Fig. 5.10. The writer process waits on binary semaphore WRITE to grant it permission to enter the critical section and to use the shared resources.
- A reader, on the other hand, goes through two critical sections, one before and one after using the resource. Their purpose is to allow a large number of readers to execute concurrently while making sure that readers are kept away when writers are active.
- An integer, READERCOUNT is used to keep track of the number of readers actively using the resource.
- In Fig. 5.11, first reader passes through MUTEX, increments the number of readers and waits on writers if any. While reader is reading data, semaphore MUTEX is free and WRITE is busy to allow multiple readers only.

- If there are writers, waiting they are prevented by busy WRITE semaphore. When READERCOUNT reaches to zero writers can enter in critical section.
- Even if this solution has high degree of concurrency it faces starvation of writer by postponing them indefinitely when readers are active.
- A strategy proposed by Hoare (1974) holds promise for both readers and writers to complete in finite time. It suggests that,
    - A new reader should not start if there is writer waiting, (prevent starvation of writer).
    - All readers waiting at the end of a write should have priority over next writer, (prevents starvation of readers).

```
/* Program readers_ writers*/
int readercount;
binary_semaphore mutex, write;
void reader( )
  {
  while(true)
  {
  wait(mutex);
  readercount ++;
  If(readercount==1)
  wait(write)
  signal(mutex);
    /* read data */
  wait(mutex)
  readercount - -;
  if(readercount==0)
  signal(write);
  }
  }
void writer( )
  {
  while(true)
  {
      wait (write);
      ..................
  /* write data */
  signal(write)
  }
  }
void parentprocess( )
  {readercount=0;
  signal(mutex);
  signal(write);
  initiate readers, writers
  }
```

**Fig. 5.11: Readers/Writers**

### 5.5.3 Dining – Philosophers Problem

- Consider five philosophers who spend their lives thinking and eating.
- The philosophers share a common circular table surrounded by five chairs, each belonging to one philosopher.
- In the center of table is a bowl of rice, and the table is laid with five single chopsticks (Fig. 5.12).
- When a philosopher thinks, she does not interact with her colleagues. From time to time, a philosopher gets hungry and tries to pick up the two chopsticks that are closest to her, (the chopsticks that are between her and her left and right neighbour).
- A philosopher may pick up only one chopstick at a time. Obviously, she cannot pick up a chopstick that is already on the hand of a neighbour.
- When a hungry philosopher has both her chopsticks at the same time, she eats without releasing her chopsticks. When she is finished eating, she puts down both of her chopsticks and start thinking again.

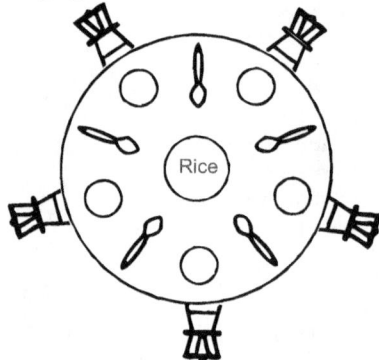

**Fig. 5.12: The Situation of Dining Philosophers**

- The dining – philosopher problem is considered a classic synchronization problem.
- One simple solution is to represent each chopstick of a semaphore.
- A philosopher tries to grab the chopstick by executing a wait operation on that semaphore. She releases her chopsticks by executing the signal operation on the appropriate semaphores.
- Thus, the shared data are,

    ```
    Semaphore chopsticks[5];
    ```
- Where all the elements of chopsticks are initialized to 1. Structure of philosopher i is shown in Fig. 5.13.

```
do{
    wait (chopsticks[i]);
    wait(chopsticks[(i+1)%5]);
    ……
    eat
    s ……
    signal(chopstick[i]);
    signal(chopstick[(i+1)%5]);
    ……
    think
    ……
} while(1)
```

**Fig. 5.13: Structure of Philosopher**

- Although this solution guarantees that no two neighbors are eating simultaneously, it nevertheless must be rejected because it has the possibility of creating a deadlock. Suppose that all five philosophers become hungry simultaneously, and each grabs her left chopstick.
- All elements of chopstick will now be equal to 0. When each tries to grabs right chopstick she will be delayed forever. We can solve this by allowing to pick chopsticks only if both are available.

## 5.6 CRITICAL SECTIONS

- A race condition on a data item arises when many processes concurrently update its value. Data consistency requires that only one process should update the value of a data item at any time, this is ensured through the notion of a Critical Section (CS).
- A critical section for a data item d is a section of code which cannot be executed concurrently with itself or with other critical section(s) for d.
- Thus, at any moment at most one process can execute a critical section for a data item. Hence, a critical section for a data item d is a mutual exclusion region with respect to d.
- Race conditions on d are avoided by performing all updates of d inside a critical section for d.
- Further, to ensure that processes see consistent values of d, references to d should also occur inside a critical section for d. If a process $p_i$ is executing a critical section on d, any other process wishing to enter a critical section of d will have to wait till $p_i$ exists from the critical section.
- A critical section is represented by a dashed rectangular box in a program.
- Fig. 5.14 shows use of critical section in airline reservation.

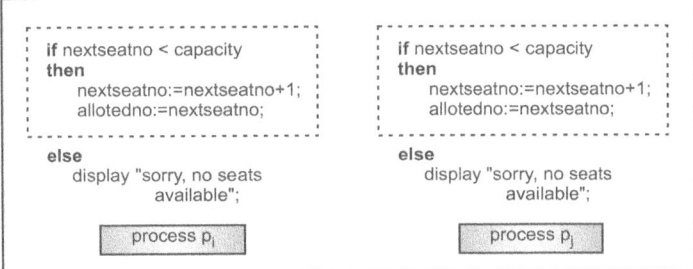

**Fig. 5.14: Critical section in Airline**

- An implementation of a critical section for a data item d must possess the following properties:
  1. **Correctness:** At most one process may execute a critical section at any given moment.
  2. **Progress:** When a critical section is not in use, one of the processes wishing to enter it will be granted entry to the critical section.
  3. **Bounded wait:** After a process $p_i$ has indicated its desire to enter a critical section, the number of times other processes gain entry to the critical section ahead of $p_i$ is bounded by a finite integer.
  4. **Deadlock freedom:** The implementation is free of deadlocks.
- Fig. 5.15 shows the typical form of a process using a critical section.
- The process is cyclic in nature. In each cycle, the process uses the critical section and also performs other computations represented by the step "remainder of the cycle".
- When the process only wishes to access shared data, the critical section is used to safeguard consistency of the data.
- When the process requires synchronization with other processes, the critical section is used to guard the consistency of some control data introduced for the purpose of synchronization.

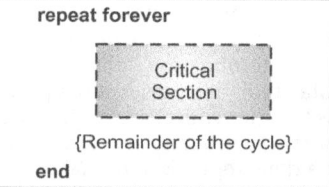

**Fig. 5.15: A typical form of a process**

### Exercise

1. What is meant by process synchronization?
2. Describe critical section problem in detail.
3. What is meant by deadlock and starvation?
4. Explain readers-writers problem in detail.
5. With suitable example describe bounded buffer problem in detail.
6. What is semaphore?
7. What is meant by binary semaphore?
8. Explain diving and philosophers problem of synchronization in detail.

# Chapter 6...

# Deadlock

## Contents ...
6.1 Introduction
    6.1.1 Principles of Deadlock
    6.1.2 System Model
6.2 Deadlock Characterization
6.3 Necessary Conditions
6.4 Resource Allocation Graph
6.5 Deadlock Prevention
6.6 Deadlock Avoidance
    6.6.1 Safe State
    6.6.2 Resource Allocation Graph Algorithm
    6.6.3 Banker's Algorithm
6.7 Deadlock Detection
6.8 Recovery from Deadlock
    6.8.1 Process Termination
    6.8.2 Resource Preemption
    Exercise

## 6.1 INTRODUCTION

- In general, high overall resource utilization and the possibility of parallel operation of many input/output devices driven by **concurrent processes**, contribute significantly to high performance potential of multitasking and multiprogramming systems.
- At the same time, concurrency and high resource utilization also provide the necessary conditions for deadlocks.

### 6.1.1 Principles of Deadlock

- Deadlock can be defined as "the permanent blocking of a set of processes that either compete for system resources or communicate with each other".
- In other words, when a process request resources, if the resources are not available at that time, the process enters a wait state.
- Waiting process may never again change state, because resources they have requested are held by other waiting processes. This situation is called **deadlock**.

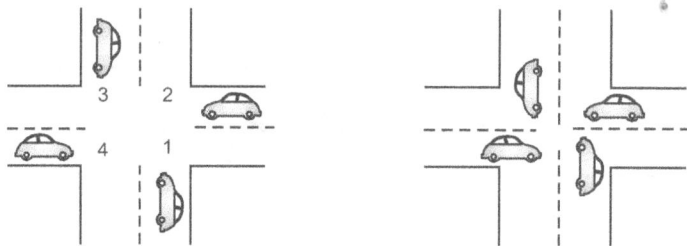

**Fig. 6.1: Illustration of Deadlock**

- All deadlocks involve conflicting needs for resources by two or more processes.
- A common example is the traffic deadlock.
- Fig. 6.1 shows a situation in which four cars have arrived at four-way stop intersections at approximately the same time.
- The four quadrants of the intersection are the resources over which control is needed.
- In particular, if all four cars wish to go straight through the intersection, the resource requirements are as follows:
    - Car travelling north needs quadrants 1 and 2.
    - Car travelling west needs quadrants 2 and 3.
    - Car travelling south needs quadrants 3 and 4.
    - Car travelling east needs quadrants 4 and 1.
- If all four cars arrive at about the same time, each will refrain from entering the intersection causing a deadlock.

## 6.1.2 System Model

- A system consists of a finite number of resources to be distributed among a number of competing processes. The resources are partitioned into several types, each of which consists of some number of identical instances.
- Memory, space, CPU cycles, files and input/output devices such as printers, tape drives are examples of resource types. If a system has two CPUs then the resources type CPU has two instances.
- A process must request a resource before using it, and must release the resource after using it. A process may request as many resources as it requires carrying out its designated task.
- Obviously, the number of resources requested may not exceed the total number of resources available in the system. For example, a process cannot request three printers if the system has only two.
- Under the normal mode of operation a process may utilize a resource in only the following sequence.
    - **Request:** If the request cannot be granted immediately, then the requesting process must wait until it can acquire the resource.
    - **Use:** The process can operate on the resource.
    - **Release:** The process releases the resource.

- A set of processes in a deadlock state when every process in the set is waiting for event that can be caused only by another process in the set. The events with which we are mainly concerned here are resource acquisition and release.

### Example of Deadlock State

- To illustrate a deadlock state, we consider a system with three tape drives.
- Suppose each of the three **processes** holds are of these tape drives. If each process now requests another tape drive, the three processes will be in a deadlock state.
- Each is waiting for the event "tape drive is released' which can be caused only by one of the other waiting processes.
- This example illustrates a deadlock involving the same resource type.
- Deadlocks may also involve different resource types. For example, consider a system with one printer and one tape drive. Suppose process $P_i$ is holding the tape drive and process $P_j$ is holding the printer.
- If $P_i$ requests the printer and $P_j$ requests the tape drive, deadlock occurs.
- A programmer who is developing multithreaded application must pay particular attention to this problem. Multithreaded programs are good candidates for deadlock because multiple threads can compete for shared resources.

## 6.2 DEADLOCK CHARACTERIZATION

- In a deadlock, processes never finish executing and system resources are tied up, preventing either jobs from starting.
- Before we discuss the various methods for dealing with the deadlock problems, we shall describe features that characterize deadlocks.
- A deadlock situation can arrive if the following four conditions hold simultaneously in a system.
    1. **Mutual Exclusion:** Atleast one resource must be held in a non-sharable mode; that is, only one process at a time can use the resource. If another process requests that resource, the requesting process must be delayed until the resource has been released.
    2. **Hold and Wait:** A process must be holding atleast one resource and waiting to acquire additional resources that are currently being held by other processes.
    3. **No pre-emption:** Resources cannot be pre-empted; that is, a resource can be released only voluntarily by the process holding it, after that process has completed its task.
    4. **Circular wait:** There must exist a set $\{P_0, P_1, ..., P_n\}$ of waiting processes must exist such that $P_0$ is waiting for a resource that is held by $P_1$, $P_1$ is waiting for a resource that is held by $P_2$, ..., $P_{n-1}$ is waiting for a resource that is held by $P_n$ and $P_n$ is waiting for a resource that is held by $P_0$.

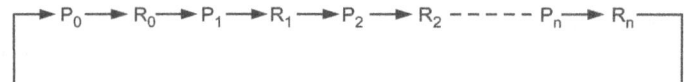

**Fig. 6.2: Circular wait**

- Above all four conditions must hold for a deadlock to occur.

## 6.3 NECESSARY CONDITIONS

- Necessary conditions of deadlock are: Mutual Exclusion, Hold and Wait, No Pre-emption and Circular Wait.
- **Mutual Exclusion:** At least one resource is held in a non sharable mode; that is only one process at a time can use the resource. Example monitor, printer etc. If another process requests that resource, the requesting process must be delayed until the resource has been released. Each resource is either currently assigned to exactly one process or is available.
- **Hold and Wait:** There must exist a process that is holding at least one resource and is waiting to acquire additional resources that are currently being held by another process. Process currently holding resources that were granted earlier can request for new resources.
- **No Pre-emption:** Resources cannot be pre-empted; i.e. resource can only be released voluntarily by the process holding it, after the process has completed its task. Resources previously granted cannot be forcibly taken away from a process. They must be explicitly released by the process holding them.
- **Circular Wait:** There exist a set ($P_o$, $P_i$, ... $P_n$) of waiting processes such that $P_o$ is waiting for a resource which is held by $P_1$, $P_1$ is waiting for a resource which is held by $P_2$. $P_{n-1}$ is waiting for resources which are held by $P_n$ and $P_n$ is waiting for a resource which is held by $P_o$. Thus, there must be a circular chain of two or more processes, each of which is waiting for a resource held by the next member of the chain.

## 6.4 RESOURCE ALLOCATION GRAPH

- Deadlock can be described more precisely in terms of a directed graph called a system resource-allocation graph. This graph consist of a set of vertices V and a set of edges E.
- The set of vertices V is partitioned into two different types of nodes:
$$P = \{P_1, P_2, P_3, ... P_n\}$$
- The set consisting of all the active processes in the system, and
$$R = [R_1, R_2, R_3, ... R_m\}$$
- The set consisting of all resource types in the system.
- A directed edge from process $P_i$ to resource type $R_j$ is denoted by:
$$P_i \rightarrow R_j - \textbf{request edge}$$
- It signifies that process $P_i$ requested an instance of resource type $R_j$ and is currently waiting for that resource.

- A directed edge from resource type $R_j$ to process $P_i$ is denoted by:
  $$R_j \rightarrow P_i - \textbf{assignment edge}$$
- It signifies that an instance of resource type $R_j$ has been allocated to process $P_i$.
- When process $P_i$ request an instance of resource type $R_j$, a request edge is inserted in the resource allocation graph.
- When this request can be fulfilled, the request edge is instantaneously transformed to an assignment edge. When the process no longer needs access to the resource, it release the resource and result is assignment edge is deleted.
- The resource allocation graph is shown in Fig. 6.3.

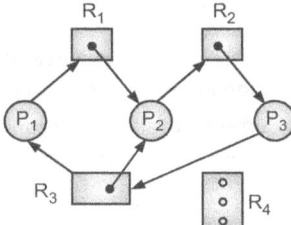

**Fig. 6.3: Resource Allocation Graph**

- Pictorially process $P_i$ is represented as a circle and each resource, $R_j$ as square since resource type $R_j$ may have more than one instance, we represent each such instance as a dot within the square.
- Also note that a request edge points to only square $R_j$, whereas an assignment edge must also designate one of the square.
  - The sets P, R and E
    - $P = \{P_1, P_2, P_3\}$
    - $R = \{R_1, R_2, R_3, R_4\}$
    - $E = \{P_1 \rightarrow R_1, P_2 \rightarrow R_3, R_1 \rightarrow P_2, R_2 \rightarrow P_2, R_2 \rightarrow P_1, R_3 \rightarrow P_3\}$
  - Resource instances
    - One instance of resource type $R_1$.
    - Two instance of resource type $R_2$.
    - One instance of resource type $R_3$.
    - Three instance of resource type $R_4$.
  - Process states
    - Process $P_1$ is holding an instance of resource type $R_2$, and is waiting for an instance of resource type $R_1$.
    - Process $P_2$ is holding an instance of $R_1$ and $R_2$ and is waiting for an instance of resource type $R_3$.
    - Process $P_3$ is holding an instance of $R_3$.

- Given the definition of resource allocation graph, it can be shown that if the graph contains no cycles, then no process in a system is deadlocked. If the graph contains a cycle, then a deadlock may exist.
- If each resource type has one instance, then a cycle implies that a deadlock has occurred. If the cycle involves only a set of resource types, each of which has only a single instance, then a deadlock has occurred. Each process involved in a cycle is deadlocked.
- In this case, cycle in the graph is both necessary and a sufficient condition for the existence of deadlock if single instance of each and every resource is there in graph.
- If each resource type has several instances, then a cycle does not necessarily imply that a deadlock has occurred. In this case, cycle is necessary but not sufficient condition for the existence of deadlock.
- To illustrate this concept, let us return to the resource-allocation graph shown in Fig. 6.3. Suppose the process $P_3$ requests an instance of resource type $R_2$.
- Since, no resource instance is currently available, a request edge $P_3 \rightarrow R_2$ is added to the graph, (Fig. 6.4). At this time, two minimal cycles exist in the system.

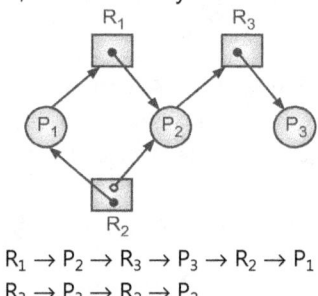

$P_1 \rightarrow R_1 \rightarrow P_2 \rightarrow R_3 \rightarrow P_3 \rightarrow R_2 \rightarrow P_1$
$P_2 \rightarrow R_3 \rightarrow P_3 \rightarrow R_2 \rightarrow P_2$

**Fig. 6.4: Resource Allocation Graph with a Deadlock**

- Process $P_1$, $P_2$, $P_3$ is deadlocked. Process $P_2$ is waiting for resource $R_3$, which is held by process $P_3$, on the other hand, is waiting for either process $P_1$ or process $P_2$ to release resource $R_2$.
- In addition, process $P_1$ is waiting for process $P_2$ to release resource $R_1$.
- Now consider the resource allocation graph in Fig. 6.5. In this example, we have a cycle.

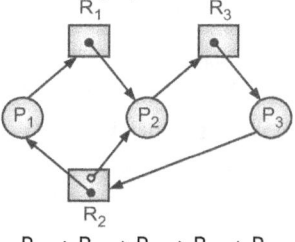

$P_1 \rightarrow R_1 \rightarrow P_3 \rightarrow R_2 \rightarrow P_1$

**Fig. 6.5: Resource-Allocation Graph with a Cycle but no Deadlock**

- However, there is no deadlock because process $P_4$ may release its instance of resource type $R_2$. That resource can be allocated to $P_3$, breaking the cycle.
- In short, if a resource allocation graph does not have a cycle, then the system is not in a deadlock state. On the other hand, if there is a cycle, then the system may or may not be in a deadlock state.

## Methods for Handling Deadlocks

- There are three ways to handle the deadlock.
    - We can use a protocol to **prevent** or **avoid deadlocks,** ensuring that the system will never enter a deadlock state.
    - We can allow the system to enter a deadlock state, **detect** it and recover.
    - We can ignore the problem altogether and pretend that deadlock never occur in the system.
- **Deadlock Prevention:** Deadlock prevention is a set of methods for ensuring that atleast one of the necessary conditions cannot hold.
- **Deadlock Avoidance:** It requires that the operating system be given in advance additional information concerning which resources a process will request and use during its lifetime. With this additional information, we can decide for each request can be satisfied or must be delayed.
- **Deadlock Detection and Recovery:** If system does not employ either a deadlock - prevention or a deadlock avoidance algorithm, then deadlock situation may occur. In this case, the system can provide an algorithm for deadlock detection and recovery.
- **Deadlock Never Occur:** In many systems, deadlock occur infrequently so no mechanism for deadlock detection and recovery is provided.
- But we may arrive at a situation where the system is in deadlock state yet has no way of recognizing what has happened. In this case, the undetected deadlock will result in the deterioration of the system performance, because resources are being held by processes that cannot run, and because more and more processes as they make requests for resources, enter a deadlock state.
- Eventually, the system will stop functioning and will need to be restarted manually. Although this method does not seem to be a viable approach to the deadlock problem, it is nevertheless used in some operating systems.

## 6.5 DEADLOCK PREVENTION

- For deadlock to occur, each of the four necessary conditions must hold.
- By ensuring that atleast one of these conditions cannot hold, we can prevent the occurrance of a deadlock.

- Now, in the following we will see how we can deny each of the four conditions.

1. **Mutual Exclusion:**
   - The mutual-exclusion condition must hold for non-sharable resources.
   - Sharable resources, on the other hand, do not require mutually exclusive access, and thus, cannot be involved in a deadlock.
   - For example, read only files. If several processes attempt to open read only file at the sametime, they can be granted simultaneous access to file.
   - Example of non-sharable resource is printer, it can not be simultaneously shared by several processes and sharable resource example is Read only files.
   - In general however, we cannot prevent deadlocks by denying the mutual exclusion condition because some resources are intrinsically non-sharable.

2. **Hold and Wait:**
   - To ensure that hold-and-wait condition never occurs in the system, we must guarantee that, whenever process requests resource, it does not hold any other resources.
   - The hold and wait condition can be eliminated by requiring or forcing a process to release all resources held by it whenever it request a resource that is not available.
   - In other words deadlocks are prevented because waiting processes are not holding any resources.
   - These are basically two possible implementations of this strategy.
     1. The process requests all needed resources prior to commencement of execution.
     2. The process requests resources incrementally in the course of execution but releases all its resources holding upon encountering a denial.
   - In first method to request all resources at the outset, a job or process must preclaim all of its resource needs. This task is somewhat easier for batch jobs, whose resource requirements are often deducible from the job control statements.
   - The overestimation problem is present whenever resource requirements must be stated in advance of execution. The overestimation problem is present whenever resource requirements must be stated in advance of execution.
   - When all resources needed by a process are acquired at the outset, they are allocated and made unavailable to other processes during the lifetime of the owner process.
   - The problem is that some of these resources may actually be used only during a portion of the execution of the related processes; say at beginning (card reader) or at end (printer).
   - Therefore, same resources can be idle for relatively large periods of time but, for the sake of deadlock prevention, they cannot be allocated to other requesting processes.
   - Deadlock prevention by means of advanced acquiring of all estimated resources can result in law resource utilization.

- In second method to acquire resources incrementally as needed and to prevent deadlocks by releasing all resources held by process when it requests a temporarily unavailable resource.
- This strategy avoids the disadvantages of preclaiming and holding all resources from the inception of a process. The disadvantage of this method is that same resources cannot easily be releaved and required at a later time.
- For example, some irreversible changes made to memory or to files may corrupt the system if not carried to completion.

3. **No Preemption:**
   - Deadlock condition can obviously be denied by allowing preemption that is by authorizing the system to revoke ownership of certain resources from blocked processes.
   - Since, preemption is involuntary from the point of view of the affected process, the operating system must be charged with saving the state and restarting it when the process is later resumed.
   - This makes preemption of resources even more difficult than voluntary release and resumption of resources.
   - Preemption is possible for certain types of resources such as CPU and main memory, since the CPU portion of process state is routinely saved during the process switch operation, and the contents of preempted memory pages can be swapped out to secondary storage.
   - However, some types of resources such as partially updated files, cannot be preempted without corruption of system.
   - Since, some resources cannot be safely preempted; this approach cannot provide complete deadlock prevention.

4. **Circular Wait:**
   - One way to prevent the circular wait condition is by linear ordering of different types of system resources. In this approach system resources are divided into different classes $C_j$ where $j = 1, ..., n$.
   - Deadlock are prevented by requiring all processes to request and acquire their resources in a strictly increasing order of the specified system resource classes.
   - Moreover, acquisition of all resources within a given class must be made with a single request, and not incrementally.
   - For example, once a process acquire a resource belonging to class $C_j$, it can only request resources of class $j + 1$ or higher thereafter.
   - Linear ordering of resource classes eliminates the possibility of circular waiting, since a process $P_i$ holding a resource in class $C_i$ cannot possibly wait for any process that is itself waiting for a resource in class $C_i$ or lower.

- A disadvantage of this approach is that resources must be acquired in the prescribed order, as opposed to being requested when actually needed.
- These may cause some resources to be acquired well in advance of their actual user, thus lowering the degree of concurrency by making unused resources unavailable for allocation to other processes.

## 6.6 DEADLOCK AVOIDANCE

- The basic idea of deadlock avoidance is to grant only those requests for available resources that can't possibly result in a state of deadlock.
- Deadlock prevention prevents deadlock by restraining how requests can be made.
- The restraints ensure that atleast one of the necessary conditions for deadlock cannot occur, and hence, that deadlock cannot hold.
- Possible side effects of preventing deadlock are low device utilization, and reduced system throughput.
- An alternative method to deadlock avoidance is to acquire additional information about how resources are to be requested.
- For example, in a system with one tape drive and one printer, we might be told that process P will request first the tape drive, and later the printer, before releasing both resources.
- Process Q, on the other hand, will request first the printer, and then the tape drive. With this knowledge of the complete sequence of requests and releases for each process, we can decide for each request whether or not the process should wait.
- Each request requires that the system consider the resources currently available, the resources currently allocated to each process, and the future requests and releases of each process, to decide whether the current request can be satisfied or must wait to avoid a possible future deadlock.
- The various algorithms are available to handle this situation.
- The simplest and most useful model requires that each process declare the maximum number of resources of each type that it may need.
- Given a priori information about the maximum number of resources of each type that may be requested for each process, it is possible to construct an algorithm that ensures that the system will never enter a deadlock state. This algorithm defines the **deadlock-avoidance approach**.
- A deadlock-avoidance algorithm dynamically examines the resource-allocation state to ensure that a circular wait condition can never exist.
- The resource-allocation state is defined by the number of available and allocated resources, and the maximum demands of the processes.

### 6.6.1 Safe State

- A state is **safe** if the system can allocate resources to each process in some order and still avoid a deadlock.
- A system is in safe state only if there exists a **safe sequence.**
- A sequence of processes <$P_1, P_2, ..., P_n$> is a safe sequence for the current allocation state if for each $P_i$, the resource that $P_i$ can still request can be satisfied by the currently available resources plus the resources held by all the $P_j$, with j < i. In this situation, if the resources that process $P_i$ needs are not immediately available, then $P_i$ can wait until all $P_j$ have finished.
- When they have finished, $P_i$ can obtain all of its needed resources, and complete its task. After completion of task $P_i$ returns all allocated resources and then terminates.
- When $P_i$ terminates, $P_{i+1}$ can obtain its required resources, and so on. If no such sequence exist then the system is said to be **unsafe**.
- A safe state is not a deadlock state.
- A deadlock state is an unsafe state, however all unsafe states are not deadlocks.
- An unsafe state can result in deadlock. As long as the state is safe, the operating system can avoid unsafe states.
- In an unsafe state, the operating system cannot prevent processes from requesting resources such that a deadlock occurs.
- The behaviour of the processes controls unsafe states.
- Fig. 6.6 shows safe states unsafe state and deadlock state spaces.

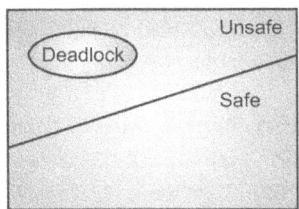

**Fig. 6.6: Safe, Unsafe and Deadlock States Spaces**

- For example, consider a system with 12 magnetic tape drives and there are three processes $P_0$, $P_1$ and $P_2$. Process $P_0$ requires 10 tape drives, process $P_1$ may need as many as 4 and process $P_2$ may need upto 9 tape drives. Suppose that, at time $t_0$ process $P_0$ is holding 5 tape drives, process $P_1$ is holding 2, and process $P_2$ is holding 2 tape drives.

| Maximum Needs | | Current Needs |
|---|---|---|
| $P_0$ | 10 | 5 |
| $P_1$ | 4 | 2 |
| $P_2$ | 9 | 2 |

- Currently, there are 3 tape drives free. At time $t_0$, the system is in safe state. The sequence <$P_1$, $P_0$, $P_2$> satisfies the safety condition.
- Process $P_1$ can immediately be allocated all its tape drives and then after finishing it can return them.
- The system will have now 5 tapes drives available then process $P_0$ can get all its tape drive as it needs 5 tape drives.
- After $P_0$ finishes it will return all tape drives allocated to it. Thus, now system has 10 free tape drives that can be finally allocated to process $P_2$. After $P_2$ finishes system will have all 12 tape drives free.
- A system may go to a unsafe state from a safe state.
- For example, suppose that at time $t_1$, process $P_2$ requests and is allocated 1 more tape drive. The system is no longer in safe state. At this point, only process $P_1$ can be allocated all its tape drives since there are only two tape drives free. When it finishes and return tape drives, the system will have only 4 available tape drives. Since, process $P_0$ is allocated 5 tape drives, but has a maximum of 10, it may then request 5 more tape drives. Since, they are unavailable, process $P_0$ must wait. Similarly, process $P_2$ may request an additional 6 tape drives and have to wait, resulting in a deadlock.
- The problem arised because the request from process $P_2$ for 1 more tape drive is satisfied. If we had made $P_2$ wait until either of the other processes had finished and released its resources, then we could have avoided deadlock.
- Given a concept of a safe state, we can define avoidance algorithms that ensures that the system will never deadlock. The idea is simply to ensure that the system will always remain in a safe state.
- In this scheme, if a process requests a resource that is currently available, it may still have to wait. Thus, resource utilization may be lower than it would be without a deadlock avoidance algorithm.

### 6.6.2 Resource Allocation Graph Algorithm
- If we have a resource allocation system with only one instance of each resource type, a variant of the resource allocation defined in section 6.4 can be used for deadlock avoidance.
- In addition to the request and assignment edges, we introduce a new type of edge called a **claim edge**.
- A claim edge $P_i \rightarrow R_j$ indicates that process $P_i$ may request resource $R_j$ at some time in the future. This edge resembles a request edge in direction, but is represented by a dashed line.
- When process $P_i$ requests resource $R_j$, the claim edge $P_i \rightarrow R_j$ is converted to request edge.
- Similarly, when a resource $R_j$ is released by $P_i$ the assignment edge $R_j \rightarrow P_i$ is reconverted to a claim edge $P_i \rightarrow R_j$. We note that the resource must be claimed a priori in the system.

- That is, before process $P_i$ starts executing all its claim edges must already appear in the resource-allocation graph.
- We can relax this condition by allowing a claim edge $P_i \to R_j$ to be added to the graph only if all the edges associated with process $P_i$ are claim edges.
- Suppose that process $P_i$ requests resource $R_j$. The request can be granted only if converting the request edge $P_i \to R_j$ to an assignment edge $R_j \to P_i$ does not result in the formation of a cycle in the resource allocation graph.
- Note that we check for safety by using a cycle-detection algorithm.
- An algorithm for detecting a cycle in this graph requires an order of $n^2$ operations, where n is the number of processes in the system.
- If no cycle exists, then the allocation of resource will leave the system in a safe state. If a cycle is found, then the allocation will put the system in an unsafe state. Therefore, process $P_i$ will have to wait for its requests to be satisfied.

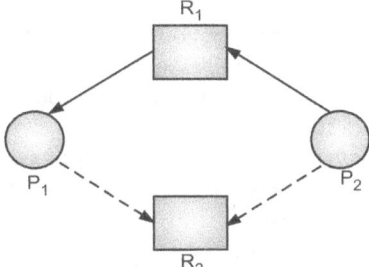

**Fig. 6.7: Resource Allocation Graph for Deadlock Avoidance**

- To illustrate this algorithm, we consider the resource allocation graph of Fig. 6.7.
- Suppose that $P_2$ requests $R_2$. Although $R_2$ is currently free, we cannot allocate it to $P_2$, since this action will create a cycle in the graph, (Fig. 6.8).
- A cycle indicates that the system is in an unsafe state. If $P_1$ requests $R_2$, and $P_2$ requests $R_1$ the deadlock will occur.

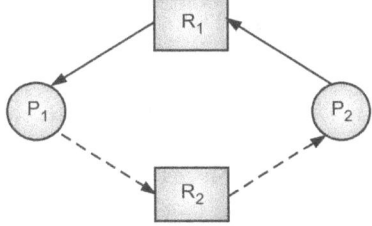

**Fig. 6.8: An Unsafe State in a Resource-Allocation Graph**

### 6.6.3 Banker's Algorithm

- The resource-allocation graph algorithm is not applicable to a resource allocation system with multiple instances of each resource type.
- The deadlock avoidance algorithm that we describe next is applicable to such a system, but is less efficient than the resource-allocation graph scheme this algorithm is commonly known as the Banker's algorithm.
- The name was chosen because this algorithm could be used in banking system to ensure that the bank never allocates its available cash such that it can no longer satisfy the needs of all its customers.
- When a new process enters the system, it must declare the maximum number of instances of each resource type that it may need. This number may not exceed the total number of resources in the system.
- When a user requests a set of resources, the system must determine whether the allocation of these resources will leave the system in a safe state. If it will, the resources are allocated; otherwise, the process must wait until some other process releases enough resources.
- Several data structures must be maintained to implement the Banker's algorithm. These data structures encode the state of the resource allocation system. Let n be the number of processes in the system and m be the number of resource types.
- We need the following data structures.

    **Available:** A vector of length m indicates the number of available resources of each type. If Available [j] = k, there are k instances of resource type $R_j$ available.

    **Max:** An n × m matrix defines the maximum demand of each process. If Max [i,j] = k, then process $P_i$ may request at most k instances of resource type $R_j$.

    **Allocation:** An n × m matrix defines the number of resources of each type currently allocated to each process.
    If Allocation[i, j]=k, then process $P_i$ is currently allocated k instances of resource type $R_j$.

    **Need:** An n × m matrix indicates the remaining resource need of each process.
    If Need[i, j]=k, then process $P_i$ may need k more instances of resource type $R_j$ to complete its task. Note that Need[i, j] = Max[i, j] − Allocation[i, j].
    These data structures vary over time in both size and value.
    To simplify the presentation of the Banker's algorithm, let us establish some notation. Let X and Y be vectors of length n. We say that X ≤ Y if and only if X[i] ≤ Y[i] for all i = 1, 2, 3, ..., n.
    For example, if X = (1, 7, 3, 2) and Y = (0, 3, 2, 1) then Y ≤ X. Y < X if Y ≤ X and Y ≠ X.

- We can treat each row in the matrices **Allocation** and **Need** as vectors and refer to them as **Allocation$_i$**, and **Need$_i$**, respectively.
- The vector Allocation$_i$ specifies the resources currently allocated to process $P_i$; the vector Need$_i$ specifies the additional resources that process $P_i$ may still request to complete its task.

## Safety Algorithm

- The algorithm for finding out whether or not a system is in a safe state can be described as follows:
  1. Let Work and Finish be vectors of length m and n, respectively.
     Initialize Work:= Available and
     Finish[i]:= false for i = 1, 2, ..., n
  2. Find an i such that both
     (a) Finish[i] = false
     (b) $Need_i \leq Work$
     If no such i exists, go to Step 4.
  3. Work:= Work + $Allocation_i$
     Finish[i]:= true
     go-to Step 2
  4. If Finish[i] = true for all i,
     then the system is in safe state.
- This algorithm may require an order of $m \times n^2$ operations to decide whether a state is safe.

## Resource-Request Algorithm

- Let $Request_i$ be the request vector for process $P_i$. If $Request_i[j]=k$, then process $P_i$ wants k instances of resource type $R_j$.
- When a request for resources is made by process $P_i$, the following action are taken.
  1. If $Request_i \leq Need_i$, go to Step 2. Otherwise, raise an error condition, since the process has exceeded its maximum claim.
  2. If $Request_i \leq Available$, go to Step 3.
     Otherwise, $P_i$ must wait, since the resources are not available.
  3. Have the system pretend to have allocated the requested resources to process $P_i$ by modifying the state as follows:
     ```
     Available:= Available - Request_i;
     Allocation:= Allocation_i + Request_i;
     Need_i:= Need_i - Request_i;
     ```
- If the resulting resource-allocation state is safe, the transaction is completed and process $P_i$ is allocated its resources.
- However, if the new state is unsafe, then $P_i$ must wait for **$Request_i$** and the old resource-allocation state is restored.

**Ex. 1:** Consider a system with five processes $P_0$ through $P_4$ and three resource types A, B, C. Resource type A has 10 instances, resource type B has 5 instances, and resource type C has 7 instances. Suppose that at time $T_0$, the following snapshot of the system has been taken.

| Resources Type | Instances |
|---|---|
| A | 10 |
| B | 5 |
| C | 7 |

|  | Allocation<br>A B C | Max<br>A B C | Available<br>A B C |
|---|---|---|---|
| $P_0$ | 0 1 0 | 7 5 3 | 3 3 2 |
| $P_1$ | 2 0 0 | 3 2 2 | |
| $P_2$ | 3 0 2 | 9 0 2 | |
| $P_3$ | 2 1 1 | 2 2 2 | |
| $P_4$ | 0 0 2 | 4 3 3 | |

**Allocation** indicates number of resources allocated by each process.
**Max** indicates maximum number of resources required by each process.
**Available** indicates, after allocation, how many total resources are available.
The content of the matrix **Need** is defined to be Max-Allocation and is,

|  | Need | | |
|---|---|---|---|
| $P_0$ | 7 | 4 | 3 |
| $P_1$ | 1 | 2 | 2 |
| $P_2$ | 6 | 0 | 0 |
| $P_3$ | 0 | 1 | 1 |
| $P_4$ | 4 | 3 | 1 |

We claim that the system is currently in a safe state. Indeed, the sequence, <$P_1$, $P_3$, $P_4$, $P_2$, $P_0$> satisfy the safety criteria.

Suppose now that process $P_1$ requests one additional instance of resource type A and two instances of resource type C so $Request_1$ = (1, 0, 2).

To decide whether this request can be immediately granted, we first check that,

$$Request_1 \leq Available$$

i.e. $(1, 0, 2) \leq (3, 3, 2)$

which is true. We then pretend that this request has been fulfilled, and we arrive at the following new state.

|       | Allocation | | | Need | | | Available | | |
|-------|---|---|---|---|---|---|---|---|---|
|       | A | B | C | A | B | C | A | B | C |
| $P_0$ | 0 | 1 | 0 | 7 | 4 | 3 | 2 | 3 | 0 |
| $P_1$ | 3 | 0 | 2 | 0 | 2 | 0 |   |   |   |
| $P_2$ | 3 | 0 | 2 | 6 | 0 | 0 |   |   |   |
| $P_3$ | 2 | 1 | 1 | 0 | 1 | 1 |   |   |   |
| $P_4$ | 0 | 0 | 2 | 4 | 3 | 1 |   |   |   |

We must determine whether this new state is safe. To do so, we execute our safety algorithm and find that the sequence,

$$<P_1, P_3, P_4, P_0, P_2>$$

satisfies our safety requirement. Hence, we can immediately grant the request of process $P_1$. You should be able to see, however, that when the system is in this state, a request for (3, 3, 0) by $P_4$ cannot be granted, since the resources are not available. A request for (0, 2, 0) by $P_0$ cannot be granted, even though the resources are available, since the resulting state is unsafe.

**Ex. 2:** Consider the total amount of resources $R_1$, $R_2$ and $R_3$ are 9, 3 and 6 units. In the current state allocation have been made to the four processes, leaving 1 unit of resource 2 and 1 unit of resource 3 available. Now, we will find whether the system is in safe state. We need to find whether the difference between the current allocation and maximum requirement. In any process be met with the available resources clearly, this is not possible for $P_1$, which has only 1 unit of $R_1$ and require 2 more unit of $R_1$ 2 units of $R_2$ and 2 units of $R_3$. However, by assigning one unit of $R_3$ to process $R_2$, $P_2$ has its maximum required resources allocated and can run to completion. Let us assume that this is accomplished.

|       | $R_1$ | $R_2$ | $R_3$ |
|-------|---|---|---|
| $P_1$ | 3 | 2 | 2 |
| $P_2$ | 6 | 1 | 3 |
| $P_3$ | 3 | 1 | 4 |
| $P_4$ | 4 | 2 | 2 |

Need Matrix

|       | $R_1$ | $R_2$ | $R_3$ |
|-------|---|---|---|
| $P_1$ | 1 | 0 | 0 |
| $P_2$ | 6 | 1 | 2 |
| $P_3$ | 2 | 1 | 1 |
| $P_4$ | 0 | 0 | 2 |

Allocation Matrix

| $R_1$ | $R_2$ | $R_3$ |
|---|---|---|
| 9 | 3 | 6 |

Resource Vector

| $R_1$ | $R_2$ | $R_3$ |
|---|---|---|
| 0 | 1 | 1 |

Available Vector

**(a) Initial State**

**Sol.:**

|       | $R_1$ | $R_2$ | $R_3$ |
|-------|---|---|---|
| $P_1$ | 3 | 2 | 2 |
| $P_2$ | 0 | 0 | 0 |
| $P_3$ | 3 | 1 | 4 |
| $P_4$ | 4 | 2 | 2 |

Need Matrix

|       | $R_1$ | $R_2$ | $R_3$ |
|-------|---|---|---|
| $P_1$ | 1 | 0 | 0 |
| $P_2$ | 0 | 0 | 0 |
| $P_3$ | 2 | 1 | 1 |
| $P_4$ | 0 | 0 | 2 |

Allocation Matrix

| $R_1$ | $R_2$ | $R_3$ |
|---|---|---|
| 6 | 2 | 3 |

Available Vector

**(b) $P_2$ runs to completion**

|   | $R_1$ | $R_2$ | $R_3$ |
|---|---|---|---|
| $P_1$ | 0 | 0 | 0 |
| $P_2$ | 0 | 0 | 0 |
| $P_3$ | 3 | 1 | 4 |
| $P_4$ | 4 | 2 | 2 |

Need Matrix

|   | $R_1$ | $R_2$ | $R_3$ |
|---|---|---|---|
| $P_1$ | 0 | 0 | 0 |
| $P_2$ | 0 | 0 | 0 |
| $P_3$ | 2 | 1 | 1 |
| $P_4$ | 0 | 0 | 2 |

Allocation Matrix

| $R_1$ | $R_2$ | $R_3$ |
|---|---|---|
| 7 | 2 | 3 |

Available Vector

**(c) $P_1$ runs to completion**

|   | $R_1$ | $R_2$ | $R_3$ |
|---|---|---|---|
| $P_1$ | 0 | 0 | 0 |
| $P_2$ | 0 | 0 | 0 |
| $P_3$ | 0 | 0 | 0 |
| $P_4$ | 4 | 2 | 3 |

Need Matrix

|   | $R_1$ | $R_2$ | $R_3$ |
|---|---|---|---|
| $P_1$ | 0 | 0 | 0 |
| $P_2$ | 0 | 0 | 0 |
| $P_3$ | 0 | 0 | 0 |
| $P_4$ | 0 | 0 | 2 |

Allocation Matrix

| $R_1$ | $R_2$ | $R_3$ |
|---|---|---|
| 9 | 3 | 4 |

Available Vector

**(d) $P_3$ runs to completion**

**Fig. 6.9: Determination of a Safe State**

When $P_2$ completes, its resources can be returned to the port of available resources. The resulting state is shown in Fig. 6.9 (b). Now, we can ask again if any of remaining processes can be completed. In tihs case, each of the remaining processes could be completed. Suppose, we choose $P_1$, allocate the required resources, complete $P_1$, and return all $P_1$'s resources to the available pool. We are left in the state shown in Fig. 6.9 (c). Next, we can complete $P_3$, resulting in state (Fig. 6.9 (d)). Finally, we can complete $P_4$. At this point, all of the processes have been run to completion. Thus, the state defined by Fig. 6.9 (a) is a safe state, and <$P_2$, $P_1$, $P_3$, $P_4$> is the safe sequence.

**Ex. 3:** The operating system contains 3 resources. The number of instances of each resource type are 7, 7, 10. The current resource allocation state is as shown as follows.

| Process | Current Allocation | | | Maximum Need | | |
|---|---|---|---|---|---|---|
|  | $R_1$ | $R_2$ | $R_3$ | $R_1$ | $R_2$ | $R_3$ |
| $P_1$ | 2 | 2 | 3 | 3 | 6 | 8 |
| $P_2$ | 2 | 0 | 3 | 4 | 4 | 3 |
| $P_3$ | 1 | 2 | 4 | 3 | 3 | 4 |

| Resources | Instances |
|---|---|
| $R_1$ | 7 |
| $R_2$ | 7 |
| $R_3$ | 10 |

(i) Is the current allocation in a safe state.

**Sol.:**

(i) First we calculate available matrix.

|  | Current Allocation | | | Max | | | Available | | |
|---|---|---|---|---|---|---|---|---|---|
|  | $R_1$ | $R_2$ | $R_3$ | $R_1$ | $R_2$ | $R_3$ | $R_1$ | $R_2$ | $R_3$ |
| $P_1$ | 2 | 2 | 3 | 3 | 6 | 8 | 2 | 3 | 0 |
| $P_2$ | 2 | 0 | 3 | 4 | 4 | 3 |  |  |  |
| $P_3$ | 1 | 2 | 4 | 3 | 3 | 4 |  |  |  |

Then, the Need matrix will be,

|  | Need | | |
|---|---|---|---|
|  | $R_1$ | $R_2$ | $R_3$ |
| $P_1$ | 1 | 4 | 5 |
| $P_2$ | 2 | 4 | 0 |
| $P_3$ | 2 | 1 | 0 |

Then, find safe sequence. Currently (2, 3, 0) resources available and need of resources of each process is given in Need matrix. So we can fulfill the requirement of $P_3$ process first. After finishing execution, $P_3$ will return all the resources to the system so new available resources will resources will be (3, 5, 4). Now the request of $P_2$ process can be satisfied after $P_2$ finishes it will also return the resources allocated to it.

Now available resources are (5, 5, 7), then the requirement of $P_1$ can be easily satisfied therefore, the safe sequence is <$P_3$, $P_2$, $P_1$> and the system is in safe state.

**Ex. 4:** Consider the following snapshot of the system.

| Process | Allocation | | | | Max | | | | Available | | | |
|---|---|---|---|---|---|---|---|---|---|---|---|---|
|  | A | B | C | D | A | B | C | D | A | B | C | D |
| $P_0$ | 0 | 0 | 1 | 2 | 0 | 0 | 1 | 2 | 1 | 5 | 2 | 0 |
| $P_1$ | 1 | 0 | 0 | 0 | 1 | 7 | 5 | 0 |  |  |  |  |
| $P_2$ | 1 | 3 | 5 | 4 | 2 | 3 | 5 | 6 |  |  |  |  |
| $P_3$ | 0 | 6 | 3 | 2 | 0 | 6 | 5 | 2 |  |  |  |  |
| $P_4$ | 0 | 0 | 1 | 4 | 0 | 6 | 5 | 6 |  |  |  |  |

Is the system safe? Justify?

If Yes, give safe sequence.

**Sol.:**

(i) Total number of instances,

| A | B | C | D |
|---|---|---|---|
| 3 | 14 | 12 | 12 |

(ii) Then Need matrix is,

|    | A | B | C | D |
|----|---|---|---|---|
| $P_0$ | 0 | 0 | 0 | 0 |
| $P_1$ | 0 | 7 | 5 | 0 |
| $P_2$ | 1 | 0 | 0 | 2 |
| $P_3$ | 0 | 0 | 2 | 0 |
| $P_4$ | 0 | 6 | 4 | 2 |

So the system is in safe state and safe sequence is,
<$P_0$, $P_2$, $P_3$, $P_4$, $P_1$>

## 6.7 DEADLOCK DETECTION

- If a system does not employ either a deadlock prevention or a deadlock avoidance algorithm, then a deadlock situation may occur.
- In this environment, the system must provide:
  - An algorithm that examines the state of the system to determine whether a deadlock has occurred.
  - An algorithm to recover from the deadlock.
- In the following discussions, we elaborate on these two requirements as they pertain to systems with only a single instance of each resource type, as well as to systems with several instances of each resource type.
- At this point, however, let us note that a detection and recovery scheme requires overhead that includes not only the run-time costs of maintaining the necessary information and executing the detection algorithm, but also the potential losses inherent in recovering from a deadlock.

1. **Single Instance of Each Resource Type:**
- If all resources have only a single instance then we can define a deadlock detection algorithm that uses a variant of the resource allocation graph, called a **wait-for graph**. We obtain this graph from the resource allocation graph by removing the nodes of type resource and collapsing the appropriate edges.
- More precisely, an edge from $P_i$ to $P_j$ in a wait-for graph implies that process $P_i$ is waiting for process $P_j$ to release a resource that $P_i$ needs. An edge $P_i \rightarrow P_j$ exists in a wait-for graph if and only if the corresponding resource allocation graph contains two edges $P_i \rightarrow R_q$ and $R_q \rightarrow P_j$ for some resource $R_q \rightarrow R_g$.
- For example, in Fig. 6.10, we present a resource-allocation graph and the corresponding wait-for graph.

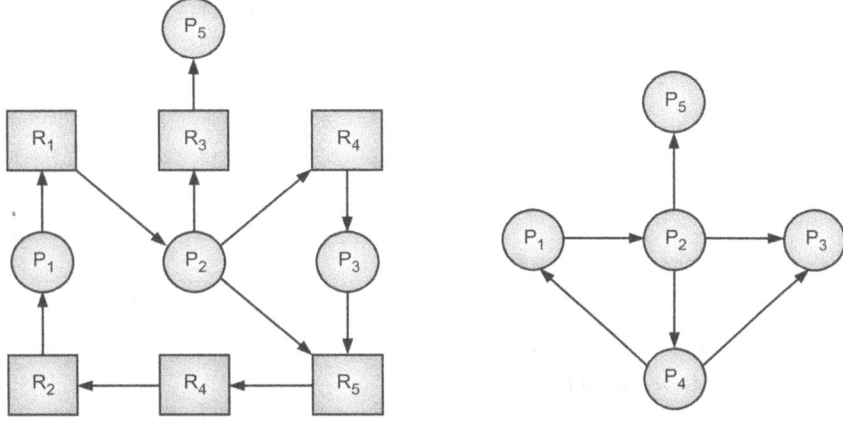

**(a) Resource-Allocation Graph**      **(b) Corresponding Wait for Graph**

**Fig. 6.10**

- As before, a deadlock exists in the system if and only if the wait-for graph contains a cycle. To detect deadlocks, the system needs to maintain the wait-for graph and periodically to invoke an algorithm that searches for a cycle in the graph.
- An algorithm to detect a cycle in a graph requires an order of $n^2$ operations, where n is the number of vertices in the graph.

2. **Several Instances of a Resource Type:**

- The wait for graph scheme is not applicable to a resource-allocation system with multiple instances of each resource type.
- The deadlock detection algorithm that we describe next is applicable to such a system.
- The algorithm employs several time-varying data structures that are similar to those used in the banker's algorithm.
    - **Available:** A vector of length m indicates the number of resources of each type.
    - **Allocation:** An n × m matrix defines the number of resources of each type currently allocated to each process.
    - **Request:** An n × m matrix indicates the current request of each process. If Request [i, j] = k, then process $P_i$ is requesting k more instances of resource type $R_j$.
- The ≤ relation between two vector is defined as in section 6.6.3. To simplify notation, we shall again treat the rows in the matrices Allocation and Request as vectors and shall refer to them as **Allocation$_i$** and **Request$_i$,** respectively.
- The detection algorithm described here simply investigates every possible allocation sequence for the processes that remain to be completed.
- Compare this algorithm with the banker's algorithm of Section 6.6.3.

1. Let Work and Finish be vectors of length m and n respectively.
   Initialize Work:= Available
   For i = 1, 2, ..., n, if Allocation i ≠ 0,
   then Finish[i]:= false;
   otherwise Finish[i]:= true
2. Find an index i such that both
   (a) Finish[i]:= false
   (b) $Request_i$ ≤ Work
   If no such i exists, go to Step 4.
3. Work:= Work + Allocation;
   Finish[i]:= true
   go to Step 2.
4. If Finish[i] = false, for some i, 1 ≤ i ≤ n,
   then the system is in deadlock state.
   Moreover, if Finish[i] = false, then processes $P_i$ is deadlocked.

- This algorithm requires an order of $m \times n^2$ operations to detect whether the system is in deadlocked state.
- You may wonder why we remain the resources of process $P_i$ (in Step 3) as soon as we determine that $Request_i$ ≤ Work (in Step 2b). We know that $P_i$ is currently not involved in a deadlock (Since, $Request_i$ ≤ Work),
- Thus, we take an optimistic attitude, and assume that Pi will require no more resources to complete its task; it will thus soon return all currently allocated resources to the system. If our assumption is incorrect, a deadlock may occur later.
- That deadlock will be detected next time that the deadlock-detection algorithm is invoked.

**Ex. 1:** To illustrate this algorithm, we consider a system with five processes $P_0$ through $P_4$ and three resource types A, B, C. Resource type A has 7 instances, resource type B has 2 instances, and resource type C has 6 instances. Suppose that at time $T_0$, we have the following resource allocation state.

|  | Allocation | | | Request | | | Available | | |
|---|---|---|---|---|---|---|---|---|---|
|  | A | B | C | A | B | C | A | B | C |
| $P_0$ | 0 | 1 | 0 | 0 | 0 | 0 | 0 | 0 | 0 |
| $P_1$ | 2 | 0 | 0 | 2 | 0 | 2 |  |  |  |
| $P_2$ | 3 | 0 | 3 | 0 | 0 | 0 |  |  |  |
| $P_3$ | 2 | 1 | 1 | 1 | 0 | 0 |  |  |  |
| $P_4$ | 0 | 0 | 2 | 0 | 0 | 2 |  |  |  |

We claim that the system is not in deadlocked state. Indeed if we execute our algorithm, we will find that sequence <$P_0$, $P_2$, $P_3$, $P_1$, $P_4$> will result in
   Finish[i] = true for all i.
Suppose now that process $P_2$ makes one additional request for an instance of type C.

The request matrix is modified as follows:

|     | Request |   |   |
|-----|---------|---|---|
|     | A       | B | C |
| $P_0$ | 0 | 0 | 0 |
| $P_1$ | 2 | 0 | 2 |
| $P_2$ | 0 | 0 | 1 |
| $P_3$ | 1 | 0 | 0 |
| $P_4$ | 0 | 0 | 2 |

We claim that the system is now deadlocked. Although we can reclaim the resources held by process $P_0$ the number of available resources is not sufficient to fulfill the request of other processes. Thus, a deadlock exists, consisting of processes $P_1$, $P_2$, $P_3$ and $P_4$.

**Ex. 2:** Apply the deadlock detection algorithm to the following data and show the results.

Available = (2, 1, 0, 0)

$$\text{Request} = \begin{matrix} P_1 \\ P_2 \\ P_3 \end{matrix} \begin{bmatrix} 2 & 0 & 0 & 1 \\ 1 & 0 & 1 & 0 \\ 2 & 1 & 0 & 0 \end{bmatrix}$$

$$\text{Allocation} = \begin{matrix} P_1 \\ P_2 \\ P_3 \end{matrix} \begin{bmatrix} 0 & 0 & 1 & 0 \\ 2 & 0 & 0 & 1 \\ 0 & 1 & 2 & 0 \end{bmatrix}$$

**Sol.:**

**Step 1:** Work := Available
= (2, 1, 0, 0)

**Step 2:** Request ≤ Work

In this Step 2 process $P_3$ fulfill the condition.

(2, 1, 0, 0) ≤ (2, 1, 0, 0)

**Step 3:**

Work : = Work + Allocation
Work : = (2, 1, 0, 0) + (0, 1, 2, 0)
= (2, 2, 2, 0)

In this way, we can finish the execution of $P_3$ Now we have (2, 2, 2, 0) available resources.

In this way, we have to repeat the procedure and finishes the execution of processes and here we will find that <$P_3$, $P_2$, $P_1$> will result in finish[i] = true for all i.

## 3. Detection Algorithm Usage:

- When should we invoke the detection algorithm? The answer depends on two factors.
  1. How often is a deadlock likely to occur?
  2. How many processes will be affected by deadlock when it happens?
- If deadlocks occur frequently, then the detection algorithm should be invoked frequently. Resources allocated to deadlocked processes will be idle until the deadlock can be broken. In addition, the number of processes involved in the deadlock cycle grow.
- Deadlocks occur only when some process makes a request that cannot be granted immediately. This request may be the final request that completes a chain of waiting processes.

- In the extreme, we could invoke the deadlock detection algorithm every time a request for allocation cannot be granted immediately. In this case, we can identify not only the set of processes i.e. deadlocked but also the specific process that "caused" the deadlock.

## 6.8 RECOVERY FROM DEADLOCK

- When a detection algorithm determines that a deadlock exists, several alternatives exist.
    1. One possibility is to inform the operator that a deadlock has occured, and to let the operator deal with the **deadlock manually.**
    2. The other possibility is to let the system recover from the deadlock automatically.
- There are two options for breaking a deadlock. One solution is simply to abort one or more processes to break the circular wait.
- The second option is to preempt some resources from one or more of the deadlocked processes.

### 6.8.1 Process Termination

- To eliminate deadlocks by aborting a process we use one of the two methods. In both methods, the system retains all resources allocated to the terminated processes.
    - **Abort all deadlocked processes:** This method clearly will break the deadlock cycle, but at a great expense, these processes may have computed for a long time, and the result of these partial computations must be discarded and probably recomputed later.
    - **Abort one process at a time until the deadlock cycle is eliminated.**
- This method incurs considerable overhead, since, after each process is aborted, a deadlock-detection algorithm must be invoked to determine whether any processes are still deadlocked.
- Aborting a process may not be easy. If the process was in the midst of updating of file, terminating it will leave that file in an incorrect state. Similarly, if the process was in the midst of printing data on the printer, the system must reset the printer to a correct state before printing the next job.
- If the partial termination method is used, then given a set of deadlocked processes, we must determine which process should be terminated in an attempt to break the deadlock.
- This determination is a policy decision, similar to CPU scheduling problems. The question is basically an economic one we should abort those processes termination of which will incur the minimum cost. Unfortunately, the term minimum cost is not a precise one.
- Many factors may determine which process is chosen including,
    1. What the priority of the process is?
    2. How long the process has computed, and how much longer the process will compute before completing its designated task?
    3. How many and what type of resources the process has used (Example whether the resources are simple to preempt)?
    4. How many more resources the process needs in order to complete?
    5. How many process will need to be terminated?
    6. Whether the process is interactive or batch?

## 6.8.2 Resource Preemption

- To eliminate deadlocks using resource preemption, we successively preempt some resources from processes and give these resources to other processes until the deadlock cycle is broken.
- If preemption is required to deal with deadlocks, then three issues need to be addressed.
    1. **Selecting a victim:** Which resources and which processes are to be preempted? As in process, termination we must determine the order of pre-emption to minimise cost. Cost factors may include such parameters as the number of resources as deadlock process is holding, and the amount of time a deadlocked process has thus far consumed during its execution.
    2. **Rollback:** If we preempt a resource from a process, what should be done with that process? Clearly, it cannot continue with its normal execution, it is missing some needed resource. We must rollback the process to same safe state, and restart it from that state.
    3. **Starvation:** How do we ensure that starvation will not occur? That is, how can we guarantee that resources will not always be preempted from the same process.
- In a system, where victim selection is based primarily on cost factors, it may happen that the same process is always picked as a victim.
- As a result this process never completes its designated task, a starvation situation that needs to be dealt with any practical system.
- Clearly, we must ensure that a process can be picked as a victim only a (small) finite number of times. The most common solution is to include the number of rollbacks in the cost factor.

## Exercise

1. What is meant by deadlock?
2. What are the principles of deadlock?
3. Describe safe state in detail.
4. Describe banker's algorithm with suitable example.
5. Explain the term resource allocation graph with example.
6. What are the necessary conditions for deadlock occurs.
7. Explain working of Banker's algorithm for deadlock avoidance with suitable example.
8. Explain deadlock detection in detail? **[Oct. 2012]**
9. Write and explain deadlock detection algorithm with suitable example.
10. Explain the following terms in detail:
    (i) Process termination
    (ii) Resource preemption
11. Describe deadlock characterization in detail.
12. Explain resource allocation graph with suitable example.
13. Enlist various deadlock handling methods in short.
14. Write short note on Recovery from deadlock.

15. For the following resource allocation graph, show that four necessary conditions for deadlock indeed hold.

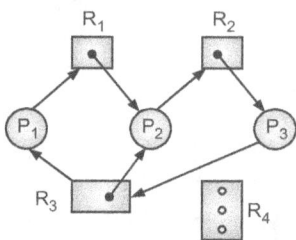

**Fig. 6.11**

16. Consider the system with 5 processes P = {P₀, P₁, P₂, P₃, P₄} and four resource types {A, B, C, D}. There are 3 instances of type A, 10 instances of type B, 15 instances of type C and 7 instances of type D. The allocation and maximum demand matrix are as follows:

| | Allocation | | | | Max | | | |
|---|---|---|---|---|---|---|---|---|
| | A | B | C | D | A | B | C | D |
| $P_0$ | 0 | 1 | 2 | 1 | 0 | 8 | 4 | 4 |
| $P_1$ | 0 | 1 | 2 | 1 | 0 | 6 | 5 | 2 |
| $P_2$ | 1 | 0 | 0 | 0 | 1 | 6 | 4 | 1 |
| $P_3$ | 1 | 3 | 5 | 3 | 2 | 3 | 7 | 5 |
| $P_4$ | 0 | 0 | 4 | 1 | 0 | 5 | 5 | 7 |

Answer the following question using Banker's Algorithm:
(i) Is the system in a Safe State?
(ii) If a request from process P4 arrives for (0, 2, 0, 2) can it be granted?

17. Consider the system with 5 processes P = {P₀, P₁, P₂, P₃, P₄} and four resources type {A, B, C, D}. There are 3 instances of type A, 14 instances of type B, 12 instances of type C and 12 instance of type D. The allocation and maximum demand matrix are as follows:

| | Allocation | | | | Max | | | |
|---|---|---|---|---|---|---|---|---|
| | A | B | C | D | A | B | C | D |
| $P_0$ | 0 | 6 | 3 | 2 | 0 | 6 | 5 | 2 |
| $P_1$ | 0 | 0 | 1 | 2 | 0 | 0 | 1 | 2 |
| $P_2$ | 1 | 0 | 0 | 0 | 1 | 7 | 5 | 0 |
| $P_3$ | 1 | 3 | 5 | 4 | 2 | 3 | 5 | 6 |
| $P_4$ | 0 | 0 | 1 | 4 | 0 | 0 | 5 | 6 |

Answer the following question using Bankers Algorithm:
(i) Is the system in a Safe State?
(ii) If a request from process P4 arrives for (0, 0, 4, 1) can the request be immediately granted. **[April 2012]**

■■■

# Chapter 7...

# Memory Management

## Contents ...

7.1 Introduction
7.2 Address Binding
    7.2.1 Dynamic Loading
    7.2.2 Dynamic Linking
    7.2.3 Overlays
7.3 Logical Versus Physical Address
7.4 Swapping
7.5 Contiguous Memory Allocation
    7.5.1 Single Partition Allocation
    7.5.2 Multiple Partitions Allocation
    7.5.3 External and Internal Fragmentations
7.6 Paging
7.7 Segmentation
7.8 Segmentation with Paging
7.9 Virtual Memory
7.10 Demand Paging
7.11 Page Replacement Algorithms
    7.11.1 FIFO (First Come First Out)
    7.11.2 NRU (Not Recently Used)
    7.11.3 LRU (Least Recently Used)
    7.11.4 LRU Approximation Using Reference Bit
    7.11.5 LFU
    7.11.6 MFU
    7.11.7 Second Chance Algorithm
7.12 Optimal Page Replacement
Exercise

## 7.1 INTRODUCTION

- The memory-management algorithms vary from a primitive bare-machine approach to paging and segmentation strategies.
- Selection of a memory-management method for a specific system depends on many factors, especially on the hardware design of the system.
- Memory is central to the operation of a modern computer system. As shown in Fig. 7.1.

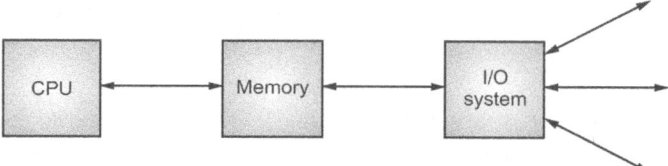

**Fig. 7.1: Central Nature of Memory in a Computer System**

- Both the CPU and I/O system interact with memory.
- Memory is a large array of words or bytes, each with its own address. Interaction is achieved through a sequence of reads or writes to specific memory addresses.
- The CPU fetches from and stores in memory.

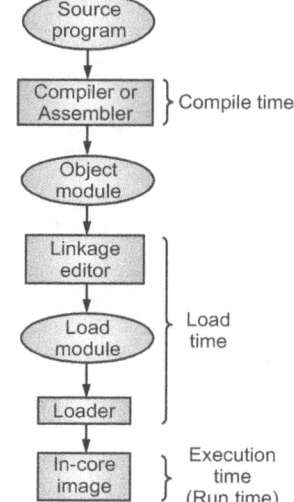

**Fig. 7.2: Multi-step Processing of a User Program**

- Addresses in the source program are generally symbolic.
- A compiler will typically bind these symbol addresses to relocatable addresses.
- The linkage editor or loader will bind these relocatable addresses to absolute addresses.
- Each binding is a mapping from one address space to another. These absolute addresses loaded into memory to be executed.

- As program executes it accesses program instructions and data from memory by generating these absolute addresses.
- Eventually, the program terminates, its memory space is declared available and the next program may be loaded and executed.

### Bare Machine

- By far the simplest memory management scheme is none. The user is provided with the bare machine and has complete control over the entire memory space.
- This approach has some advantages. It provides maximum flexibility to the user.

**Fig. 7.3: User**

- The user can control the use of memory in whatever manner desired. It has maximum simplicity and minimum cost.

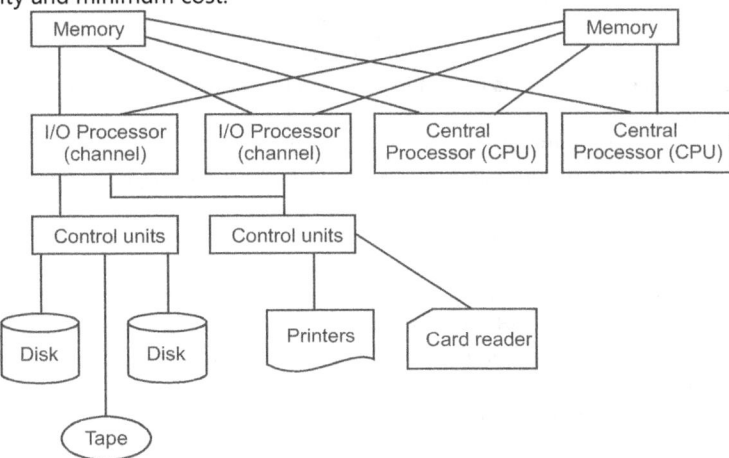

**Fig. 7.4: Basic Computer Hardware (Bare Machine)**

- There is no need for special hardware for this approach to memory management nor is there a need for operating system software.
- This system has its limitations. It provides no services. The user has complete control over the computer, but the operating system has no control over interrupts, no resident monitor to process system calls or errors.
- And no space to provide control card sequencing 32 K or job sequencing. Hence, the bare machine approach has its limitations.
- It is generally used only on dedicated systems where the users require flexibility and simplicity and are willing to program their own support routines.

## Resident Monitor

- Next simplest scheme is to divide memory into two sections, one for user and one for resident monitor of the operating system.

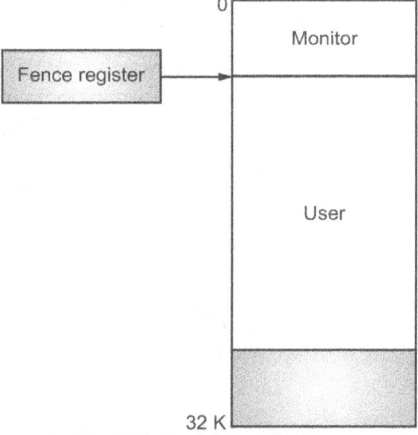

Fig. 7.5: Resident Monitor

- Commonly resident monitor is placed in low memory, and user programs are executed in high memory space.
- We need to protect the monitor code and data from changes by the user program.
- This protection must be provided by the hardware and can be implemented in several ways.
- The general approach is every address (instruction and data) generated by the user program is compared with a fence address.
- If the generated address is greater than or equal to the fence, then it is a legitimate reference to user memory and is sent to the memory unit as usual.
- If the generated address is less than the fence, then the address is an illegal reference to monitor memory.
- The reference is then intercepted and a trap to operating system is generated. The operating system will then take the appropriate action. Notice that every reference to memory by the user program must be checked.

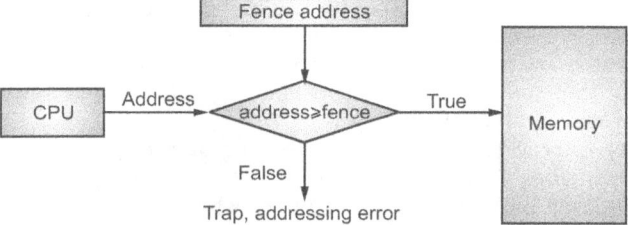

Fig. 7.6: Hardware Address Protection for a Resident Monitor

- The operating system executing in monitor mode, is generally given unrestricted access to both monitor and user memory.
- This provision allows the Operating System to load user programs into user memory, dump them out in case of errors, access and modify parameters of System Calls and so on.
- The fence register contains the address of the fence and is used to check the correctness of all user memory references.

## Relocation

- As discussed above, although the address space of computer starts at 00000 the first address of user program is not 00000, but the first address beyond the fence. This is relocation of the program.
- If the fence address is known at compile time, then absolute code address can be generated. This code will start at fence and extend up from there. In this case, the fence must be static during the execution of the program.
- In CDC 6600 computers, dynamic relocation scheme requires different hardware support.

1. **Dynamic relocation using relocation register:**
- The fence register is now called a **relocation** or **base register**.
- The value in the base register is added to every address generated by a user process at the time it is sent to the memory.

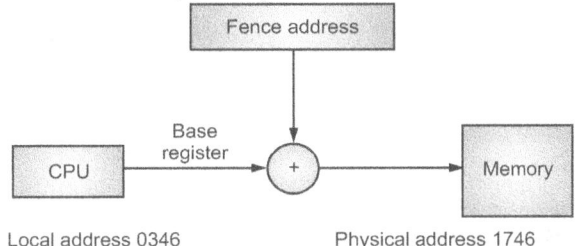

**Fig. 7.7: Dynamic Relocation**

- For example, if the fence is at 1400 then an attempt by the user to address location 0 is dynamically relocated to location 1400; an access to location 346 is relocated to location 1746.
- Notice that the user never sees the real physical addresses. The user can create a pointer to location 346, store it in memory, manipulate it, and compare it to other addresses all as the number 346. Only when it is used as a memory address, is it relocated relative to the base register. The user program deals with logical addresses. The memory mapping hardware converts logical addresses into physical addresses.

## Logical and Physical Address

- We have two different types of addresses logical addresses and physical addresses.
- The user generates only logical addresses and thinks that the program runs in locations 0 to maximum.
- The operating system knows better and can access physical memory directly in monitor mode.
- The user supplies logical addresses; these logical addresses must be mapped to physical addresses before they are used.
- The mapping of logical addresses to the physical addresses is carried out by the memory management unit of the operating system.

| Techniques | Description | Strengths | Weaknesses |
|---|---|---|---|
| Fixed Partitioning | Main memory is divided into a number of partitions at system generation time. A process may be loaded into a partition of the equal or greater size. | Simple to implement. | Inefficient use of memory due to internal fragmentation. Number of active processes is fixed |
| Dynamic Partitioning | Partitions are created dynamically, so that each process is loaded into a partition of exactly the same size as that of the process. | No internal fragmentation: more efficient use of main memory. | Inefficient use of processor due to the need for compaction to counter external fragmentation. |
| Simple Paging | Main memory is divided into a number of equal sized frames. Each process is divided into a number of equal size pages of the same length as frames. A process is loaded by loading all of the pages into available, not necessarily contiguous frames. | No external fragmentation | A small amount of internal fragmentation. |
| Simple Segmentation | Each process is divided into a number of segments. A process is loaded by loading all of its segments into dynamic partitions that need not be contiguous. | No internal fragmentation. | Improved memory utilization and reduced overhead compared to dynamic partitioning. |

*contd. ...*

| Virtual Memory Paging | Similar to simple paging except that, it is not necessary to load all of the pages of a process. Nonresident pages that are needed are brought in later automatically. | No external fragmentation: higher degree of multiprogramming: Large virtual process space. | Overhead of complex memory management. |
|---|---|---|---|
| Virtual Memory Segmentation | Similar to simple segmentation. Except that it is not necessary to load all of the segments of a process. Nonresident segments that are needed are brought in later automatically. | No internal fragmentation. Higher degree of multiprogramming. Large virtual address space: protection and sharing support. | Overhead of complex memory management. |

### Memory Management Requirements

- Operating system consist of memory management module which will have a following function:
    - Keep the track of status of Resource (Memory).
    - Decide the policy to allocate a free memory to a job or process.
    - Enforce the policy to allocate memory.
    - Allocation of free memory to a job.
    - Deallocation of allocated memory after completion of job.
- Address generated by the CPU is commonly referred as a logical address.
- Address seen by memory management unit is physical address.

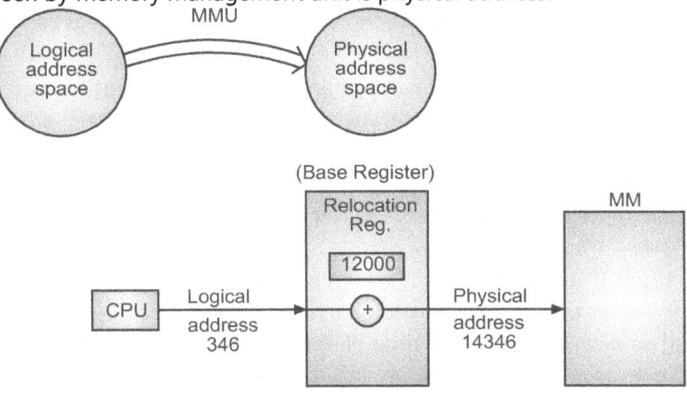

MS-DOS ──── 4 Relocation Register

**Fig. 7.8: MS-DOS – 4 Relocation Reg**

## 7.2 ADDRESS BINDING

- A program resides on a disk as a binary executable file. To be executed, the program must be brought into memory and placed within a process.
- Depending on the memory management in use, the process may be moved between memory and disk during its execution.
- The processes on the disk that are waiting to be brought into memory for execution form the input queue.
- The normal procedure is to select one of the processes in the input queue and to load that process into memory.
- As the process is executed, it accesses instructions and data from memory. Eventually, the process terminates, and its memory space is declared available.
- Number of systems allows a user process to reside in any part of the physical memory. Thus, although the address space of the computer starts of 00000, the first address of the user process need not be 00000. This approach affects the addresses that the user program can use.
- In many case, a user program will go through several steps, some of which may be optional before being executed as shown in Fig. 7.9.
- Addresses may be represented in different ways during these steps. Addresses in the source program are generally symbolic as such as count.
- A compiler will typically bind these symbolic addresses to relocatable addresses. The linkage loader will in turn bind the relocatable addresses to absolute addresses. Fig. 7.9 shows multistep processing of a user program.
- Each binding is a mapping from one address space to another.
- Classically, the binding of instructions and data to memory addresses can be done at any step along the following way:
    1. **Compile time:** If you know at compile time where the process will reside in memory, then absolute code can be generated. If you know that a user process will reside starting at location R, then the generated compiler code will start at that location and extend up from there. If, at some later time, the starting location changes, then it will be necessary to recompile this code. The MS-DOS.COM format programs are bound at compile time.
    2. **Load time:** If it is not known at compile time where the process will reside in memory, then the compiler must generate relocatable code. In this situation final binding is delayed until load time. If the starting address changes, we need only reload the user code to incorporate this changed value.
    3. **Execution time:** If the process can be moved during its execution from one memory segment to another, then binding must be delayed until run time.

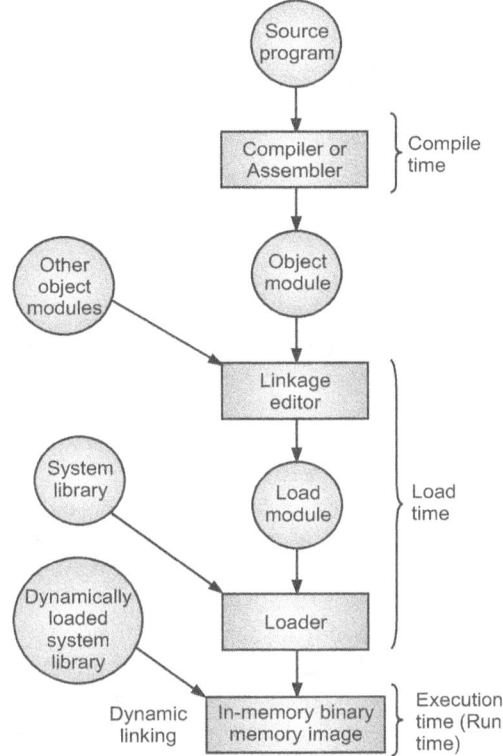

**Fig. 7.9: Address Binding**

## 7.2.1 Dynamic Loading

- It has been necessary for the entire program and all data of a process to be in physical memory for the process to execute. The size of a process has thus, been limited to the size of physical memory. To obtain better memory-space utilization, we can use dynamic loading.
- With dynamic loading approach a routine is not loaded until it is called.
- All routines in dynamic loading are kept on disk in a relocatable load format. The main program is loaded into memory and is executed.
- When a routine in dynamic loading needs to call another routine, the calling routine first checks to see whether the other routine has been loaded.
- If it has not, the relocatable linking loader is called to load the desired routine into memory and to update the program's address tables to reflect this change.
- The control is passed to the newly loaded routine.
- The advantage of dynamic loading approach is that an unused routine is never loaded.

- Dynamic loading method is particularly useful when large amounts of code are needed to handle infrequently occurring cases, such as error routines. In this condition, although the total program size may be large, the portion that is used may be much smaller.
- Dynamic loading does not require special support from the operating system.
- Dynamic loading is the responsibility of the users to design their programs to take advantage of such a method.
- Operating systems may help the programmer, however, by providing library routines to implement dynamic loading.

## 7.2.2 Dynamic Linking

- Fig. 7.9 also shows dynamically linked libraries.
- Some operating systems support only static linking. In static linking system language libraries are treated like any other object module and are combined by the loader into the binary program image.
- Dynamic linking, in contrast, is similar to dynamic loading. Here, though, linking, rather than loading, is postponed until execution time.
- This feature is usually used with system libraries, such as language subroutine libraries. Without this facility, each program on a system must include a copy of its language library in the executable image. This requirement wastes both disk space and main memory.
- With dynamic linking, a stub is included in the image for each library-routine reference.
- The stub is a small piece of code that indicates how to locate the appropriate memory resident library routine or how to load the library if the routine is not already present.
- When the stub is executed, it checks to see whether the needed routine is already in memory. If it is not, the program loads the routine into memory. Either way, the stub replaces itself with the address of the routine and executes the routine.
- Thus, the next time the particular code segment is reached, the library routine is executed directly, incurring to cost for dynamic linking.
- Under dynamic linking, all processes that use a language library execute only one copy of the library code.
- A library may be replaced by a new version, and all programs that reference the library will automatically use the new version.
- Without dynamic linking, all such programs would need to be relinked to gain access the new library, for this reason programs will not accidentally execute new, incompatible versions of libraries, version information is included in both the program and the library.

## 7.2.3 Overlays

- The entire program and data of process must be in physical memory for the process to execute. The size of a process is limited to the size of physical memory.
- So that a process can be larger than the amount of memory allocated to it, a technique called overlays is used.

- The ideas of overlays is to keep in memory only those instructions and data that are needed at any given time. When other instructions are needed, they are loaded into the space that was occupied previously by instructions that are no longer needed.
- For example, consider a two pass assembler. During pass-1, it constructs a symbol table and then during pass-2 it generates a machine language code. We may be able to partition such as assembler into pass-1 code, pass-2 code, the symbol table and common support routines used by both pass-1 and pass-2. Assume the sizes of these components are as follows:

    Pass-1              70K
    Pass-2              80K
    Symbol table        20K
    Common routines     30K

- To load everything at once we would require 200K of memory. If only 150 K is available, we cannot run our process. Notice that pass-1 and pass-2 do not need to be in memory at the same time. Thus, we define two overlays:

    Overlay A is the symbol table, common routines and pass-1

    Overlay B is the symbol table, common routines and pass-2

- We add on overlay driver (10K) and start with overlay A in memory. When we finish pass-1, we jump to the overlay driver, which reads overlay B into memory, overwriting overlay A and then transfers control to pass-2.
- **Overlays for a Two pass assembler:**

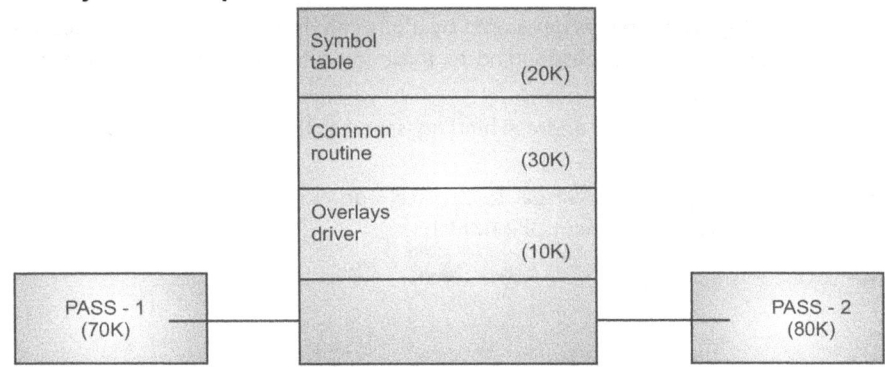

Fig. 7.10: Overlays for two pass

- Overlay A needs only 120K; whereas overlay B needs 130K we can now run our assembler in the 150K of memory.
- The code for overlay A and the code for overlay B are kept on disk as absolute memory images, and are read by the overlay driver as needed. Special relocation and linking algorithms are needed to construct the overlays.

- In dynamic loading overlays do not require any support from the operating system. They can be implemented by the user with simple file structure.
- The programmer must design and program the overlay structure properly, requiring complete knowledge of the structure of the program, its code and its data structures, because the program is by definition, large, obtaining a sufficient understanding of the program, may be difficult for these reasons.
- The use of overlays is currently limited to micro computers and other systems that have limited amounts of physical memory and take hardware support for more advanced techniques.
- Some micro computer compilers are provided to the programmer for support of overlays to make the task execution easier.

## 7.3 LOGICAL VERSUS PHYSICAL ADDRESS

- An address generated by the CPU is commonly referred to as a logical address, whereas an address seen by the memory unit i.e. the one loaded into the memory address register of the memory – is commonly referred to as a physical address.
- The compile-time and load-time address-binding methods generate identical logical and physical addresses.
- However, the execution-time addresses binding scheme results in differing logical and physical addresses. In this case, we usually refer to the logical address as a virtual address.
- The set of all logical addresses generated by a program is a logical address space; the set of all physical addresses corresponding to these logical addresses is a physical address space.
- Thus, in the execution-time address-binding scheme, the logical and physical address space differ.
- The run-time mapping from virtual to physical address is done by a hardware device called the Memory Management Unit (MMU).

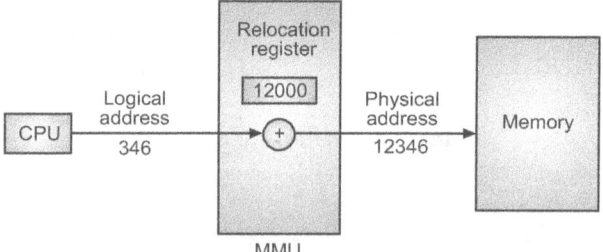

**Fig. 7.11: Virtual to physical mapping**

- Fig. 7.11 shows dynamic relocation using a relocation register.

- The base register is now called a relocation register. The value in the relocation register is added to every address generated by a user process at the time the address is sent to memory.
- The user program never sees the real physical addresses.
- The user program deals with logical addresses. The memory-mapping hardware converts logical addresses into physical addresses. This form of execution-time binding and final location of a referenced memory address is not determined until the reference is made.
- We now have two different types of addresses logical addresses and physical addresses. The user program generates only logical addresses and thinks that the process runs in location 0 to max.
- However, these logical addresses must be mapped to physical addresses before they are used.
- The concept of a logical address space that is bound to a separate physical address space is central to proper memory management.

## 7.4 SWAPPING

- The partitioned memory management scheme is categorised whether it supports swapping or not. Lifting the program from the memory and placing it on the disk is called as "swapping out". To bring the program again from the disk to main memory is called as "swapping in".
- Normally, a blocked process is swapped out to make room for a ready process to improve the CPU utilization. If more than one process is blocked, the swapper chooses a process with lowest or a process waiting for a slow I/O event for swapping out.
- The operating system has to find a place on the disk for the swapped out process image. There are two alternatives one is to create a separate swap file for each process.
- This method is flexible but can be very important due to the increased number of files and dictionary entries.
- The other alternative is to keep a common swap file on the disk and not the location of each swapped out process image within that file. In this method, the estimate, of the swap file has to be made initially.
- If smaller area is reserved for this file, the operating system may not be able to swap out processes beyond a certain limit and thus affecting the performance.
- These systems use a resident monitor with the remainder of memory available to the currently executing user.
- When the system to the next user, the current contents of user memory are written out to a backing store (a disk or a drum) and the memory of the next user is read in. This scheme is called *Swapping*.

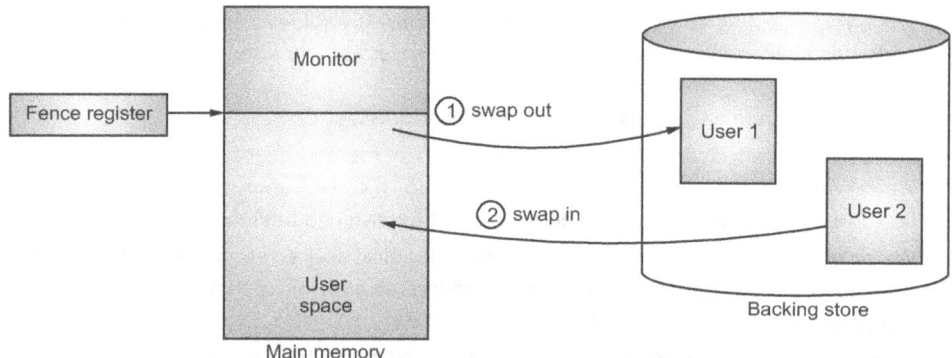

**Fig. 7.12: Swapping Two Users using a Drum as a Backing Store**

1. **Backing Store:** Swapping requires a backing store. The backing store is commonly a fast drum or disk. It must be large enough to accommodate copies of all memory images for all users, and must provide direct access to these memory images. All memory images are on the backing stores, which are ready to run. Whenever, the CPU scheduler decides to execute a process, it calls the dispatcher. The dispatcher checks to see whether that process is in memory. If not, it swaps out the process currently in memory and swaps in the desired process.

2. **Overlapped Swapping:** In this scheme, the objective is to overlap the swapping of one process with the execution of another. Thus, the CPU will not sit idle while swapping is going on. While one user program is being executed the previous users program is swapped out from buffer1 and the next user's program to be executed is swapped into buffer2, (Refer Fig. 7.13).

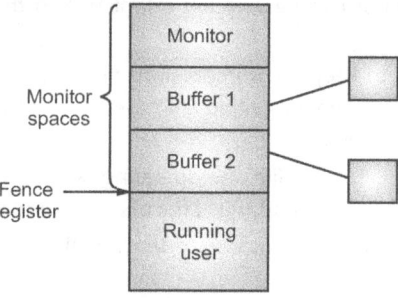

**Fig. 7.13**

Notice however that after the current user program releases the CPU, we must move the next user's program from buffer2 to the user region, before it can be executed.

The program currently in the user region must also be moved into one of the buffers for swapping. If this was not done we could only execute the program in buffer2 by moving the fence as shown in Fig. 7.14.

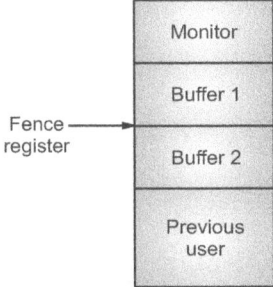

Fig. 7.14

## 7.5 CONTIGUOUS MEMORY ALLOCATION

- The memory is divided into two positions one for resident operating system and one for user processes.
- In contiguous memory allocation each process is contained in a single contiguous section of memory.
- We can place the OS in either low memory or high memory and the major factor affecting this decision is the location of the interrupt vector.
- We usually coat several user processes to reside in memory of the same time for this reason we need to consider how to allocate available memory to the processes that are in the input queue waiting to be brought into memory.

    Resident operating system port $\Rightarrow$ Low memory
    User area $\Rightarrow$ High memory area

### 7.5.1 Single Partition Allocation

- Fig. 7.15 shows single memory partition allocation.

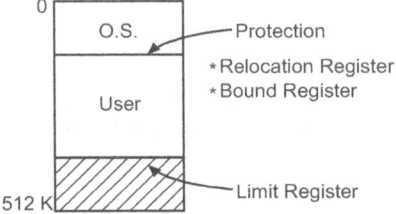

Fig. 7.15: Memory partition

- Memory management is divided into separate memory partitions. Each partition holds a separate Job's address space.

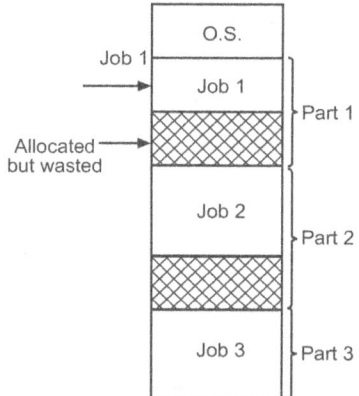

Fig. 7.16

### Fixed or Static Partitioning

| Part No. | Size | Location | Status |
|---|---|---|---|
| 1 | 8K | 312 K | In use |
| 2 | 32 K | 320 K | In use |
| 3 | 32 K | 352 K | Not in use |
| 4 | 120 K | 384 K | Not in use |
| 5 | 520 K | 504 K | In use |

- Memory is divided into partitions prior to procedure of job.
- A partition of sufficient size is then founded and assigned. Software algorithm handles allocation and deallocation.
- This technique is appropriate especially when the job size and frequency of jobs are well known.
- Considerable memory wastage if sizes and frequency are not known.
  For example,   Job size    1 K, 9 K, 33 K, 121 K, 9 K
  Part size is   8 K, 32 K, 32 K, 120 K, 520 K

| Part No. | Size | Job Size | Wasted space |
|---|---|---|---|
| 1 | 8K | 1 K | 7 K |
| 2 | 32 K | 9 K | 23 K |
| 3 | 32 K | 9 K | 23 K |
| 4 | 120 K | 33 K | 87 K |
| 5 | 520 L | 121 K | 399 K |
| Total | 712 K | 173 K | 539 K |

### First Fit Algorithm

- **Free table sorted by location:** Start the search for allocating partition form lower memory area and once it get enough large partition, allocates the job to it ("First Fit").
- **Advantages:**
  1. Approximately you have to search half the free table to get allocated.
  2. You will get a large free area at higher memory address.

- **Disadvantages:**
  o Memory utilization is poor.
  For example, If we want to allocate a job 24 K, but free table is having partition of 32K, then 8K is get wasted.

## Best Fit Algorithm

  o Free table is kept sorted by partition size.
  o Thus, the first free area, we find that is large enough for the desired partition is the "Best Fit".
- **Advantages:**
  1. On average the best fit free area can be found by searching only half the table.
  2. If there is a free area of exactly desired size, it will be selected. This is not true for "First Fit".
  3. Lower memory wastage than "First Fit".
- **Disadvantages:**
  o Fragmentation problem
      Very small parts of memory remain unutilised which is called "Fragmentation".

## Worst Fit Algorithm

- It allocates the largest hole and we must search the entire list unless it is sorted by size. This approach produces the largest leftover hole which may be more useful than the smaller leftover hole from a best-fit approach.
- **Relocatable Partitioned Memory Management:**

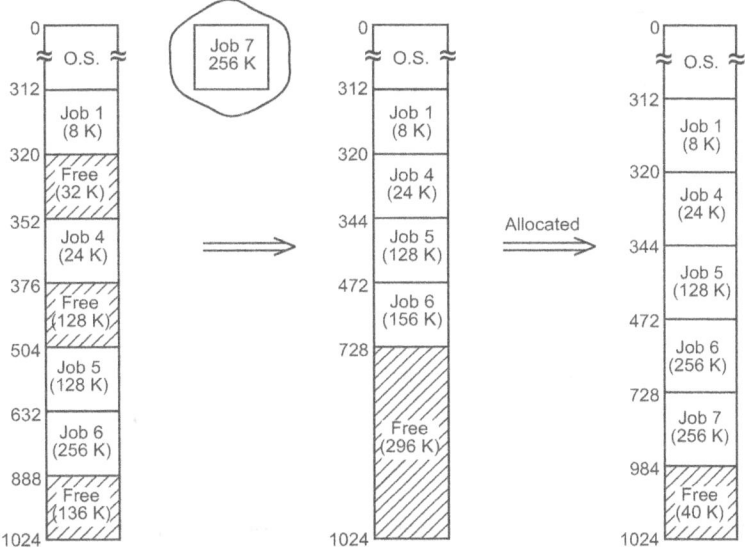

(a) Initial state    (b) After compaction    (c) After allocating portion for Job 7

Fig. 7.17: Relocatable partition

- Solution to problem of "fragmentation" Process of "compaction".
- Although conceptually simple, moving job partition doesn't guarantees that the job will run correctly because:
    1. Base register's, Limiting Reg.
    2. Memory referencing instrument.
    3. Parameter lists.
    4. Data structures (lists, chains, etc.)
- For example, Job 4 is moved from,
    
    352 K $\xrightarrow{To}$ 320 K
- All the address of Job 4 must be decreased by 32 K (Relocation).
    - Another solution for relocation, reloading all jobs to be relocated and restart from beginning. "Restart is not feasible in certain situation".
- **Dynamic Partition Allocation:**

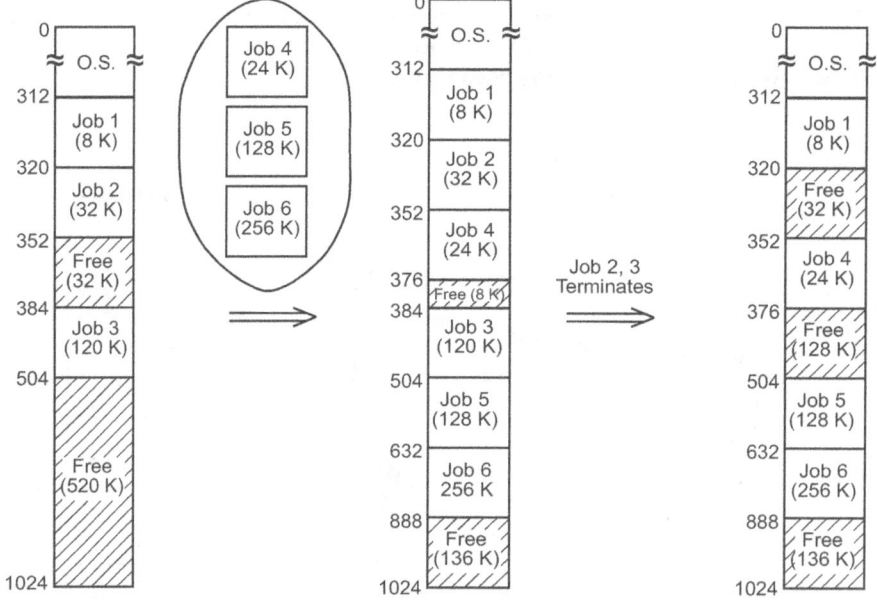

(a) Initial state  (b) Job 4, 5, 6 allocated partition  (c) Job's 2, 3, terminated

Fig. 7.18: Dynamic partition

- Hardware support for Relocation Reg and Limit Reg,

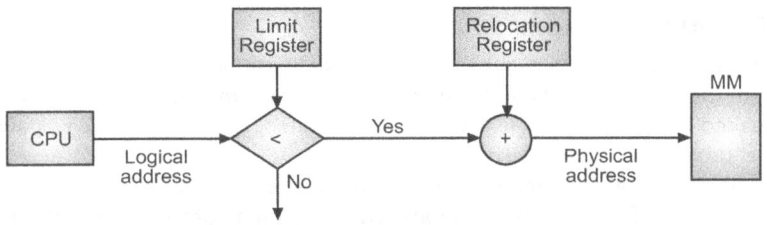

Trap addressing err
Dispatcher – Loads – Limits – Relocation

**Fig. 7.19**

- **Advantages:**
  - Simplicity
  - Great expertise
- **Disadvantages:**
  - Memory utilisation.
  - Poor utilisation of processes.
  - User job is limited to the size of available memory.
  - Multiprogramming not possible.

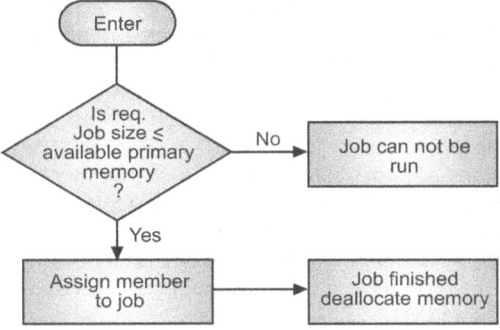

**Fig. 7.20**

- **Algorithm:**
  1. Keep the track of status of each location of primary memory, i.e. each location is either "allocated" or "free".
  2. Determine allocation policy for memory i.e. decides:
     (i) Whom should get it?
     (ii) How much
     (iii) When and Where.
  3. Allocation, once it is decided, specific location must be selected and allocation information updated.
  4. Reclamation of memory and updating its status.

## 7.5.2 Multiple Partitions Allocation

- Memory is divided into a number of regions or partitions. Each region may have one program to be executed. When a region is free, a program is selected from the job queue and loaded into the free region. When it terminated, the region becomes available for another program.
- Two major memory management schemes are possible. Each approach divides memory into a number of regions or partitions. These schemes are multiple contiguous fixed partition allocation and multiple contiguous variable partition allocation.
- The most widely known examples of these algorithms are the:
  1. MFT (Multiprogramming with a Fixed number of Tasks).
  2. MVT (Multiprogramming with a Variable number of Tasks).

**1. Fixed Regions Partitioning (MFT)**

- In MFT the region sizes are fixed and do not change as the system runs. For example a memory of 32K words might be divided into regions of the following sizes:

   Resident Monitor = 10K
   Very small jobs = 4K
   Average jobs = 6K
   Large jobs = 12K

- **MFT Job Scheduling:** As jobs enter the system, they are put into a job queue. The job scheduler takes into account the memory requirement of each job and the available regions in determining which jobs are to be allocated to what memory space. When a job is allocated space, it is loaded into a region. It can then compete for the CPU. When the job terminates, it releases its memory region, which the job scheduler may then fill with another job from the job queue.
- A number of variations are possible in allocation of memory to jobs. One strategy is to classify all jobs on entry to the system, according to its memory requirements. User specifies the maximum amount of memory required.
- The system can attempt to determine memory requirements automatically.
- For example, if we have three user memory regions of sizes 2K, 6K and 12K we need three queues: Q2, Q6 and Q12.

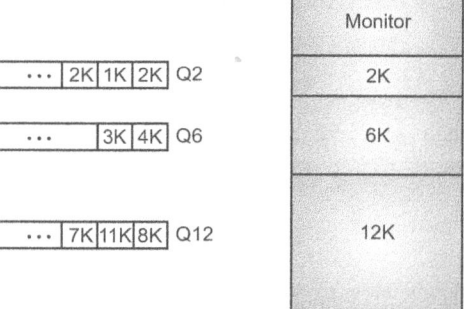

**Fig. 7.21: MFT with Separate Queues for Each Region**

- An incoming job requiring 5K of memory would be appended to Q6, a new job needing 10K would be put in Q12, a job of 2K would go in Q2. Each queue is scheduled separately. Since, each queue has its own memory region, there is no competition between queues for memory.
- Another approach is to throw all jobs into one queue. The job scheduler selects the next job to be run and waits until a memory region of that size is available.

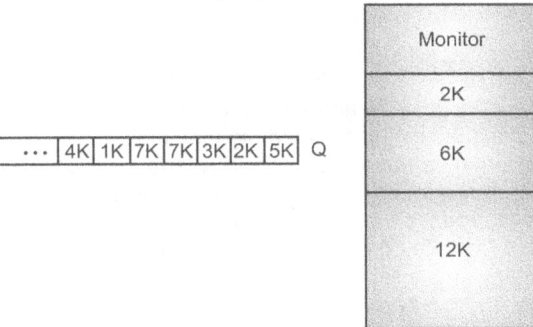

**Fig. 7.22: MFT with a Unified Queue**

- Suppose that we had FCFS job scheduler, the job queue of Fig. 7.22. And regions of 2K, 6K and 12K. We would first assign job1 (5K) to the 6K regions and job2 (2K) to the 2K regions. Since, our next job requires 3K, we need the 6K regions.
- Since, 6K regions are being used by job1, we must wait until job1 terminates, and then job3 will be allocated the 6 K regions. Job4 is then allocated to 12K regions and so on.

2. **Variable Partitions (MVT)**

- The problem with MFT is determining the best region sizes in order to minimize internal and external fragmentation. Suppose 120K of memory is available for user programs and all user jobs are 20K except one big job of 80K, which runs once a day.
- We must allocate an 80K region to allow this program to run, but all other jobs are 20K. We are faced with 60K of internal fragmentation, except when that one big job is run once a day.
- The solution to the problem is to allow region sizes to vary dynamically. This approach is called **Multiple Contiguous Variable Partition Allocation**. We use MVT to denote this class of memory management algorithms.
- MVT memory management is fairly simple. The operating system keeps a table indicating which parts of memory are available and which are occupied. Initially all memory is available for user programs and is considered as one large block of available memory, a hole. When a job arrives and needs memory, we search for a hole large enough for this job. If we find one, we allocate only as much as is needed, keeping the rest available to satisfy future requests.
- For example, assume 256K memory available and a resident monitor of 40K. This situation leaves 216K for user programs.

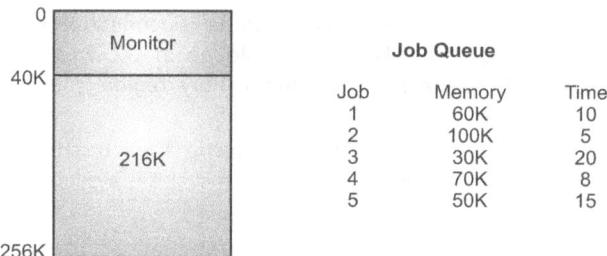

Fig. 7.23: MVT

- Given the job queue in Fig. 7.23 and FCFS job scheduling, we can immediately allocate memory to job1, 2 and 3 creating the memory map of Fig. 7.24 (a).
- We have 26K of external fragmentation. Job2 will terminate at time 5 units, releasing its memory allocation shown in Fig. 7.24 (b). We then return to our job queue and schedule the next job, job4 to produce the memory map of Fig. 7.24 (c). Job1 will terminate at time 10 units to produce Fig. 7.24 (d) and job5 is then scheduled, producing Fig. 7.24 (e).
- In MVT there is at any time a set of holes, of various sizes, scattered throughout memory. When a job arrives and needs memory, we search this set for a hole that is large enough for this job.
- If the new hole is adjacent to other holes, we would merge these adjacent holes to form one large hole. Once, a block of memory has been allocated to a job, its program can be loaded into that space and executed.
- Here the software determines the difference between MFT and MVT. As with MFT, MVT interacts strongly with job scheduling.
- Memory utilization is generally better for MVT than for MFT.
- There is little or no internal fragmentation in MVT, since the regions are created to be the size requested by the job. However, we can have external fragmentation.

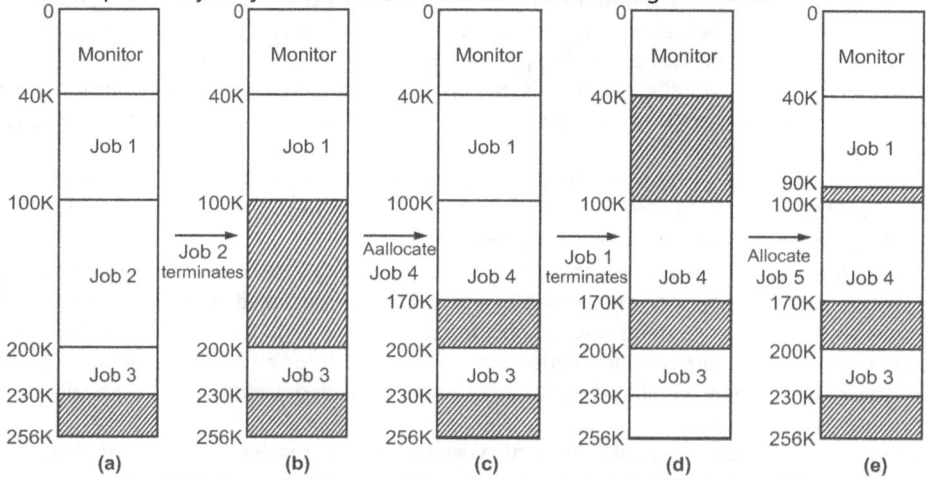

Fig. 7.24: Example Memory Allocation and Job Scheduling for MVT

- Compaction is to shuffle the memory contents to place all free memory spaces together in one large block. For example, the memory map of (e) can be compacted as shown in Fig. 7.25.

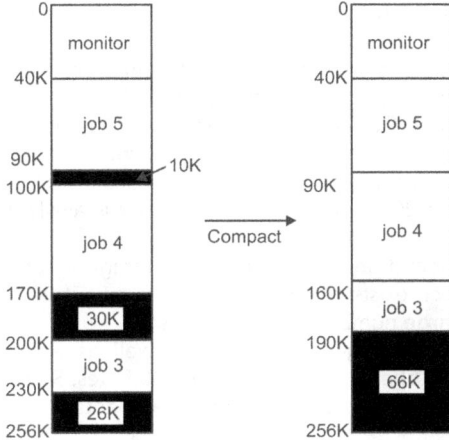

**Fig. 7.25: Compaction**

- The three holes of sizes 10K, 30K and 26K can be compacted into one hole of 66K. Compaction is not always possible.
- In Fig. 7.25, if we move job4 and job3, for these programs to work in their new locations, all internal addresses must be relocated.
- Compaction is possible only if relocation is dynamic, at execution time, using base and limit registers.
- The simplest compaction algorithm is to simply move all jobs towards one end of the memory, all holes move in the other direction, producing one large hole of available memory. This scheme can be quite expensive.
- Compaction changes the allocation of memory to make free space contiguous and hence useful.

### 7.5.3 External and Internal Fragmentation
- A job which needs m words of memory; may be run in a region of n words where n>=m. The difference between these two numbers (n-m) is **Internal Fragmentation, memory which is internal to a region, but is not being used.**
- **External Fragmentation occurs when a region is unused and available, but too small for any waiting job.**
- Both types of fragmentation are sources of memory wastage in MFT.
- For example, suppose that we break a 22K user space into a 10K region; and three 4K regions. If our job queue contains job-requiring 7K, 3K, 6K and 6K, we can allocate the 7K jobs to the 10K region (producing 3K of internal fragmentation) and the 3K job to one of the 4K regions. (Producing 1K of internal fragmentation) Since, the two remaining jobs

are too large for the two available regions, we are left with two unusable regions of 4K each, a total of 8K of external fragmentation. Our total fragmentation both internal and external is 12K, more than half our memory.
- Several factors must be considered in selecting a partitioned memory algorithm. Speed and simplicity are among them.
- More important concern is the effect of fragmentation, the development of a large number of separate free areas. i.e. total free memory is fragmented into small pieces.
- By referring the following Fig. 7.26. Say two jobs are terminated and total of say 200 k of memory is free. In Fig. 7.26, Job1 and Job 5 are terminated. If request were made for a partition of size 175 K it could not be possible to allocate such a partition.
  - Although a total of 200 K bytes of free memory is available there is no single area larger than 150 K.
  - This type of fragmentation is called as external fragmentation. It exists, when enough total memory space exists to satisfy a request, but it is not contiguous, storage is fragmented into large number of small pieces.
  - Memory fragmentation can be internal as well as external. Consider a multiple partition allocation scheme with a partition 500 bytes. Suppose that the next process request 480 bytes. In such case we left with fragments 20 bytes.

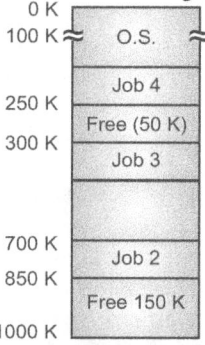

**Fig. 7.26: Fragmentation**

  - The overhead to keep track of this fragment will be larger than fragment itself.
  - The general approach is to break the physical memory into fixed sized blocks and allocate memory in unit of block size. With this approach, the memory allocated to a process may be slightly larger than the requested memory. The difference between these two numbers is internal fragmentation i.e. memory which is internal to a portion but is not being used.

## 7.6 PAGING

- Each job's address space is divided into equal pieces, called **"pages"**, and likewise, physical memory is divided into pieces of same. Size, called **"blocks"** or **"Frames"**. Then by providing suitable hardware mapping facility any **"page"** can be mapped to any **"block"**.

- The page remains logically contiguous but the corresponding blocks are not necessarily contiguous.

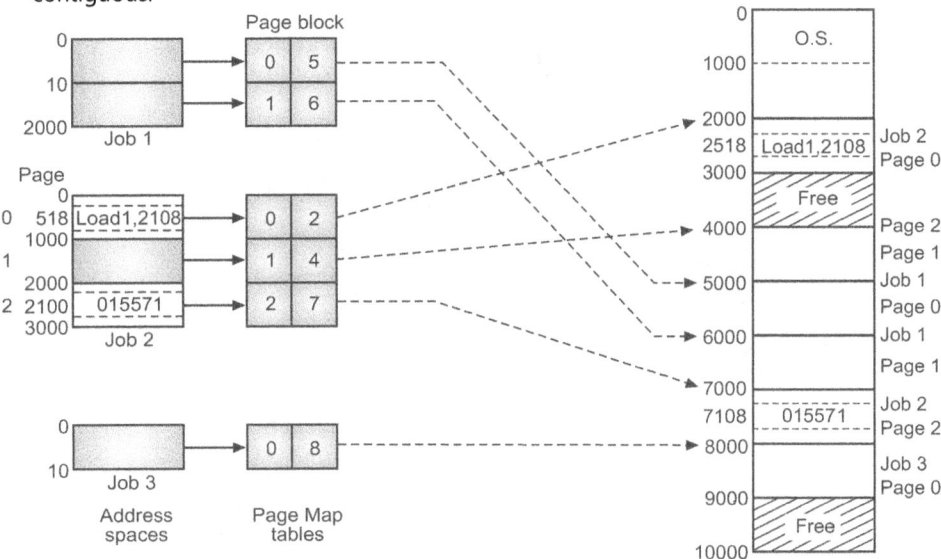

**Fig. 7.27: Paging**

- Paging permits a programs memory to be non-contiguous, thus allowing a program to be allocated physical memory wherever it is available.
- Paging model of logical and physical memory.

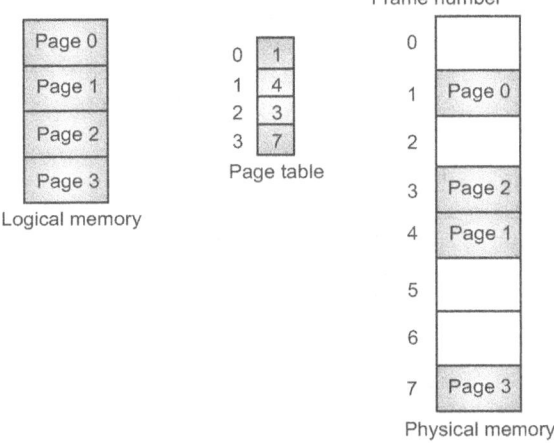

**Fig. 7.28: Paging Model of Logical and Physical Memory**

- Every address generated by the CPU is divided into two parts: A page number (p) and a page offset (d). The page number is used as an index into a page table. The page table contains the base address of each page in physical memory.
- This base address is combined with page offset to define the physical address that is sent to memory unit.

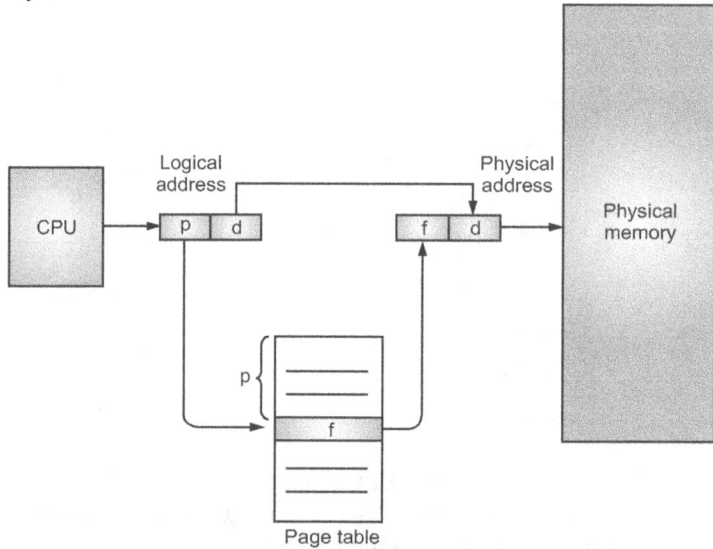

**Fig. 7.29: Paging Hardware**

- Physical memory is broken into fixed size blocks called **frames**. Logical memory is also broken into blocks of the same size called **pages**.
- When a program is to be executed, its pages are loaded into any available frames and the page table is defined to translate from user pages to memory frames.
- For example, using a page size of 4 words and physical memory of 32 words (8 pages) we show how the user's view of memory can be mapped into physical memory. Logical address 0 is page 0 offset 0. We find that page 0 is in frame 5. Thus, logical address 0 maps to physical address $(5 \times 4 + 0) = 20$. Logical address 4 is page1, offset 0. Logical address 4 maps to physical address $(6 \times 4 + 0) = 24$.
- Paging itself is a form of dynamic relocation. Every logical address is mapped by paging hardware to some physical address.
- Each user page needs one frame. Thus, if the job requires n pages, there must be n frames available in memory.
- The page of job is loaded into one of the allocated frames and the frame number is put in the page table for this job and so on.
- Using a paging scheme, we have no external fragmentation, any free frame can be allocated to a job that needs it. Each job has its own page table. The page table is implemented as a set of dedicated registers.

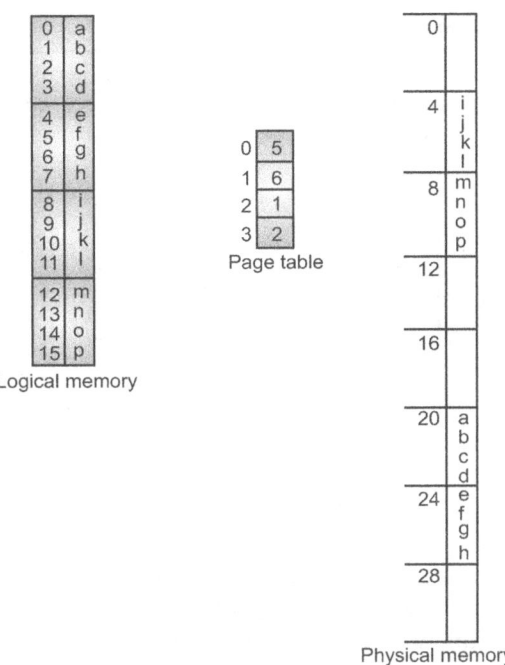

**Fig. 7.30: Paging example for a 32-word memory with 4-word pages**

- **Allocation of Free Frames:**

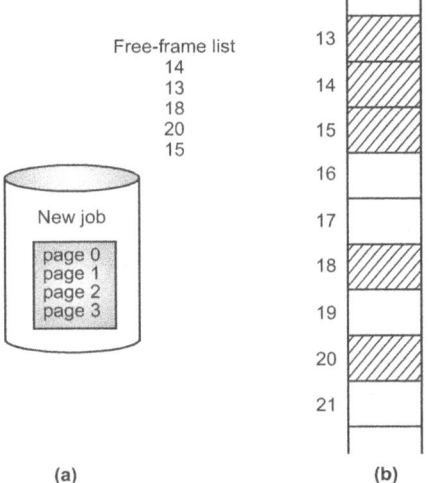

**Fig. 7.31: Allocation of Free Frames (a) Before and (b) After**

## 7.7 SEGMENTATION

- Here, the user does not view the memory as a linear array of words. Instead, the user views the memory as a collection of variable sized segments with no necessary ordering among segments.

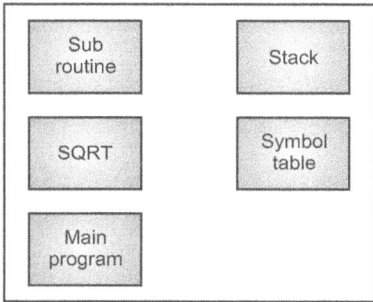

Fig. 7.32

- Each of these segments (tables, arrays, stacks, programs, subroutines, procedures functions or modules etc.) are of variable lengths.
- Elements within a segment are identified by their offset from the beginning of the segment i.e. the first statement of the program.
- Segmentation is a memory management scheme which supports user's view of Memory. A logical address space is a Collection of segments. Each segment has a name and a length.
- Address specifies both the segment name and the offset within the segment. The user specifies each address by two quantities: a segment name and an offset.
- A logical address consists of two parts a segment number 's' and an offset into that segment 'd'. The segment number is used as an index into segment table.
- Each entry of segment table has a segment base and a segment limit.
- The offset 'd' of the logical address must be between 0 and the segment limit. If it is not, a trap is generated to the operating system. If this offset is legal, it is added to the segment base to produce the address in physical memory of the desired word.
- The segment table is thus essentially an array of base/limit register pairs.
- **Advantages:**
    1. Segmentation eliminates internal fragmentation.
    2. Segmentation is usually visible, unlike paging which is invisible to the programmer.
    3. It provides a convenient way of organizing programs and data to the programmer.
- **Disadvantages:**
    1. It suffers from external fragmentation.
    2. Address translation i.e. conversion from logical address to physical address is not a simple function, as regards to paging.

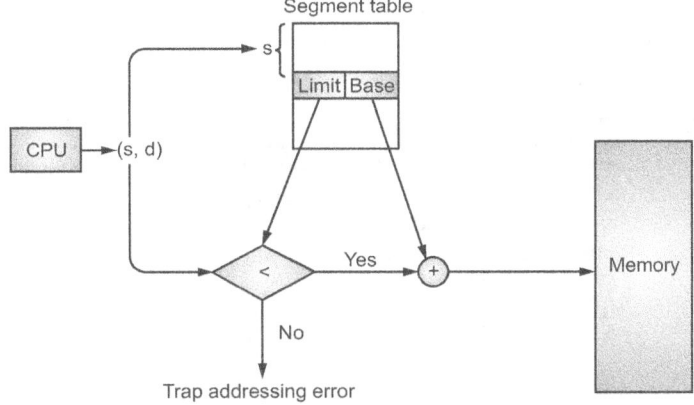

**Fig. 7.33: Segmentation Hardware**

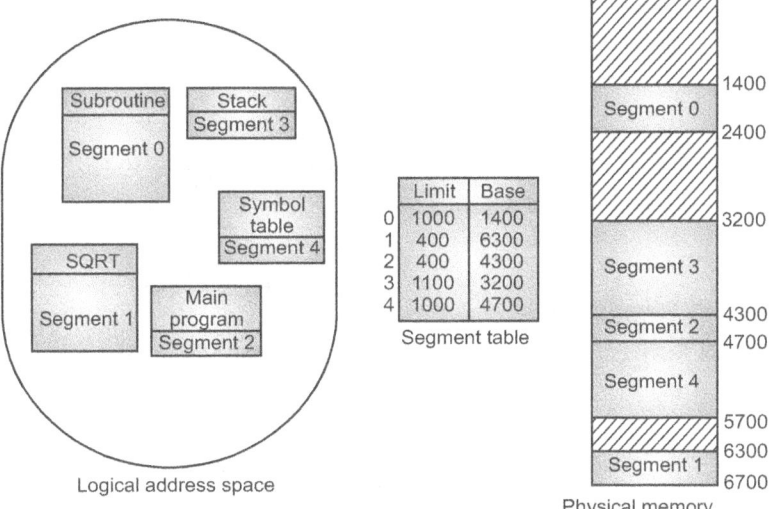

**Fig. 7.34: Example Segmentation**

- As an example consider the situation shown in Fig. 7.34.
- We have five segments numbered from 0 through 4. The segments are actually stored in physical memory as shown in Fig. 7.34.
- The segment table has a separate entry for each segment, giving the beginning address of the segment in physical memory (the base) and the length of that segment (the limit) for example, segment 2 is 400 words long, beginning at location 4300. Thus, reference to word 53 of segment 2 is mapped on to location 4300 + 53 = 4353.

- A reference to segment 3, word 852 is mapped to 3200 (the base of segment 3) + 852 = 4052. A reference to word 1222 of segment 0 would result in a trap to the operating system, since this segment is only 1000 words long.

## 7.8 SEGMENTATION WITH PAGING

- The 80386 uses segmentation with paging for memory management. In 80386, maximum number of segmentation per process is 16 KB and each segment can be as large as 4 gigabytes. While the page size is 4 KB.
- A simple mode of Intel 80386 address translation is shown in Fig. 7.35.

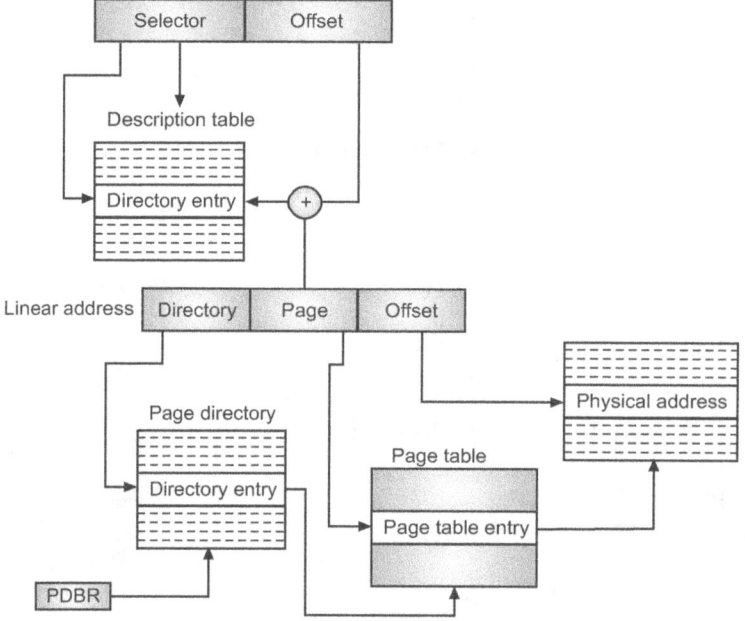

Fig. 7.35: PDBR – Page directory base register

## 7.9 VIRTUAL MEMORY

- Virtual memory is the separation of user logical memory from physical memory.
- This separation allows an extremely large virtual memory to be provided for programmers when only a smaller physical memory is available.
- Virtual memory makes the task of programming much easier because the programmer no longer needs to worry about the amount of physical memory available.
- Virtual memory is commonly implemented by demand paging, it can also be implemented in a segmentation system.
- Virtual memory also allows files and memory to be shared by several different processes through page sharing.

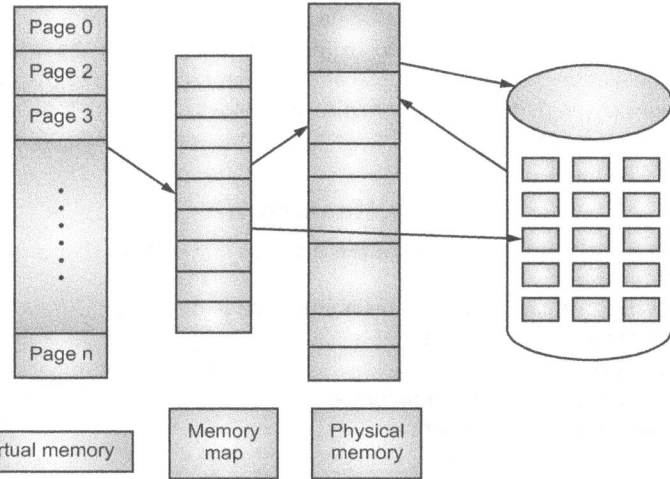

**Fig. 7.36: Diagram showing Virtual Memory that is larger than Physical Memory**

- Virtual memory is a technique which allows the execution of processes that may not be completely in memory.
- Virtual memory is the separation of user logical memory from physical memory. This separation allows an extremely large virtual memory to be provided for programmers when only a smaller physical memory is available.
- Virtual memory makes the task of programming much easier because the programmer no longer needs to worry about the amount of physical memory available.
- Virtual memory is commonly implemented by demand paging. It can also be implemented in a segmentation system. It is not easy to implement, and may decrease performance, if it is used carelessly.
- The basic idea behind virtual memory is that the combined size of the program, data and stack may exceed the amount of physical memory available for it.
- The operating system keeps those parts of the program currently in use in main memory and the rest on the disk.

## Page Fault

- The pages are mapped on to physical memory.
- The pages that mapped are shown by a cross. In the actual hardware a present / absent bit keeps track of which page are physically present in the memory.
- If any program tries to use an unmapped page, the MMU notices that the page is unmapped and causes the CPU notifies to the operating system by generating a trap interrupt. This trap is called a **page fault**.

## Page Tables

- The virtual address is split into a virtual page number (high order bits) and a offset (low order bits).
- The virtual page number is used as an index into the page table to find the entry for that virtual page.

- From the page table entry, the page frame number is found.
- The page frame number is attached to the high order end of the offset, replacing the virtual page number, to form a physical address that can be sent to the memory.
- The purpose of the page table is to map virtual pages onto page frames. Mathematically speaking, the page table is a function, with the virtual page number as argument, and the physical frame number as result.

### Hashing

- This is the technique for handling address spaces larger than 32-bits in which a hashed page table is used.
- The hash value in a hashed page table is virtual-page number.
- Each element having three fields:
  1. a virtual page number.
  2. the value of the mapped page frame.
  3. a pointer to the next element.

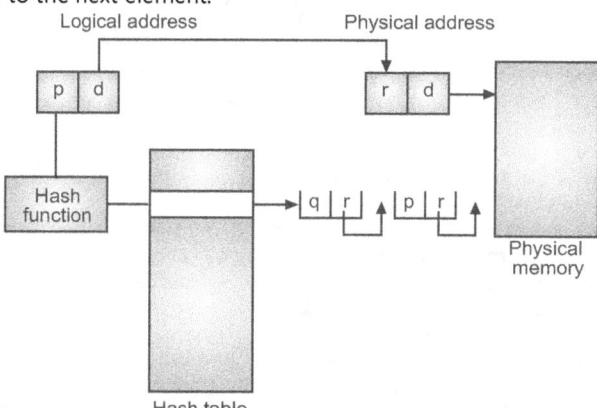

Fig. 7.37: Hash Page table

## 7.10 DEMAND PAGING

- A demand paging system is similar to a paging system with swapping where processes reside in secondary memory.
- When we want to execute a process then we swap into memory.
- Rather than swapping the entire process into memory we use lazy swapper and it never swaps a page into memory unless that page will be needed.
- When a program starts with a list of available option from which the user is to select. Loading the entire program into memory results in loading the executable code for all options regardless of whether an option is ultimately selected by the user or not. An alternative approach is to load pages only as they needed this technique is known as demand paging.
- Fig. 7.38 shows transfer of a paged memory to contiguous disk space.

# Memory Management

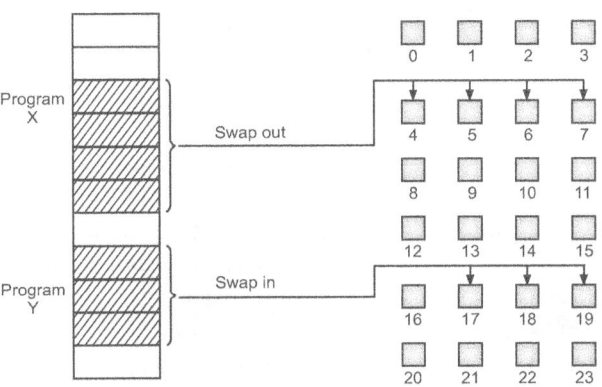

Fig. 7.38

## Pure Demand Paging:

- We start executing a job with no pages in memory. When operating system points towards first instrumentation first page fault occurs. Subsequent page faults occurs and the necessary pages will be brought in memory.

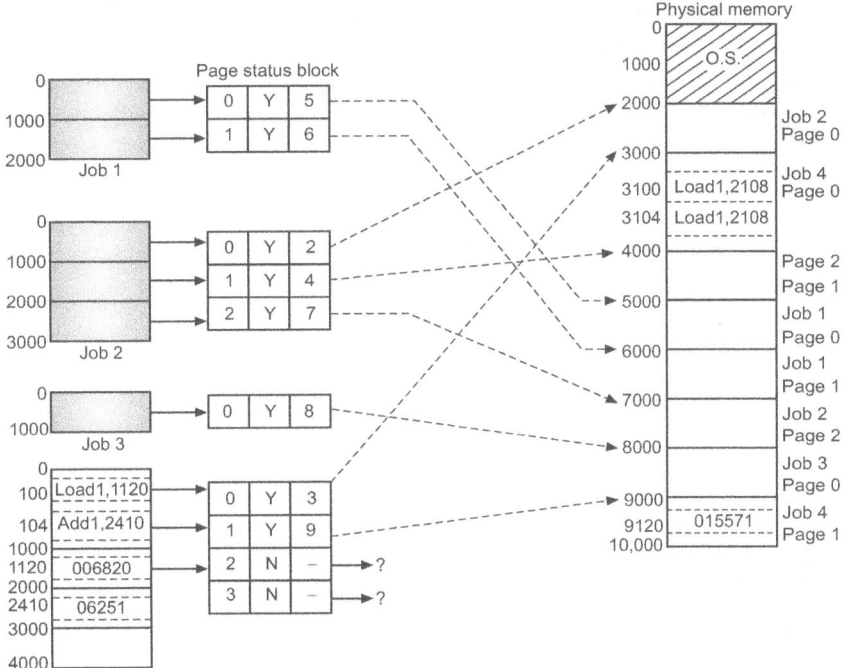

Fig. 7.39: Page Map Table (PMT)

## 7.11 PAGE REPLACEMENT ALGORITHMS

- When a page fault occurs, the operating system has to choose a page to remove from memory to make room for the page that has to be brought in. This is known as **page replacement**.
- Page replacement algorithms should have the lowest page fault rate.
- For a given page size, we need to consider only the page number, not the entire address.
- If we have a reference to a page p, then any immediately following references to page p will never cause a page fault. Page p will be memory after the first reference; hence, the immediately following references will not cause a page fault.
- As the number of frames increases, the numbers of page faults are minimized.
- Page replacement is basic to demand paging. It completes the separation between logical memory and physical memory. With this mechanism an enormous virtual memory can be provided for programmers on a smaller physical memory.
- Every operating system usually has its own page replacement scheme.
- "What is the best page to remove"? It is the page that will not need again or at least, not for a long time.
- Some of the algorithm for page replacements are:
  1. FIFO (First In First Out).
  2. LRU (Least Recently Used).
  3. Optimal.
  4. MFU
  5. LFU, etc.
- Basic idea behind the replacement analogy "Incharge of super market".
  Now product, where do you put it you have to replace a product already on your shelf.
  1. Replace the product that has been on your shelves longest (FIFO).
  2. Blow a dust off the product. Replace the product with the most dust on it (LRU).
  3. Replace the product which is for a long time and having a most dust on it (Optimal).

### 7.11.1 FIFO (First In First Out)

- The simplest page replacement algorithm is a FIFO.
- A FIFO replacement algorithm associates with each page the time when that page was brought into the memory. When a page must be replaced, the oldest page is chosen.
- FIFO queue is created to hold all pages in the memory. We replace the page at the head of the queue. When a page is brought into memory, we insert it at the tail of the queue.
- The FIFO page replacement algorithm is easy to understand and program.
- Its performance is not always good.
- For example consider the following reference string:
  7, 0, 1, 2, 0, 3, 0, 4, 2, 3, 0, 3, 2, 1, 2, 0

- Our three frames are initially empty. The first three references (7, 0, 1) cause page faults and are brought into these empty frames.
- The next reference (2) replaces page 7, because page 7 was brought in first. Since, 0 is the next reference and 0 is already in memory, we have no fault for this reference.
- The first reference to 3 results in page 0 being replaced, since it was the first of the three pages in memory (0, 1 and 2) to be brought in.
- Because of this replacement, the next reference 0 will cause page fault. Page 1 is then replaced by 0. This process continues. There are 15 faults altogether.

**Reference String:**

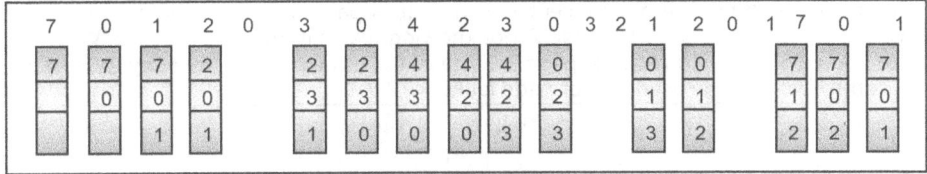

**Fig. 7.40: FIFO**

- The number of faults for four frames (10) is greater than the number of faults for three frames (9).
- This most unexpected result is known as Belady's anomaly: for some page replacement algorithms, the page fault rate may increase as the number of allocated frames increases.

## 7.11.2 NRU (Not Recently Used)

- The Not Recently Used (NRU) page replacement algorithm is an algorithm that favors keeping pages in the memory that have been recently used.
- This algorithm works on the following principle: when a page is referenced, a referenced bit is set for that page, marking it as referenced.
- Similarly, when a page is modified (written to), a modified bit is set.
- The setting of the bits is usually done by the hardware, although it is possible to do so on the software level as well.
- At a certain fixed time interval, the clock interrupt triggers and clears the referenced bit of all the pages, so only pages referenced within the current clock interval are marked with a referenced bit.
- When a page needs to be replaced, the operating system divides the pages into four classes:
   o  Class 0: not referenced, not modified.
   o  Class 1: not referenced, modified.
   o  Class 2: referenced, not modified.
   o  Class 3: referenced, modified.
- Although it does not seem possible for a page to be not referenced yet modified, this happens when a category 3 page has its referenced bit cleared by the clock interrupt.
- The NRU algorithm picks a random page from the lowest category for removal. Note that this algorithm implies that a referenced page is more important than a modified page.

## 7.11.3 LRU (Last Recently Used)

- If we use the recent past as an approximation of the near future, then LRU replaces the page which has not been used for the longest period of time. This is the least recently used algorithm.
- LRU replacement associates with each page the time of its last use. When a page is to be replaced, LRU chooses that page which has not been used for the longest period or time.
- For example, consider the following reference string
  7, 0, 1, 2, 0, 3, 0, 4, 2, 3, 0, 3, 2, 1, 2, 0, 1, 7, 0, 1
- By applying LRU, the first five faults are same as the optimal replacement. When the reference to page 4 occurs, LRU sees out of the three frames in memory, page 2 was used least recently. The most recently used page is page 0, and just before that page 3 was used. Thus, LRU replaces page 2, not knowing that it is about to be used. When fault for page 2 occurs, LRU replaces page 3. Since of the three pages in memory (0, 3, 4) page 3 is the least recently used. No. of page faults = 12.

| 7 | 0 | 1 | 2 | 0 | 3 | 0 | 4 | 2 | 3 | 0 | 3 | 2 | 1 | 2 | 0 | 1 | 7 | 0 | 1 |
|---|---|---|---|---|---|---|---|---|---|---|---|---|---|---|---|---|---|---|---|
| 7 | 7 | 7 | 2 |   | 2 |   | 4 | 4 | 4 | 0 |   |   | 1 |   | 1 |   | 1 |   |   |
|   | 0 | 0 | 0 |   | 0 |   | 0 | 0 | 3 | 3 |   |   | 3 |   | 0 |   | 0 |   |   |
|   |   | 1 | 1 |   | 3 |   | 3 | 2 | 2 | 2 |   |   | 2 |   | 2 |   | 7 |   |   |

**Fig. 7.41 (a)**

- Two implementation of LRU are:

**1. Counters:**
- Each page table entry has a time of use of the register and adds to the CPU a logical clock or counter. The clock is incremented for every memory reference.
- Whenever, a reference to a page is made, the contents of the clock register are copied to the time of use of the register in the page table for that page.
- Thus, we always have the "time" of the last reference to each page. We replace the page with the smaller time value i.e. the least recently used.
- Associate each PMT entry a "Time of use" field and add to a CPU a logical counter or clock.
- The clock is incremented on every memory reference. Whenever a reference to page is made the contents of logical clocks are copied to "time-of-use" field.
- In this way we exactly know the time of last reference of a particular page. We replace the page with smallest time value.

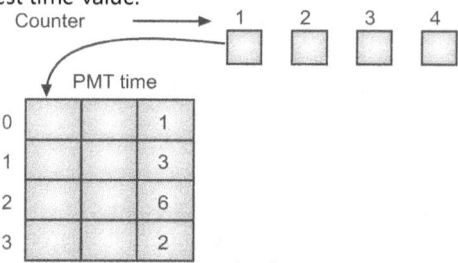

**Fig. 7.41 (b)**

This requires a search of page map table to find LRU candidate.

2. **Stack:**
   - This implementation keeps a stack of page numbers. Whenever a page is referenced, it is removed from the stack and put on the top.
   - It uses a stack of memory pages. Whenever, a page is referenced, it is removed from a stack and put on the stack top. In this way the "top" of the stack is always "MRU" member while "bottom" contains LRU page. There is no search for LRU page, only it has to manage the different address pointers.
   - Thus, the top of the stack is always the most recently used page and the bottom is the least recently used page.

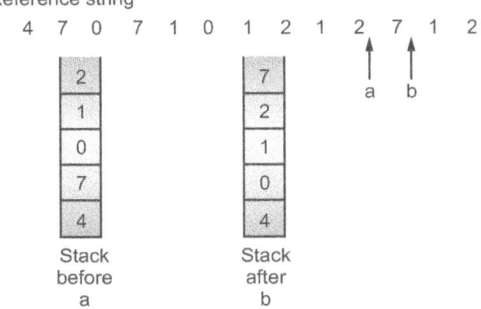

- Least Recently Used Removal (LRU) selects a page for removal that has not been referenced for the longest time.
- FIFO in contrast removes the page that has been in the memory for the longest time, regardless of how often and when it is referenced.
- LRU is based on theory that if a page is referenced, it is liked to be referenced again. This is according to a "theory of locality of references".
- **Temporal locality:** Once a data, instrumentation is referenced, it is often referenced again very soon. For example: Program constructs such as loop, variables or subroutines.
- **Spatial locality:** Probability that once a location is referenced a nearby location referenced a nearby.
  
  e.g. Program constructs such as sequential instrumentation sequencing, linear data structures like array.
- Most recently used pages are top of memory list.
- Candidate of removal are at bottom.
- Increasing memory size can never cause number of page faults increased.
- m (p, c, t) c m (p, c + 1, t)
  
  inclusion properly
  
  when p = page trace, c = memory size, t = reference time t.

## M = 3

| | 1 | 2 | 3 | 4 | 5 | 6 | 7 | 8 | 9 | 10 | 11 | 12 |
|---|---|---|---|---|---|---|---|---|---|---|---|---|
| P = | 4 | 3 | 2 | 1 | 4 | 3 | 5 | 4 | 3 | 2 | 1 | 5 |
| | | 4+ | 3+ | 2+ | 1+ | 4+ | 3+ | 5+ | 4 | 3 | 2+ | 1+ | 5+ |
| M = 3 | | | 4 | 3 | 2 | 1 | 4 | 3 | 5 | 4 | 3 | 2 | 1 |
| | | | | ④ | ③ | ② | ① | 4 | 3 | ⑤ | ④ | ③ | ② |
| F = | | + | + | + | + | + | + | + | S | S | F | + |

m = 3    F = 10

$$S = \frac{10}{12} \approx 83\%$$

## M = 4

| | 1 | 2 | 3 | 4 | 5 | 6 | 7 | 8 | 9 | 10 | 11 | 12 |
|---|---|---|---|---|---|---|---|---|---|---|---|---|
| P = | 4 | 3 | 2 | 1 | 4 | 3 | 5 | 4 | 3 | 2 | 1 | 5 |
| | | 4+ | 3+ | 2+ | 1+ | 4 | 3 | 5+ | 4 | 3 | 2+ | 1+ | 5+ |
| M = 4 | | | 4 | 3 | 2 | 1 | 4 | 3 | 5 | 4 | 3 | 2 | 1 |
| | | | | 4 | 3 | 2 | 1 | 4 | 3 | 5 | 4 | 3 | 2 |
| | | | | | 4 | 3 | ② | 1 | 1 | ① | ⑤ | ④ | 3 |
| F = | | + | + | + | + | S | S | + | S | S | + | + | + |

m = 4    F = 8

$$F = \frac{8}{12} \approx 67\%$$

m (p, c, t) C M (p, c + 1, t)

---------> time

| | 1 | 2 | 3 | 4 | 5 | 6 | 7 | 8 | 9 | 10 | 11 | 12 | 13 | 14 | 15 | 16 | 17 | 18 | 19 | 20 |
|---|---|---|---|---|---|---|---|---|---|---|---|---|---|---|---|---|---|---|---|---|
| P = | 7 | 0 | 1 | 2 | 0 | 3 | 0 | 4 | 2 | 3 | 0 | 3 | 2 | 1 | 2 | 0 | 1 | 7 | 0 | 1 |
| | 7+ | 6+ | 1+ | 2+ | 0 | 3+ | 0 | 4+ | 2+ | 3+ | 0+ | 3 | 2 | 1+ | 2 | 0+ | 1 | 7+ | 0 | 1 |
| M = 3 | | 7 | 0 | 1 | 2 | 0 | 3 | 0 | 4 | 2 | 3 | 0 | 3 | 2 | 1 | 2 | 0 | 1 | 7 | 0 |
| | | | ⑦ | 0 | ① | 2 | ② | ③ | | 4 | 2 | 2 | | 3 | ③ | 1 | ② | 0 | 1 | 7 |
| F = | + | + | + | + | S | + | S | + | + | F | F | S | S | F | S | F | S | + | S | S |

$$S = 8 \quad F = 12 \quad F = \frac{6}{10} \quad 0.6 = 60\%$$

---------> time

| | 1 | 2 | 3 | 4 | 5 | 6 | 7 | 8 | 9 | 10 | 11 | 12 | 13 | 14 | 15 | 16 | 17 | 18 | 19 | 20 |
|---|---|---|---|---|---|---|---|---|---|---|---|---|---|---|---|---|---|---|---|---|
| P = | 7 | 0 | 1 | 2 | 0 | 3 | 0 | 4 | 2 | 3 | 0 | 3 | 2 | 1 | 2 | 0 | 1 | 7 | 0 | 1 |
| | 7+ | 0+ | 1+ | 2+ | 0 | 3+ | 0 | 4+ | 2 | 3 | 0 | 3 | 2 | 1+ | 2 | 0 | 1 | 7+ | 0 | 1 |
| | | 7 | 0 | 1 | 2 | 0 | 3 | 0 | 4 | 2 | 3 | 0 | 3 | 2 | 1 | 2 | 0 | 1 | 7 | 0 |
| M = 4 | | | 7 | 0 | 1 | 2 | 2 | 3 | 0 | 4 | 2 | 2 | 0 | 3 | 3 | 1 | 2 | 0 | 1 | 7 |
| | | | | 7 | ⑦ | 1 | ① | 2 | 3 | 0 | 4 | 4 | ④ | 0 | 0 | 3 | ③ | 2 | 2 | 2 |
| F = | + | + | + | + | S | + | S | + | S | S | S | S | + | S | S | S | + | S | S |

$$S = 12 \quad F = 8 \quad F = \frac{4}{10} \quad 0.4 = 40\%$$

## 7.11.4 LRU Approximation using Reference Bit

- Few computer systems provide sufficient hardware support for true LRU page replacement while some computer systems provide no hardware support and other page-replacement algorithms (FIFO) must be used.
- Number of computer systems provide some help, however in the form of a reference bit. The reference bit for a page is set by the hardware whenever, that page is referenced.
- Reference bits are associated with each entry in the page table.
- Initially, all bits are cleared (to 0) by the operating system. As a user process executes, the bit associated with each page referenced is set (to 1) by the hardware.
- PMT entry contains a reference bit, which indicates a reference is made to any address within the page.
- Initially all bits are cleared (tool) by operating system. As a user process executes, the bit associated with each page referenced is set (to 1) by hardwork.
- By examining the bits we can identify which page have been used and which not but we don't get any ordering information.

### Additional-Reference-Bits Algorithm

- We can gain additional ordering information by recording the reference bits at regular intervals. We can keep an 8-bit byte for each page in a table in memory.
- At regular intervals, a timer interrupt transfers control to the operating system. The operating system shifts the reference bit for each page into the high-order bit of its 8-bit byte, shifting the other bits right by 1 bit and discarding the low-order bit.
- These 8-bit shift registers contain the history of page use for the last eight time periods. If the shift register contains 00000000, for example, then the page has not been used for eight time periods a page that is used at least once in each period has a shift register value of 11111111. A page with a history register value of 11000100 has been used more recently than one with a value of 01110111. If we interpret these 8-bit bytes as unsigned integers, the page with the lowest number is the LRU page and it can be replaced.
- The number of bits history included in the shift register can be varied, of course, and is selected to make the updating as fast as possible. In the extreme case, the number can be reduced to zero, leaving only the reference bit itself. This algorithm is called the second-chance page-replacement algorithm.

## 7.11.5 LFU

- The **Least Frequently Used (LFU) page-replacement algorithm** requires that the page with the smallest count be replaced. The reason for this selection is that an actively used page should have a large reference count.
- A problem arises, however, when a page is used heavily during the initial phase of a process but then is never used again.
- Since, it was used heavily, it has a large count and remains in memory even though it is no longer needed. One solution of this problem is to shift the counts right by 1 bit at regular intervals, forming an exponentially decaying average usage count.

## 7.11.6 MFU
- The **Most Frequently Used** (MFU) **page-replacement algorithm** is based on the argument that the page with the smallest count was probably just brought in and has yet to be used.
- As you might expect, neither MFU nor LFU page replacement is common. The implementation of these (MFU and LFU) algorithms is expensive and they do not approximate OPT replacement well.

## 7.11.7 Second-Chance Algorithm
- The basic algorithm of second-chance replacement is a FIFO replacement algorithm.
- When a page has been selected, however, we inspect its reference bit. If the values is 0, we proceed to replace this page, but if the reference bit is set to 1, we give the page a second chance and move on to select the next FIFO page.
- When a page gets a second chance, its reference bit is cleared and its arrival time is reset to the current time for this reason, a page that is given a second chance will not be replaced until all other pages have been replaced.
- If a page is used often enough to keep its reference bit set, it will never be replaced.
- One way to implement the second-chance algorithm is as a circular queue.
- A pointer indicates which page is to be replaced next. When a frame is needed, the pointer advances until it finds a page with a 0 reference bit.
- Fig. 7.42 show Second-chance (clock) Page-Replacement Algorithm

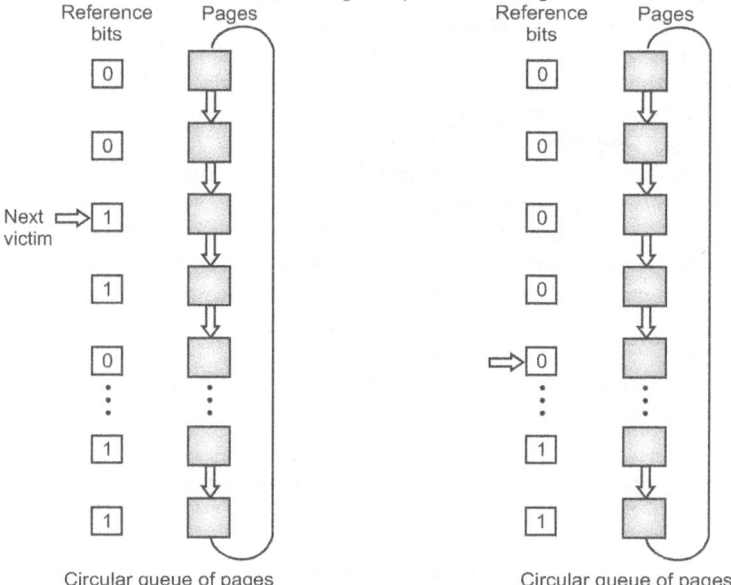

**Fig. 7.42**

- As it advances, it clears the reference bits as shown in Fig. 7.42.
- Once, a victim page is found, the page is replaced, and the new page is inserted in the circular queue in that position.
- Second-chance replacement degenerates to FIFO replacement if all bits are set.

### Enhanced Second-Chance Algorithm

- We can enhance the second-chance algorithm by considering the reference bit and the modify bit as an ordered pair. With these two bits, we have the following four possible classes:
  1. **(0, 0) neither recently used nor modified:** best page to replace.
  2. **(0, 1) not recently used but modified:** Not quite as good, because the page will need to be written out before replacement.
  3. **(1, 0) recently used but clean:** Probably will be used again soon.
  4. **(1, 1) recently used and modified:** Probably will be used again soon and the page will be need to be written out to disk before it can be replaced.

## 7.12 OPTIMAL PAGE REPLACEMENT

- An optimal page replacement algorithm has the lowest page fault rate of all algorithms and does not suffer from Belady's anomaly.
- Optimal replacement algorithm state that replaces the page which will not be used for the longest period of time.
- For example, consider the following reference string.
  7, 0, 1, 2, 0, 3, 0, 4, 2, 3, 0, 3, 2, 1, 2, 0, 1, 7, 0, 1
- The first three reference' cause faults which fill the three empty frames.
- The reference to page 2 replaces page 7, because 7 will be used until reference 18, whereas page 0 will be used at 5 and page 1 at 14, the reference to page 3 replaces page 1, as page 1 will be the last of the three pages in memory to be referenced again.
- With only nine page faults, optimal replacement is much better than a FIFO algorithm, which had 15 faults. The optimal page replacement algorithm is difficult to implement, because it requires future knowledge of the reference string.

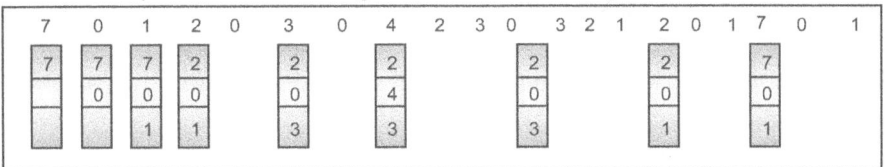

**Fig. 7.43**

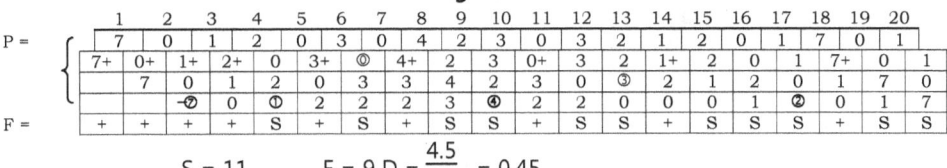

$S = 11 \qquad F = 9 \quad D = \dfrac{4.5}{10} = 0.45$

Failure frequency = 45%

{Replace the page that will not be used for the longest time}

- It requires future knowledge of the page trace.
- The major problems arises in implementation of LRU. It requires either hardware assistance or software method to determine whether a page is most recently used of least recently used.

**Exercise**

1. What is meant by memory management?
2. What is swapping? What is need of swapping?
3. Explain MVT & MFT Job Scheduling in Detail.
4. Explain page replacement algorithms with their advantages and disadvantages.
5. Describe the basic concept of paging.
6. Define page fault and page table.
7. What is meant by logical and physical address?
8. What is segmentation? How to use it with paging?
9. Define NRU, MFU, LFU page replacement algorithms.
10. Explain the term virtual memory in detail.
11. Explain FIFO, LRU page replacement algorithms for the reference string 7 0 1 2 0 3 0 4 2 3 1 0 3.
12. With the help of diagram describe demand paging.
13. Describe second chance algorithm with example.
14. What is meant by fragmentation?
15. State advantages and disadvantages of segmentation.
16. Differentiate between Internal and External fragmentation.
17. Explain optional page replacement algorithm with example.
18. Consider the following reference string:
    2 3 2 1 5 2 4 5 3 2 5 2
    Calculate the page fault for number of frames = 3 for the following algorithms.
    (i) LRU
    (ii) FIFO
19. Why demand paging approach is preferred over segmentation?
20. Compare paging and segmentation.
21. What is meant by memory partition? Explain single and multiple partition in short.
22. What is meant by dynamic loading and dynamic linking?
23. Consider the following page reference string:
    4, 3, 2, 1, 4, 3, 5, 4, 3, 2, 1, 5
    The number of frame are 3. Show page trace and calculate page
    Faults for the following page replacement schemes:
    (i) FIFO
    (ii) MFU
24. Write a Short note on Overlays.

■■■

# Chapter 8...

# File System

## Contents ...
8.1 Introduction and File Concepts
    8.1.1 File Attributes
    8.1.2 Operations on File
    8.1.3 Types of Files
8.2 Access Methods
    8.2.1 Sequential Access
    8.2.2 Direct Access
8.3 File Structure
8.4 File Allocation Methods
    8.4.1 Contiguous Allocation
    8.4.2 Linked Allocation (Chained Allocation)
    8.4.3 Indexed Allocation
8.5 Free Space Management Techniques
    8.5.1 Bit Vector
    8.5.2 Linked List
    8.5.3 Grouping
    8.5.4 Counting
    Exercise

## 8.1 INTRODUCTION AND FILE CONCEPTS

- All computer applications need to store and retrieve information while a process is running; it can store a limited amount of information within its own address space.
- However, the storage capacity is restricted to the size of the virtual memory.
- For some applications, this size is enough, but is far others, such as banking, railway reservation, it is far too small.
- A second problem with keeping information within a process address space is that when process terminates the information is lost.
- For many applications must be retained for long period. This situation is unacceptable.
- A third problem is that it is frequently necessary for multiple processes to access the information at the same time.

- Thus, we have three essential requirements for long-term information storage:
  1. It must be possible to store a very large amount of information.
  2. The information must survive the termination of the process using it.
  3. Multiple processes must be able to access the information concurrently.
- The usual solution to all the problems is to store information on disks and other external media in units called files.
- Files are managed by the operating system.
- How they are structured, named, accessed, used, protected, and implemented are major topics in monitoring system design.
- As a whole that part of the operating system dealing with files is known as the file system.
- Computers can store information on several different storage media such as magnetic disks, magnetic tapes. In order to make the computer system convenient to use, the operating system provides a uniform logical view of information storage.
- The operating system extracts from the physical properties of its storage devices to define a logical storage unit, the file.
- Files are mapped by the operating system onto the physical devices.
- A file is a named collection of related information that is recorded on a secondary storage. Commonly, files represent programs (source and object forms) and data.
- Data files may be numeric, alphabetic, alphanumeric or binary.
- Files may be of free form such as text files or may be formatted rigidly.
- In general a file is a sequence of bits, bytes, lines or records whose meaning is defined by the file's creator and user.
- The information in a file is defined by its creator.
- Many different types of information may be stored in a file: Source programs, Object programs, Executable programs, Numeric Data, Text, Payroll records, Graphic Images, Sound recording and so on. A file has a certain defined structure according to its type.
- A text file is a sequence of characters organized into lines.
- A source file is a sequence of subroutines and functions etc.

### 8.1.1 File Attributes

- A file is needed for the convenience of its human users and is referred to by its name, such as "example.c".
- A file has certain other attributes, which vary from one operating system to another, but typically consist of these:
  1. **Name:** The symbolic file name is the only information kept in human readable form.
  2. **Type:** This information is needed for those systems that support different file types.
  3. **Location:** This information is a pointer to a device and to the location of the file on that device.

4. **Size:** The current size of the file (in bytes, words or blocks) and possibly the maximum allowed size are included in this attribute.
5. **Protection:** Access control information controls that can do reading, writing, executing and so on.
6. **Time, Date and User Identification:** This information specifies the date of creation, Last modification and last use. These data items can be useful for protection, security and usage monitoring.

## 8.1.2 Operations on File
- A file is an abstract data type. To define a file properly, we need to consider the operations that can be performed on files.
- The operating system provides system calls to create, write, read, reposition, delete and truncate files.
    1. **Creating a file:** Two steps are necessary to create a file. First space in the file system must be found for the file. Second an entry for the new file must be made in the directory. The directory entry records the name of the file and the location in the file system.
    2. **Writing a file:** To write a file, we make a system call specifying both the name of the file and the information to be written to the file. Given the name of the file, the system searches the directory to find the location of file then the write pointer must be updated whenever, a write occurs.
    3. **Reading a file:** To read from a file, we use a system call that specifies the name of the file and where, (in memory) the next block of the file should be put. System needs to keep a read pointer to location in the file where the next read is to take place. Once, the read has taken place, the read pointer is updated.
    4. **Repositioning within a file:** The directory is searched for the appropriate entry, and the current file position is set to a given value. Repositioning within a file does not need to involve any actual I/O. This file operation is also known as a **file seeks**.
    5. **Deleting a file:** To delete a file, we search the directory for the named file. Having found the associated directory entry, we release all file space and erase the directory entry.
    6. **Truncating a file:** Instead of deleting a file and then recreate it, this function allows all attributes to remain unchanged except for the file to be reset to length zero, if the user wants to erase the contents of the file.
- Other common operations include appending new information to the end of an existing file, and renaming an existing file.

## 8.1.3 Types of Files
- To operate on the file in reasonable way an operating system recognizes the type of a file.
- A common technique for implementing file types is to include the type as a part of the file name.

- The name is split into two parts a name and an extension. In this way the user and the operating system can tell from the name alone what the type of a file is, for example, in MS-DOS a name can consist of up to eight characters followed by period and terminated by an up to three-character extension.
- The system uses the extension to indicate the type of the file and the type of operations that can be done on that file.
- For instance only a file with a ".com", ".exe", or ".bat" extension can be executed.
- The ".com" and ".exe" files are two forms of binary executable files, whereas a ".bat" file is a batch file containing information in ASCII format i.e. commands to the operating system.

| File Type | Usual Extensions | Function |
|---|---|---|
| Executable | exe, com, bin or none | Ready to run machine language program |
| Object | obj, o | Compiled, machine language, not linked |
| Source Code | c, p, pas, as, a, f77 | Source code in various languages |
| Text | txt, doc | Textual data documents |
| Batch | bat, sh | Commands to the command interpreter |
| Word Processor | wp, rrf, tex, etc | Various word processor formats |
| Library | lib, a | Libraries of routines for programmers |
| Print or View | ps, gif, dvi | ASCII or binary file in a format for printing or viewing |
| Archive | arc, zip, tar | Related files grouped into one file, sometimes compressed, for archiving or storage. |

## 8.2 ACCESS METHODS

- File stores information.
- When it is used, this information must be accessed and read into the computer's memory.
- There are several ways that the information in the file can be accessed. Some systems provide only one access method for files.

### Serial File

- The least complicated form of file organization is the serial file or pile.
- Here, the data items are collected in the order in which they arrive.
- The purpose of this file is simply to accumulate the mass of data that arrives and save it.
- Records may have different fields, or similar fields in different orders.
- Thus, each field should be self describing including a field name as well as a value.

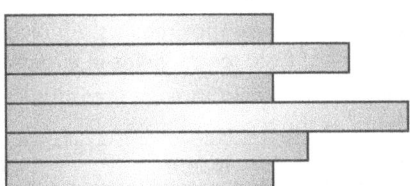

**Fig. 8.1: Variable Length Records, Variable Set of Fields, Chronological Order**

**Advantages:**
1. Simple organization.
2. Data items are usually stored prior to processing.
3. Less complexity and good efficiency for variable sized records.
4. Utilizes space very well for varying data structures.

**Disadvantages:**
1. Because there is no structure to these files, record access is very difficult.
2. Requires more Searching time.
3. Records are not arranged in proper manner.

## 8.2.1 Sequential Access

- The most common form of file structure is the sequential file. In this type of file, a fixed format is used for records.
- All records are of same length, consisting of the same number of fixed-length fields in a particular order.
- Usually first field in each record is referred to as the key field. The key field uniquely identifies the record.
- In sequential access method information in the file is processed in order, one record after the other.
- The most of the operations on a file is read or writes. A read operation read the next portion of file and advances a file pointer, which tracks the I/O location. Similarly, a write appends to the end of the file.
- The simplest access method is sequential access. Information in the file is processed in order, one record after the other. The bulk of the operations on a file are reads and writes.
- A read operation reads the next portion of the file and automatically advances a file pointer, which tracks the I/O location.
- Similarly, a write appends to the end of the file and advances to the end of the newly written material. Such a file can be reset to the beginning and on some systems a program may be able to skip forward or backward 'n' records for some integer 'n'.

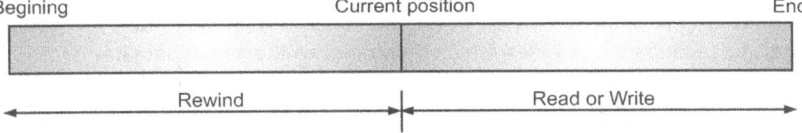

**Fig. 8.2: Sequential Access**

- In this type of file, a fixed format is used for records. All records are of the same length consisting of the same number of fixed length fields in a particular order.
- One particular field usually the first field in each record is referred to as the **key field**. The key field uniquely identifies the record.

| Roll No. | Name | Marks |
|---|---|---|
|  |  |  |
|  |  |  |
|  |  |  |
|  |  |  |
|  |  |  |
|  |  |  |

**Advantages:**
1. Easy to access the next record.
2. Data organization is very simple.
3. Absence of data structures.
4. Sequential files are typically used in batch applications where they are involved in the processing of all the records such as payroll, billing etc.
5. They are easily stored on tapes as well as disks.
6. Automatic backup copy is created.

**Disadvantages:**
1. Wastage of memory space because of master file and transaction file.
2. For interactive applications that involve queries and/or updates of individual records, the sequential file provides poor performance.

### Indexed Sequential File

- These additional methods generally involve the construction of an index for the file.
- The index, like an index of a book, contains pointers to the various blocks. To find an entry in the file, we first search the index and then use the pointer to directly access the file and find the desired entry.
- From this search, we would know exactly which block contains the desired entry and access that block. This structure allows us to search a large file with very little effort.
- With large files, the index file itself may become too large to be kept in the memory. One solution is then to create an index for the index file. The primary index file would contain pointers to secondary index files, which then point to the actual data items.
- The indexed sequential file maintains the key characteristics of the sequential file. Two features are added, first an index to the file to support random access, and an overflow file. The index file provides a quick lookup for victim record.

- The overflow file is a log file, to add new records. The records in overflow file are located by following a pointer from their predecessor record.
- In the simplest indexed sequential structure, a single level of indexing is used. Each record in index file consists of two fields.
- Key field, which is same as the key field in main file, and a pointer into the main file. To find specific field, the index is searched to find the highest key value that is equal to or precedes the desire key value.
- The search continues in the main file at the location indicated by the pointer.
- In case of additions to the file, each record in the main file contains an additional field not visible to application, which is a pointer to the overflow file.
- The indexed sequential file greatly reduces the time required to access a single record, without sacrificing a sequential nature of the file.
- The process the entire file sequentially, the records of main file are processed in sequence until a pointer to overflow file is found, then accessing continues in the overflow file until a null pointer is encountered.
- To provide greater efficiency in access, multiple levels of indexing can be used.

**Advantages:**
1. Variable length records are allowed.
2. Indexed sequential file may be updated in sequential or random mode.
3. Very fast operation.

**Disadvantages:**
1. The major disadvantage of the indexed sequential file is that, as the file grows, a performance deteriorates rapidly because of overflows and consequently there arises the need for periodic reorganization. Reorganization is an expensive process and the file becomes unavailable during reorganization.
2. When a new record is added to the main file, all of the index files must be updated.
3. Consumes large memory space for maintaining index files.

### 8.2.2 Direct Access
- For direct access, the file is viewed as a number of sequential blocks of records.
- A block is generally a fixed length quantity, defined by an operating system.
- A block may be 512 bytes long, 1024 bytes long or some other length, depending upon the system.

Block 0   Block 2   Block 2         Block n   Block n+1

**Fig. 8.3: Direct Access**

- A direct access file allows arbitrary blocks to be read or written. Thus, we may read block 14, then read block 50 and then write block 7. There are no restrictions on the order of reading or writing for a direct access file.

- Direct access files are of great use for immediate access to large amounts of information.
- When a query concerning a particular subject arrives, we compute which block contains the answer and then read the block directly to provide the desired information.
- For example, in an airline reservation system, we store all the information about a particular flight in the block identified by the flight by number (flight 710). Thus, the number of available seats for flight 710 is stored in block 710 of the reservation file.
- The block number provided by the user to the operating system is normally relative block number.
- A relative block number is an index relative to the beginning of the file. Thus, the first relative block of the file is 0; the next is 1 and so on.
- The use of relative block numbers allows the operating system to decide where the file should be placed. Not all the operating system support both sequential and direct access of files.
- Some systems allow only sequential file access, others allow only direct access.

## Hashing

- The basic idea of Hash addressing is that each record is placed in the database at a location whose address (SRA) Stored Record Address may be computed as some function (Called as Hash function) of a value usually the primary key value.
- Thus, to store the record initially, the DBMS computes SRA and instructs the access method to place the occurrence at that position, and to retrieve the occurrence, the DBMS performs the same computation as before and then requests the access method to fetch the occurrence at the computed position.
- What address is generated by the Hashing function? There are a number of ways of converting a key to a numeric value. Most of the keys are numeric, but if the keys are alphabetic or alpha numeric we can use the bit representation of the alphabet to generate the numeric equivalent key.
- A number of simple hashing methods are given below.
  1. Use the low order part of the key.
  2. For long keys, we identify start, middle and end regions, such that the sum of the lengths of the start and end regions equals the length of the middle region. The start and end digits are combined and the combined string of digits is added to the middle region digits. The (new number) mod (the upper limit of the hash function) gives the bucket address.
  3. Square all or part of the key and take a part from the result. The whole or some defined part of the key is squared and a number of digits are selected from the square as being part of the hash result.
  4. Division can be used to form the address. The key can be divided by a number (consider it as a prime number) and the remainder is taken as the bucket address usually a prime number is used for division because if keys are in some multiples, this would produce a poor result.

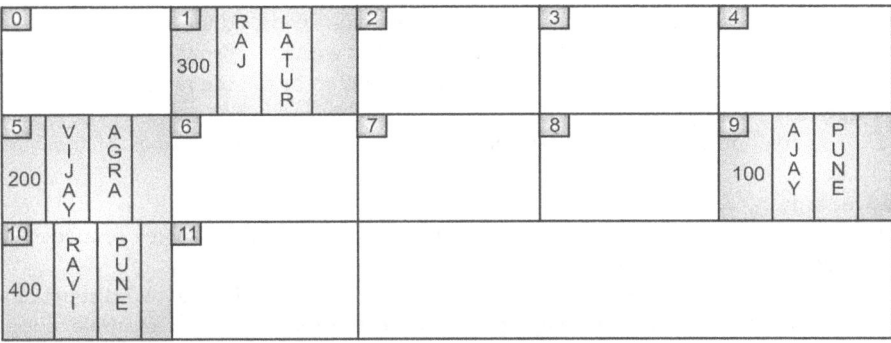

**Fig. 8.4: Hashing**

- There are a number of possible methods for generating a hash function but it has been found that hash functions using division or multiplication perform quite well under most conditions.
- We will take a simple hashing function:

$$H(k) = k \bmod s$$

- Where h (k) produces an address and h is a hash function that maps the key value k to the value h (k) and k is the numeric representation of the key.
- To explain the above hashing function we will take an example of a Table supplier.

**Table 8.1: Supplier**

| S_no | S_name | Address |
|------|--------|---------|
| 100  | Ajay   | Pune    |
| 200  | Vijay  | Agra    |
| 300  | Raj    | Latur   |
| 400  | Ravi   | Pune    |

For hash function S_no is used as a key.

| 0 | 1 | 2 | 3 | 4 |
|---|---|---|---|---|
|   | 300 |   |   |   |

**Fig. 8.5**

SRA = S_no Mod 13

- The SRA = Stored record address is the remainder of the above operation example for S_no 100, SRA = 9, next is 5, 1, 10.
- It would be theoretically possible to use an "identity" hash function i.e. to use the primary key value for any given occurrence directly as the SRA for that occurrence. This is practically inadequate, because the range of primary key values is generally much wider than the range of available SRA.

- For example, if the supplier numbers are in three digits wide, (1000), whereas in practice there may be a maximum of only ten. To reduce this wastage of space, we require a hash function that will reduce any value in the range 0-999 to one in the range 0-9.

**Advantages:**
1. This method provides very fast direct access on the basis of values of the hashed field.

**Disadvantages:**
1. The sequence of stored record occurrence will not be a primary key sequence i.e. it has no particular sequence.
2. Another disadvantage of hashing is the possibility of collision i.e. two distinct stored record occurrences whose keys may hash to the same SRA. For example, suppose that the sample data also included a supplier with S_no = 1400. This would produce SRA = 9 which is the SRA of S_no = 100. This supplier 1400 would then collide at SRA = 9 where S_no= 100 is stored. The solution for this is we go to SRA 9, and search for from this position for the first free location and insert the record for S_no = 1400 there. Collisions are handled in a number of ways. The colliding records may be assigned to the next available free space or they may be assigned to an overflow area.

## File Directories

- To keep track of file, file system normally have directories or folders, which in many systems, are themselves files.
- The directory can be viewed as a symbol table translates file names into their directory entries. If we take such a view, we see that the directory itself can be organized in many ways.
- When we are considering a particular directory structure, the operations that are performed on a directory are:
    - **Search for a file:** We need to be able to search a directory structure to find the entry for particular file.
    - **Create a file:** New files need to be created and added to directory.
    - **Delete a file:** When a file is deleted, an entry must be removed from directory.
    - **List directory:** We need to be able to list the files in directory and contents of the directory entry for each file in the list.
    - **Update directory:** Because some file attributes are stored in the directory a change in one of these attributes requires a change in the corresponding directory entry.
    - **Single level directory:** The simplest directory structure is the single level directory. All files are contained in a same directory, which is easy to support and understand.

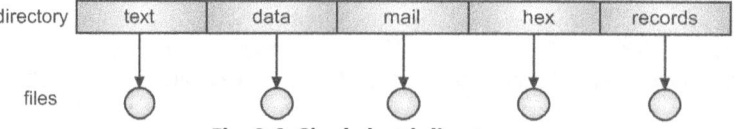

**Fig. 8.6: Single level directory**

- A single-level directory has significant limitation, however, when number of files increases or when the system has more than one user. Since all files are in the same directory, they must have unique names.

## Two-level Directory

- A single-level directory have problem of filenames using by different users. The solution is to create separate directory for each user.
- In the two-level directory structure, each user has own User File Directory (UFD) when user log in, the system's Master File Directory (MFD) is searched. The MFD is indexed by user name or account number and each entry points to the UFD for that user, (Fig. 8.7).

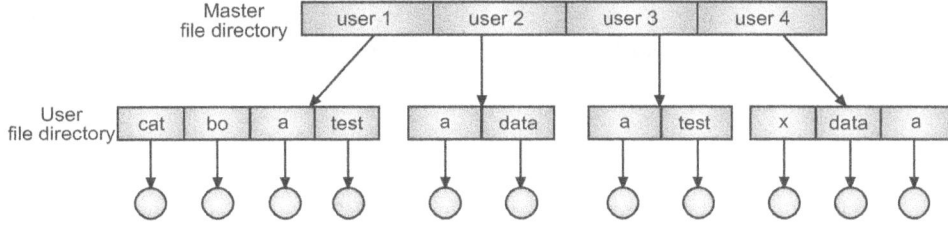

**Fig. 8.7: Two level directory**

- To create file for a user, the operating system searches only that user's UFD to ascertain whether another file of that name exists. To delete file, the operating system continues its search to the local UFD. The user directories themselves must be created and deleted as necessary.
- The two-level directory solves the name-collision problem, it still has disadvantage. This structure isolates one user from another. This isolation is an advantage when the user is completely independent but is disadvantage when the user wants to co-operate on same task and to access one another's file.

## Tree-structured Directories

- The two-level hierarchy eliminates name conflicts among users but is not satisfactory for user with large number of files. We have to extend the two-level tree into the directory structure to tree of arbitrary height, (Fig. 8.8).
- This generalization allows user to create their own subdirectories and to organise their file accordingly.
- The MS-DOS system is structured as a tree.
- The tree has a root directory. Every file in the system has a unique path name.
- A path name is the path from the root, through all the subdirectories to specified file.
- A directory (or subdirectory) contains a set of files or subdirectories. A directory is simply another file, but it is treated in a special way. In normal use, each user has a current directory. The current directory should contain most of the files that are of current interest to the user.

- When reference is made to file, the current directory is searched. If a file is needed that is not in current directory, then the user must either specify a path name or change the current directory to be the directory holding that file.

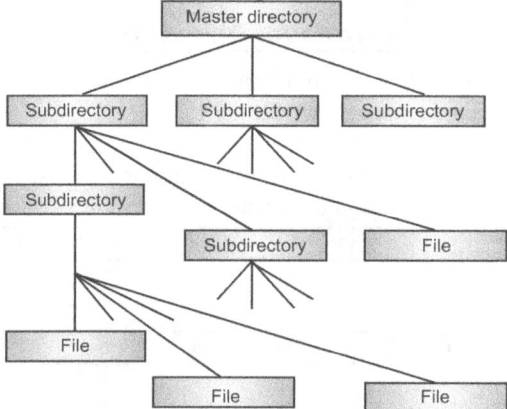

**Fig. 8.8: Tree structure directory**

## Acyclic-Graph Directories

- Consider two programmes who are working on a joint project.
- The files associates with that project can be stored in a subdirectory, separating them from other projects and files of the two programmers.
- But since both the programmes are equally responsible for the project both want the subdirectory to be in their own directories. The common subdirectory should be shared.
- A shared directory or file will exist the file system in two places at once.
- A tree structure prohibits the sharing of files or directories.
- An acyclic graph allows directories to have shared subdirectories of files, (Fig. 8.9).

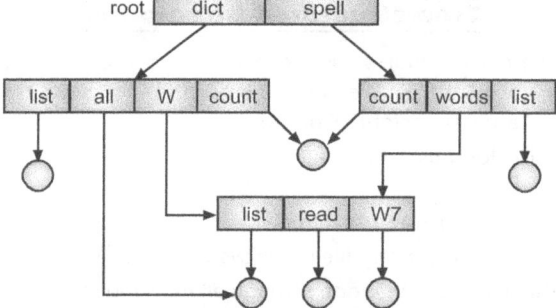

**Fig. 8.9: A cyclic graph directory**

- The same file subdirectory may be in two different directories. An acyclic graph, that is, a graph with no cycles is a natural generation of tree structured directory schemes.

## 8.3 FILE STRUCTURE

- Files can be structured in any of the several ways. The three common possibilities are depicted in Fig. 8.10.
  1. **Stream of Bytes (See Fig. 8.10 (a)).**
     - OS (Operating System) considers a file to be unstructured.
     - Simplifies file management for the OS. Applications can impose their own structure.
     - Used by UNIX, Windows and most modern Operating Systems.
  2. **Records (See Fig. 8.10 (b))**
     - A file is a sequence of fixed length record, each with some internal structure.
     - Collection of bytes is treated as a unit.
       For example: employee record.
     - Operations are at the level of records (read_rec, write_rec).
     - File is a collection of similar records. OS can optimize operations on records.
  3. **Tree of Records (see Fig. 8.10 (c))**
     - A file consists of a tree of records, not necessarily all the same length.
     - Records can be of variable length.
     - Each record has an associated key. The record retrieval is based on the key.

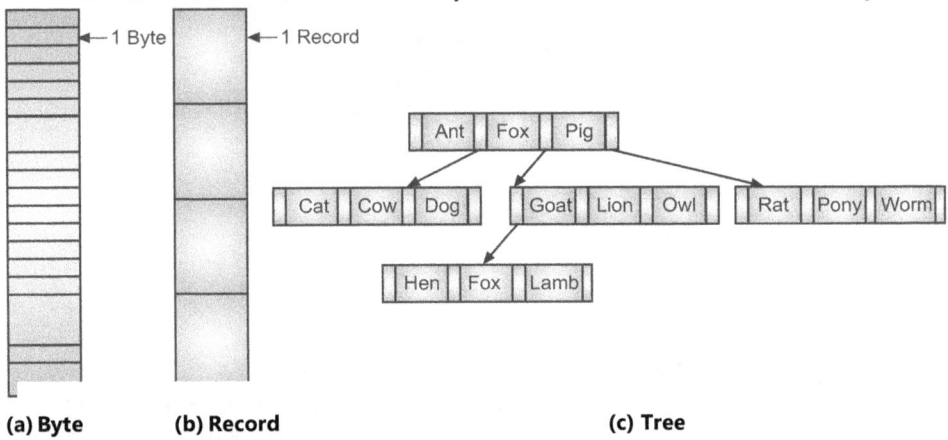

(a) Byte Sequence  (b) Record Sequence  (c) Tree

**Fig. 8.10: File structure**

1. **Tape Based Systems:** A Disk is divided into tracks. The number of tracks varies from disk drive to disk drive. Each track is further divided into sectors. A sector is the smallest unit of information which can be read from or written to the disk. Depending upon disk drive, sectors vary from 32 bytes to 4096 bytes. There are

upto 4 to 32 sectors per track and from 75 to 500 tracks per disk surface. Large disk systems may have several platters. Each platter has two surfaces. To access a sector we must specify the surface, track and sector. The read/write heads are moved to the correct track, electronically switched to the correct surface and then we wait for the requested sector to rotate below the heads. A cylinder is a set of tracks, which are at the same track position of the disk but on different platter surfaces.

Addressing a particular sector requires a track number, a surface number and a sector number. Thus, the disk can be viewed as three-dimensional array of sectors. If 's' is the number of sectors per track and 't' is the number of tracks per cylinder, then we can convert from a disk address of cylinder 'i', surface 'j', sector 'k' to a one dimensional block number 'b' by:

$$b = k + s \times (j + i \times t)$$

| Capacity of Hard Disk = Number of usable surface × Bytes stored per sector × Sectors per track × Tracks per surface |
|---|

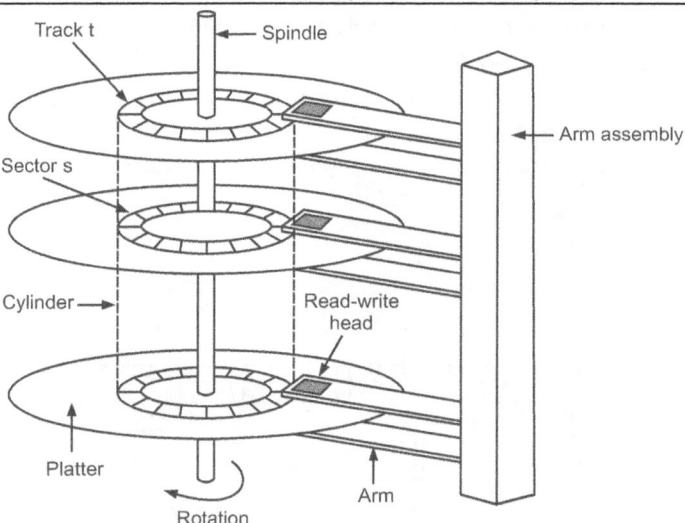

Fig. 8.11: Moving Head Disk Mechanism

2. **Blocking:** Disk systems typically have a well-defined block size determined by the size of a sector. All disk input/output is in units of one block (physical record) and all blocks are of the same size. With tape or disks, physical record size will exact match the length of the desired logical record.

Knowledge of the logical size, physical block size and packing technique determines how many logical records are packed into each physical block. The packing can be done either by the user's application program or by the operating system.

The file may be considered to be a sequence of blocks. All of the basic I/O functions operate in terms of blocks. Notice that always allocating disk space in blocks means that in general some portion of the last block of each file may be wasted. If each block is 512 bytes, then a file of 1949 bytes would be allocated 4 blocks (2048 bytes) the last 99 byte would be wasted. The wasted bytes represent internal fragmentation. All file systems suffer from ***internal fragmentation***. In general larger block sizes cause more internal fragmentation.

## 8.4 FILE ALLOCATION METHODS

- From the user's point of view, a file is an abstract data type. It can be created, opened, written, read, closed and deleted without any real concern for its implementation.
- The implementation of a file is a problem for the operating system.
- On a tape based system, we can map each file to a separate tape or several files on to the same tape. The main problem is how to allocate space to these files so that disk space is effectively utilized and files can be quickly accessed.
- Three major methods of allocating disk space widely in use are:
  o Contiguous allocation.
  o Linked allocation (Chained allocation), and
  o Indexed allocation.
- Several issues are involved in file allocation:
  1. When a new file is created, is the maximum space required for the file allocated at once?
  2. Space is allocated to file as one or more contiguous units. What size of portion should be used for file allocation?
  3. What sort of data structure is used to keep track of the blocks to a file? Such a table is typically referred to as File Allocation Table (FAT).

### Static Versus Dynamic Allocation

- A static allocation requires that the maximum size of file be declared at the time of file creation request.
- In number of cases the value can be reliably estimate, but many cases, it is difficult.
- In those cases users and application programmers would tend to over estimate file size.
- This clearly is wasteful from the point view of secondary storage allocation.
- Thus, there are advantages to the use of dynamic allocation, which allocates space to a file in blocks are needed.

### 8.4.1 Contiguous Allocation

- With this method a single contiguous set of blocks is allocated to a file creation (Fig. 8.12). Thus, this is the static allocation method, using variable-size portion.
- The FAT needs just a one entry. For each file, showing starting block and the length of file. Contiguous allocation is best for sequential file.
- Contiguous allocation has some problems. External fragmentation will occur, making it difficult to find contiguous blocks of space of sufficient length.

- For time to time, it is necessary to do a compaction algorithm to tree up additional space of disk, (Fig. 8.13).

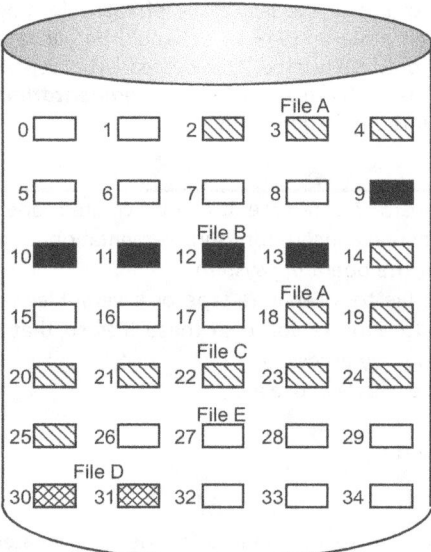

Fig. 8.12: Contiguous File Allocation

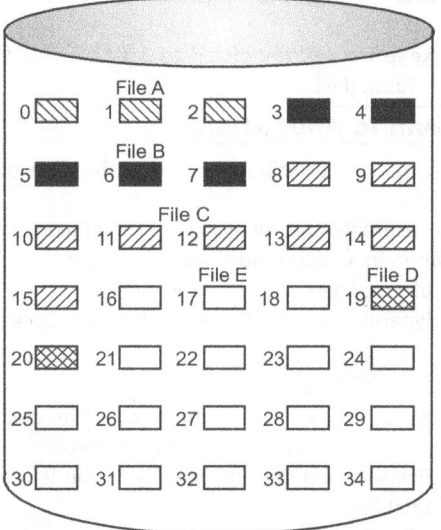

Fig. 8.13: Contiguous File Allocation (After Compaction)

**Advantages:**
1. Supports both sequential and direct access methods.
2. Contiguous allocation is the best form of allocation for **sequential files**. Multiple blocks can be brought in at a time to improve I/O performance for sequential processing.
3. It is also easy to retrieve a single block from a file. For example, if a file starts at block 'n' and the $i^{th}$ block of the file is wanted, its location on secondary storage is simply n + i.

**Disadvantages:**
1. Suffers from external fragmentation.
2. Very difficult to find contiguous blocks of space.
3. Also with pre-allocation, it is necessary to declare the size of the file at the time of creation which many times is difficult to estimate.

## 8.4.2 Linked Allocation (Chained Allocation)

- Linked allocation solves all the problem of contiguous allocation (Fig. 8.14). With chained allocation, each file is a linked list of disk blocks; the blocks may be scattered anywhere on the disk. Again, the file allocation table needs just a single entry for each file, showing starting block and length of file.
- Although static allocation is possible, it is more common simply to allocate block as needed. There is no external fragmentation because only one block at a time is needed.
- The major problem is that it can be used efficiently only for sequential file. To find its block, we must start at the beginning of that file and follow the pointer until we get to the ith block.
- Linked allocation is inefficient to support a direct access files. Another disadvantage to chained allocation is the space required for the pointers.

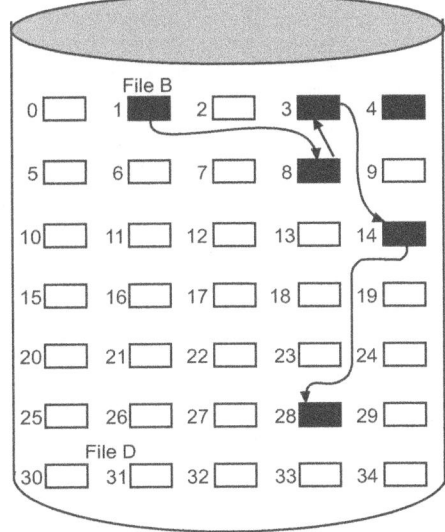

**Fig. 8.14: Chained Allocation**

**Advantages:**
1. Any free blocks can be added to a chain.
2. There is no external fragmentation.
3. Best suited for sequential files that are to be processed sequentially.

**Disadvantages:**
1. There is no accommodation of the principle of locality that is series of accesses to different parts of the disk are required.
2. Space is required for the pointers. 1.5% of disk is used for the pointers and not for information. If a pointer is lost or damaged or bug occurs in operating system or disk hardware failure occur, it may result in picking up the wrong pointer.
3. This method cannot support direct access.

### 8.4.3 Indexed Allocation

- Linked allocation solves the external fragmentation and size declaration problem and contiguous allocation.
- However, chained allocation cannot support efficient direct access, since pointers are scattered with the blocks themselves all over the disk and need to be retrieved in order.
- Indexed allocation solves this problem by bringing all the pointer is together into one location: the index block. In this case, the FAT contains a separate one-level index for each file, the index has one entry for each portion allocated to file.
- File indexes are not physically stored as part of the FAT, but it is kept in a separate block and entry for the file in the FAT points to that block.
- Allocation may be on the basis of either fixed-sized blocks (Fig. 8.15) or variable-size partitions, (Fig. 8.16). Allocation by blocks eliminates external fragmentation, whereas allocation by variable size portions improve locality.
- Indexed allocation supports both sequential and direct access to the file and thus is the most popular form of file allocation.

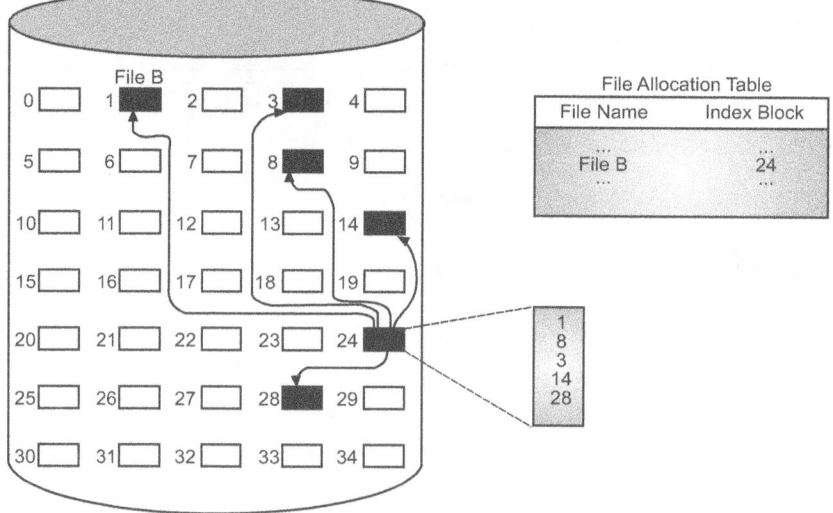

**Fig. 8.15: Indexed Allocation with Block Portions**

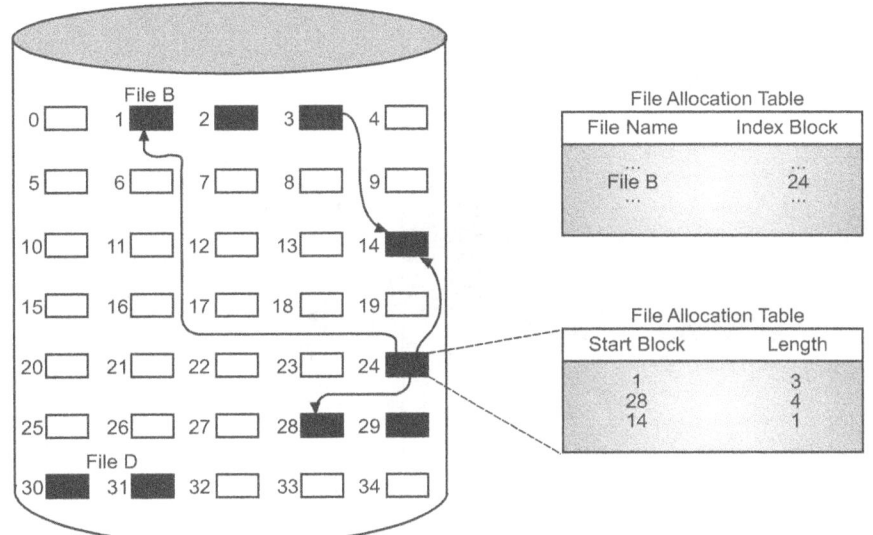

**Fig. 8.16: Indexed Allocations with Variable-Length Portions**

**Advantages:**
1. Does not suffer from external fragmentation.
2. Support both sequential and direct access to the file.

## 8.5 FREE SPACE MANAGEMENT TECHNIQUES

- Files are created and deleted frequently during the operation of a computer system.
- Since, there is only a limited amount of disk space, it is necessary to reuse the space from deleted files for new files. To keep track of free disk space, the file system maintains a free space list.
- The free space list records all disk blocks, which are free. To create a file, we search the free space list for the required amount of space and allocate it to the new file.
- This space is then removed from the free space list. When a file is deleted, its disk space is added to the free space list.

### 8.5.1 Bit Vector

- The free space list may not be implemented as a list; it is implemented as a Bit Map or Bit Vector.
- Each block is represented by one bit. If the block is free, the bit is '0', if the block is allocated the bit is '1', for example, consider a disk where blocks 2,3,4,5,8,9,10,11,12,13,17,18,25,26 and 27 are free, the free space bit map would be,

' 11000011000000111001111110001111 - - - - - - - - - - - - - - '

- **Advantage** of bit vector are:
  1. It is very simple approach.
  2. It is very efficient method.

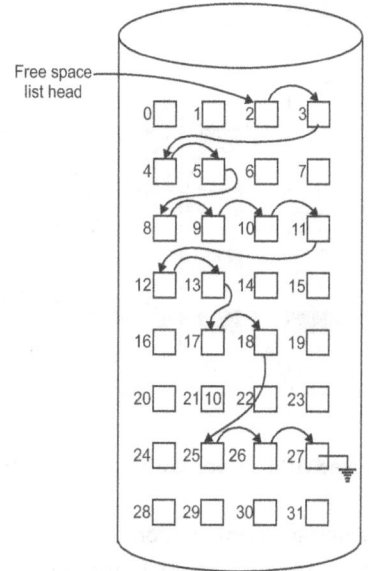

**Fig. 8.17: Linked Free Space List on Disk**

## 8.5.2 Linked List

- Another important approach to free-space management is to link together all the free disk blocks, keeping a pointer to the first free block in a special location on the disk and caching it in memory.

- This first block contains a pointer to the next free disk block, and so on. Recall our earlier example in which blocks 2, 3, 4, 5, 8, 9, 10, 11, 12, 13, 17, 18, 25, 26 and 27 were free and the rest of the blocks were allocated. In this condition, we would keep a pointer to block 2 as the first free block.

- Block 2 would contain a pointer to block 3, which would point to block 4, which would point to block 5, which would point to block 8 etc. as shown in Fig. 8.17.

- This scheme is not efficient; to traverse the list, we must read each block, which requires substantial I/O time. Fortunately, however, traversing the free list is not a frequent action.

Usually, the operating system simply needs a free block so that it can allocate that block to a file, so-the first block in the free list is used.

- The FAT method incorporates free-block accounting into the allocation data structure. No separate method is needed.

### 8.5.3 Grouping

- A modification of the free-list approach stores the addresses of n free blocks in the first free block. The first n − 1 of these blocks are actually free and the last block contains the addresses of other n free blocks, and so on.
- The addresses of a large number of free blocks can now be found quickly, unlike the situation when the standard linked-list approach is used.

### 8.5.4 Counting

- Another important approach takes advantage of the fact that, generally, several contiguous blocks maybe allocated or freed simultaneously, particularly when space is allocated with the contiguous-allocation algorithm or through clustering.
- Thus, rather than keeping a list of n free disk addresses, we can keep the address of the first free block and the number (n) of free contiguous blocks that follow the first block.
- Each entry in the free-space list then consists of a disk address and a count. Although each entry requires more space than would a simple disk address, the overall list is shorter, as long as the count is generally greater than 1.

### Exercise

1. Define the term file.
2. State various attributes of files.
3. What are the types of files?
4. What is meant by file allocation?
5. Enlist various operations and files.
6. What are the different types of access methods?
7. With suitable diagram describe direct access method.
8. Describe the term Indexed allocation in detail.
9. With the help of diagram describe file structure.

10. Define bit vector.
11. Explain the following terms:
    (i) Linked list
    (ii) Grouping
12. With the help of diagram describe sequential access method.
13. What is meant by free space management?
14. Write short note on linked allocation.
15. Compare sequential access and direct access.

# Chapter 9...

# I/O System

## Contents ...
9.1 Introduction
9.2 I/O Hardware
9.3 Application I/O Interface
9.4 Kernel I/O Subsystem
9.5 Disk Scheduling
    9.5.1 FCFS (First Come First Serve)
    9.5.2 Shortest Seek Time First (SSTF)
    9.5.3 SCAN (Elevator Disk Algorithm)
    9.5.4 C-SCAN
    9.5.5 C-LOOK
    Exercise

## 9.1 INTRODUCTION

- The control of devices connected to the computer is a major concern of operating-system designers because I/O devices vary so widely in their function and speed varied methods are needed to control them and these methods form the I/O subsystem of the kernel, which separates the rest of the kernel from the complexities of managing I/O devices.
- The role of the operating system in computer I/O is to manage and control I/O operations and I/O devices.
- I/O device technology exhibits two conflicting trends one hand, we see increasing standardization of software and hardware interfaces. This trend helps us to incorporate improved device generations into existing computers and operating systems and on the other hand, we see an increasingly broad variety of I/O devices.
- Some new devices are so unlike previous devices that it is a challenge to incorporate them into our computers and operating systems. This challenge is met by a combination of hardware and software techniques.
- The basic I/O hardware elements, such as buses, ports and device controllers, accommodate a wide variety of I/O devices. To encapsulate the details and oddities of different devices, the kernel of an operating system is structured to use device driver modules.

- The device drivers present a uniform device-access interface to the I/O subsystem, much as system calls provide a standard interface between the application and the operating system.

## I/O Devices

- The I/O devices with computer system can be roughly group into three categories.
  - **Human readable:** Use for communicating with the computer uses. **Examples:** printer, keyboard.
  - **Machine readable:** Use for communicating with electronic equipment. **Examples:** disk and tape drives, sensors, controllers.
  - **Communication:** Use for communicating with remote devices. Example: modems.
- There are differences between classes and some differences within classes. The key differences are as follows:
  - **Data rate:** There may be differences of several orders of magnitude between data transfer rates.
  - **Application:** The use to which device is put has an influence on the software and policies in the operating system and supporting utilities. For example, a disk used for files requires supporting of file system. A disk used as backing store for pages in virtual memory scheme.
  - **Complexity of control:** A printer requires a relatively simple control interface. A disk is much more complex. The effect of these differences on operating system is filtered to some extent by the complexity of the I/O module that controls the device.
  - **Unit of transfer:** Data may be transfer as a stream of bytes or characters or in larger blocks.
  - **Data representation:** Different data encoding schemes are used by different devices.
  - **Error conditions:** The nature of errors, the way in which they are reported, their consequences and available range of responses different widely from one device to another.

## Organisation of the I/O Functions

- These are three techniques for performing I/O.
  - **Programmed I/O:** The processor issues an I/O command, on behalf of process, to an I/O module; that process then busy waits for the operation to be completed before proceeding.
  - **Interrupt-driven I/O:** The processor issues an I/O command, on behalf of process, continues to execute next instructions, and is interrupted by the I/O module when the latter has completed its work.
  - **Direct Memory Access (DMA):** A DMA module controls the exchange of data between main memory and an I/O module. The processor sends a request for the transfer of a block of data to the DMA module and is interrupted only after the entire block has been transferred I/O system organisation.

- In modern operating system, device management is implemented either through the interaction of device driver and interrupt routine called interrupt driven I/O or wholly within device driver if interrupt are not used called direct I/O with polling.
- Fig. 9.1 shows the unit involved in I/O operation for both approaches.

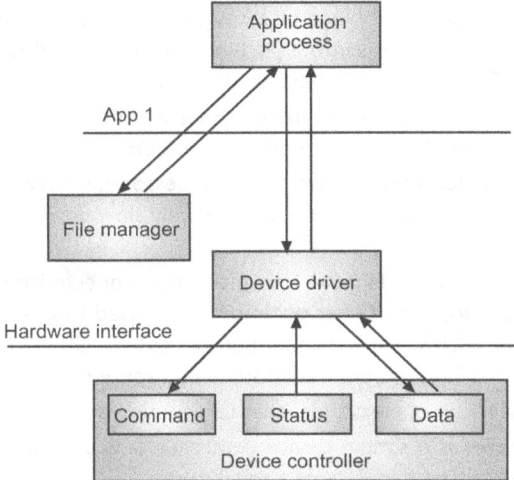

**Fig. 9.1: I/O Operations**

- An application process uses device by issuing commands and exchanging data with the device management device drives. The device driver has two major responsibilities.
    o Implement an abstract application programming interface (API) to the application process.
    o Provide device dependent operations to issue appropriate command to implement functions defined on the API.

## 9.2 I/O HARDWARE

- Basically, computers operate a great many kinds of devices. Most fit into the general categories of storage devices such as disks, tapes etc. transmission devices such as network cards, modems etc. and human-interface devices such as screen, keyboard, mouse and so on.
- Other computer devices are more specialized, such as those involved in the steering of a military fighter jet or a space shuttle. In these aircraft, a human gives input to the flight computer via a joystick and foot pedals, and the computer sends output commands that cause motors to move rudders, flaps and thrusters.
- A computer device communicates with a computer system by sending signals over a cable or even through the air. The device communicates with the machine via a connection point, or port (a serial port).

- When devices use a common set of wires, the connection is called a bus. A bus is a set of wires and a rigidly defined protocol that specifies a set of messages that can be sent on the wires. In terms of the electronics, the messages are conveyed by patterns of electrical voltages applied to the wires with defined timings.
- When device A has a cable that plugs into device B, and device B has a cable that plugs into device C, and device C plugs into a port on the computer, this arrangement is called a daisy chain. A daisy chain usually operates as a bus.
- Buses in computers are used widely in computer architecture and vary in their speed, signaling methods, throughput and connection methods.
- Fig. 9.2 shows a PCI bus that connects the processor–memory subsystem to the fast devices and an expansion bus that connects relatively slow devices, like the keyboard and serial and USB ports.
- In the upper-right portion of Fig. 9.2 four disks are connected together on a SCSI bus plugged into a SCSI controller. Other common buses used to interconnect main parts of a computer include PCI-X, with throughput up to 4.3 GB; PCI Express (PCIe), with throughput up to 16 GB; and HyperTransport, with throughput up to 20 GB.
- A controller is a collection of electronics that can operate a port, a bus or a device.
- A serial port controller is a simple device controller. It is a single chip in the computer that controls the signals on the wires of a serial port.

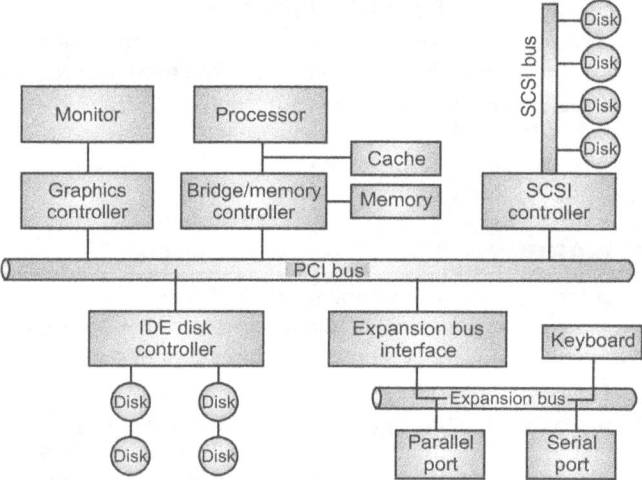

**Fig. 9.2: I/O Hardware**

- By contrast, a SCSI bus controller is not simple, because the SCSI protocol is complex, the SCSI bus controller is often implemented as a separate circuit board or a host adapter that plugs into the computer.

- Host adapter typically contains a processor, microcode and some private memory to enable it to process the SCSI protocol messages.
- Some devices have their own built-in controllers. If you look at a disk drive, you will see a circuit board attached to one side. This circuit board is the disk controller and it implements the disk side of the protocol for some kind of connection—SCSI or ATA, for instance.
- This circuit board has microcode and a processor to do many tasks, such as bad-sector mapping, prefetching, buffering, caching and so on.
- How can the processor give commands and data to a controller to accomplish an I/O transfer? The controller has more than one registers for data and control signals.
- The processor communicates with the controller by reading and writing bit patterns in these registers. One way in which this communication can occur is through the use of special I/O instructions that specify the transfer of a byte or word to an I/O port address.
- The I/O instruction triggers bus lines to select the proper device and to move bits into or out of a device register. Alternatively, the device controller can support memory-mapped I/O. In this condition, the device-control registers are mapped into the address space of the processor and the CPU executes I/O requests using the standard data-transfer instructions to read and write the device-control registers.
- Some computer systems use both techniques. For instance, PCs use I/O instructions to control some devices and memory-mapped I/O to control others.
- Fig. 9.3 shows the usual I/O port addresses for PCs. The graphics controller has I/O ports for basic control operations, but the controller has a large memory mapped region to hold screen contents.
- The process sends output to the screen by writing data into the memory-mapped region then the controller generates the screen image based on the contents of this memory. This technique is simple and easy to use.

| I/O address range (hexadecimal) | Device |
|---|---|
| 000-00F | DMA controller |
| 020-021 | Interrupt controller |
| 040-043 | Timer |
| 200-20F | Game controller |
| 2F8-2FF | Serial port (Secondary) |
| 320-32F | Hard-disk controller |
| 378-37F | Parallel port |
| 3D0-3DF | Graphics controller |
| 3F0-3F7 | Diskette-drive controller |
| 3F8-3FF | Serial port (primary) |

**Fig. 9.3: Device I/O port locations on PCs (partial)**

- An I/O port typically consists of four registers, called, status, control, data-in, and data-out registers.
- **The data-in register:** It is read by the host to get input.
- **The data-out register:** It is written by the host to send output.
- **The status register:** It contains bits that can be read by the host. These bits indicate states.
- **The control register:** It can be written by the host to start a command or to change the mode of a device.
- The data registers are typically 1 to 4 bytes in size. Some controllers have FIFO chips that can hold several bytes of input or output data to expand the capacity of the controller beyond the size of the data register.

### Direct I/O with Polling

- In direct I/O method, to do I/O, the CPU is responsible for transferring the data between the primary memory and the device controller data registers.
- While managing I/O, the device manager may poll the device busy-done flags or use interrupts to detect the operations completion. The step required to do an input operation using polling (Refer Fig. 9.4).
    1. The application process requests a read operation.
    2. The device driver queries the status register to determine if the device is idle. If the device is busy, the driver waits for it to become idle.
    3. The driver stores an input command into the controller's command register, thereby starting the device.
    4. The driver repeatedly reads the status register while waiting for the device to complete its operations.
    5. The driver copies the contents of the controller's data registers into the user process space. The steps to perform an output operation are as follows:
        (i) The application process requests a write operation.
        (ii) The device driver queries the status register to determine if the device is idle. If device is busy, the driver waits for it to become idle.
        (iii) The driver copies data from user space memory to the controller's data registers.
        (iv) The driver stores an O/P command into the command register, thereby starting the device.
        (v) The driver repeatedly read the status register while waiting for the device to complete its operation.

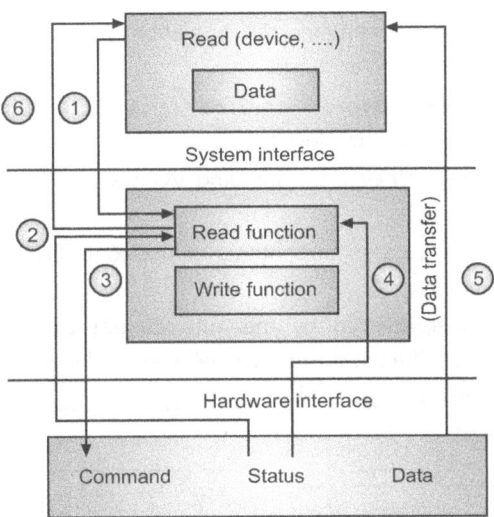

**Fig. 9.4: I/O operations using polling**

### Interrupt - Drive I/O

- The motivation for incorporating interrupt into the computer hardware is to eliminate the need for the device driver to constantly poll the controller status register.
- In the scenario using interrupts, the device management functionality is partitioned into four different parts:
  o "Top half" of the driver that initiates the operation.
  o Device status table.
  o Interrupt-handler.
  o Device handle.
- The following are the steps for performing an input instruction in a system by using interrupts, (Refer Fig. 9.5).
  1. The application process requests a read operation.
  2. The top half of device driver queries the status register to determine if device is idle. If the device is busy, the driver waits for the device to become idle.
  3. The driver stores an input command into the controllers command register, thereby starting the device.
  4. When the top half of the device driver completes it work, it saves information regarding the operation that it began in the device status table. This table contains an entry for each device in the system. The top half of the driver writes information into the entry for the device it is using such as the return address of the original call and any special parameters for the I/O operation. The CPU then can be used by another program, so the device manager invokes the scheduler past of the process manager. It then terminates.

5. Eventually the device completes the operation and interrupts the CPU, thereby causing the interrupt handler to run.
6. The interrupt handler determines which device causes the interrupt. It then branches to the device handler for that device.
7. The device handler retrieves the pending I/O status information from the device status table.
8. The device handler copies the contents of the controller's data registers into the user processes space.
9. The device handler invoked by the application process return control to the application process. The output process behaves similarly.

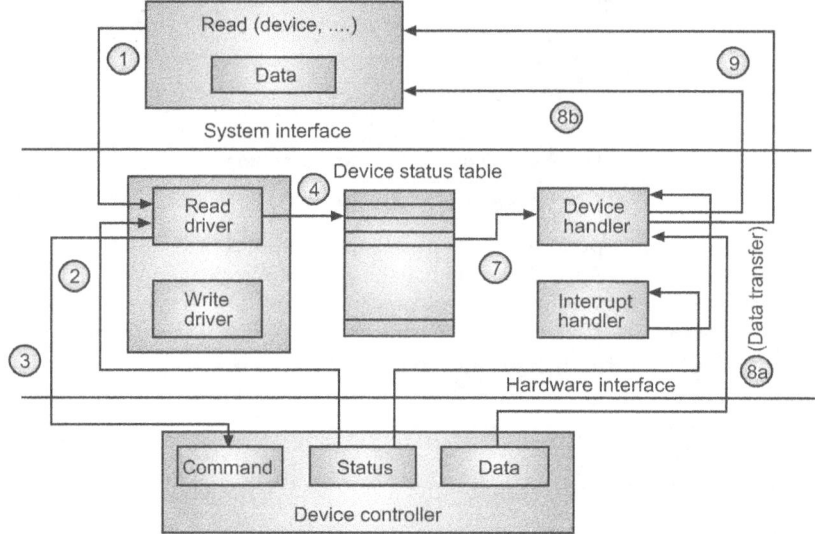

Fig. 9.5: I/O operations using interrupt

## Direct Memory Access (DMA)

- For a device that does large transfer, such as disk drive, it seems, useful to use an expensive general purpose processor to watch status bit and to feed data into controller register 1 byte at a time.
- Many computers avoid burdening the main CPU by off loading some of this work to a special purpose processor called Direct Memory Access (DMA) controller.
- The DMA controller has access to system bus independent of the CPU as shown in Fig. 9.6.

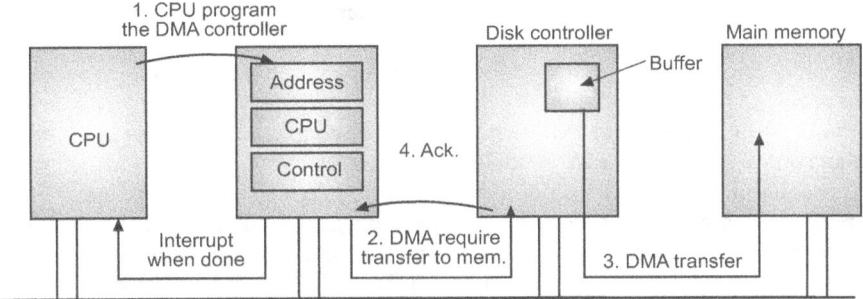

**Fig. 9.6: DMA controller**

- DMA contains several registers that can be written and read by the CPU.
- This includes a memory address register, a byte count register and one or more control registers.
- The control registers specify the I/O port to use, the direction of the transfer, the transfer unit and the number of bytes to transfer in one burst.
    1. The CPU programs the DMA controller by setting its registers, so it knows what to transfer. It also issues a command to the disk controller to read data from the disk into it internal buffer and verify the checksum. When valid data are in the disk controller's buffer, DMA can begin.
    2. The DMA controller initiates the transfer by issuing read request over the bus to the disk controller.
    3. The memory address to write to is on the bus address lines so when the disk controller fetches the next word from its internal buffer. It knows where to write it. The write to memory is another standard bus cycle.
    4. When the write is complete, the disk controller sends an acknowledgement signal to the disk controller, also over the bus.
- The DMA controller then increments the memory address to use and decrements the byte count. If the byte count is still greater than 0, step 2 through 4 are repeated until the count reaches 0.
- At that time, the DMA controller interrupts the CPU to let it know that the transfer is now complete.
- The DMA mechanism can be configured in a variety of ways. Some possibilities are shown in Fig. 9.7. In the first example, all modules share the same system bus.
- The DMA module, acting as a surrogate processor, uses programmed I/O to exchange data between memory and I/O module through DMA module.
- This configuration may be inexpensive but is inefficient. As with processor controlled programmed I/O, each transfer of a word consumes two bus cycles.

- The number of required bus cycles can be substantially by integrating the DMA and I/O functions.
- As in Fig. 9.7 indicates, this means that there is a path between the DMA module and one or more I/O modules that does not include the system bus.
- The DMA logic may actually be a part of an I/O module, or it may be separate module that controls one or more I/O modules.
- This concept can be taken on one step further by connecting I/O modules to the DMA module using an I/O bus, (Fig. 9.7 (c)). This reduces the number of I/O interfaces in the DMA module to one and provides for an easily expandable configuration.

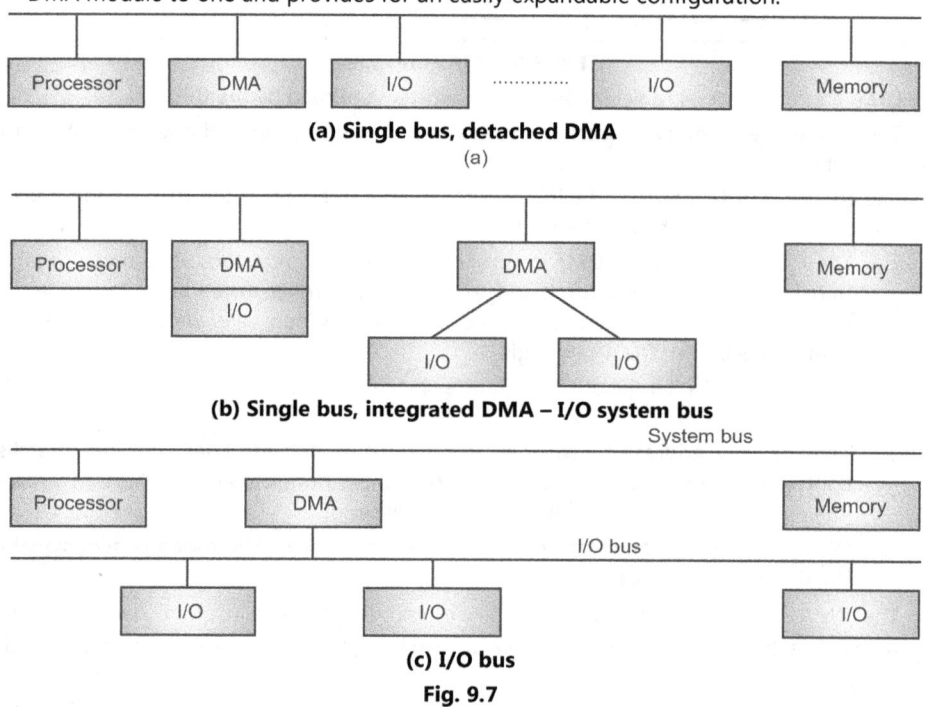

Fig. 9.7

## 9.3 APPLICATION I/O INTERFACE

- In this section, we will learn structuring techniques and interfaces for the operating system that enable I/O devices to be treated in a standard, uniform way.
- We also explain, for instance, how an application can open a file on a disk without knowing what kind of disk it is and how new disks and other devices can be added to a computer without disruption of the operating system.
- Like other complex and critical software-engineering problems, the approach here involves encapsulation, abstraction and software layering.

- Specifically, we can abstract away the detailed differences in I/O devices by identifying a few general kinds and each general kind is accessed through a standardized set of functions an interface.
- The differences are encapsulated in kernel modules called device drivers which internally are custom-tailored to specific devices but that export one of the standard interfaces.
- Fig. 9.8 shows the I/O-related portions of the kernel are structured in software layers.
- The purpose of the device-driver layer is to hide the differences among device controllers from the I/O subsystem of the kernel, much as the I/O system calls encapsulate the behavior of devices in a few generic classes that hide hardware differences from applications.
- Making the I/O subsystem independent of the hardware simplifies the job of the operating-system developer. It also benefits the hardware manufacturers.
- They either design new devices to be compatible with an existing host controller interface or they write device drivers to interface the new hardware to popular operating systems for this reason we can attach new peripherals to a computer without waiting for the operating-system vendor to develop support code.

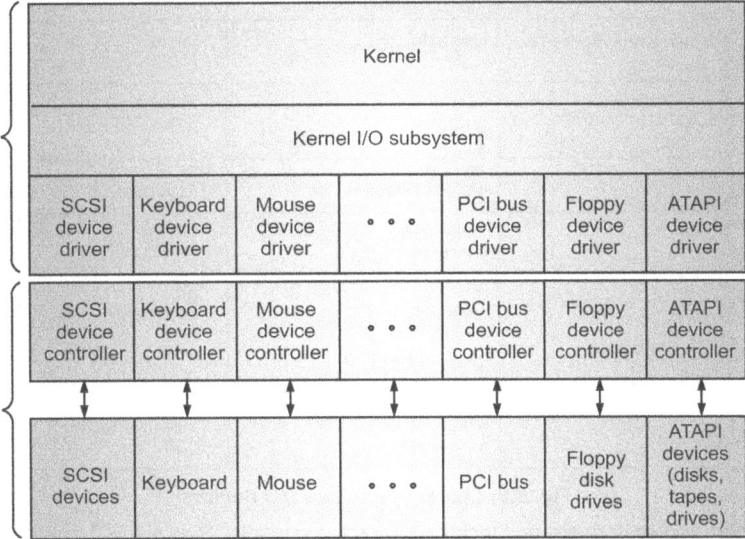

**Fig. 9.8: A kernel I/O structure**

- Unfortunately, for device-hardware manufacturers, each and every type of operating system has its own standards for the device-driver interface.
- A given device may ship with multiple device drivers for instance, drivers for Windows NT/2000, MS-DOS, Windows 95/98/2000 and Solaris. Devices vary on many dimensions, as shown in Fig. 9.9.

1. **Character-stream or Block:** This device transfers bytes one by one, whereas a block device transfers a block of bytes as a unit.
2. **Sequential or Random access:** This device transfers data in a fixed order determined by the device, whereas the user of a random-access device can instruct the device to seek to any of the available data storage locations.
3. **Synchronous or Asynchronous:** This device performs data transfers with predictable response times. An asynchronous device exhibits irregular response times.
4. **Sharable or Dedicated:** This device can be used concurrently by several processes or threads; a dedicated device cannot.
5. **Speed of operation:** Device speeds range from a few bytes per second to a few gigabytes per second.
6. **Read-write, Read only or Write only:** Some devices perform both input and output, but others support only one data transfer direction.

| aspect | variation | example |
|---|---|---|
| data-transfer mode | character<br>block | terminal<br>disk |
| access method<br>transfer schedule<br>haring | sequential<br>random | modem<br>CD-ROM |
| | synchronous<br>asynchronous | tape<br>keyboard |
| | dedicated<br>sharable | tape<br>keyboard |
| device speed<br><br>I/O direction | latency<br>seek time<br>transfer rate<br>delay between operations | tape<br>keyboard |
| | read only<br>write only<br>read-write | CD-ROM<br>graphics controller<br>disk |

**Fig. 9.9: Characteristics of I/O devices**

- The major access conventions include character-stream I/O, block I/O, memory-mapped file access and network sockets.
- Operating systems also provide special system calls to access a few additional devices, such as a time-of-day clock and a timer. Some operating systems provide a set of system calls for graphical display, video and audio devices.
- Number of operating systems also have an escape or back door that transparently passes arbitrary commands from an application to a device driver.

## Block and Character Devices

- This devices captures all the aspects necessary for accessing disk drives and other block-oriented devices.
- The device is expected to understand commands such as read() and write (); if it is a random-access device, it is also expected to have a seek() command to specify which block to transfer next.
- Computer applications normally access such a device through a file-system interface. We can see that read(), write() and seek() capture the essential behaviors of block-storage devices, for this reason the applications are insulated from the low-level differences among those devices.
- Memory-mapped file access can be layered on top of block-device drivers.
- A keyboard is an example of a device that is accessed through a character-stream interface. The basic system calls in this interface enable an application to get () or put() one character.

## Network Devices

- Because the addressing and performance characteristics of network I/O differ significantly from those of disk I/O, number of operating systems provide a network I/O interface that is different from the read(), write(), seek() interface used for disks. One interface available in number of operating systems, including UNIX and Windows NT, is the network socket interface.
- Think of a wall socket for electricity, any electrical appliance can be plugged in. By analogy of OS, the system calls in the socket interface enable an application to create a socket, to connect a local socket to a remote address to listen for any remote application to plug into the local socket and to send and receive packets over the connection.
- To support the implementation of servers, the socket interface also provides a function called select(). This function manages a set of sockets and a call to select() returns information about which sockets have a packet waiting to be received and which sockets have room to accept a packet to be sent.
- The use of select() eliminates the polling and busy waiting that would otherwise be necessary for network I/O.
- These functions encapsulate the essential behaviors of networks, greatly facilitating the creation of distributed applications that can use any underlying network hardware and protocol stack.
- Number of other approaches to interprocess communication and network communication has been implemented.
- Windows NT provides one interface to the network interface card and a second interface to the network protocols while in UNIX, which has a long history as a proving ground for network technology, we find half-duplex pipes, full-duplex STREAMS, full-duplex FIFOs, message queues and sockets.

## Clocks and Timers

- Number of computers have hardware clocks and timers that provide following basic functions:
  1. Give the current time.
  2. Give the elapsed time.
  3. Set a timer to trigger operation X at time T
- Above functions are used heavily by the operating system, as well as by time-sensitive applications. Unfortunately, the operating system calls that implement these functions are not standardized across operating systems.
- The hardware to measure elapsed time and to trigger operations is called a programmable interval timer.
- This timer can be set to wait a certain amount of time and then generate an interrupt and it can be set to do this once or to repeat the process to generate periodic interrupts.
- The scheduler uses this mechanism to generate an interrupt that will preempt a process at the end of its time slice.
- The disk I/O subsystem uses it to invoke the periodic flushing of dirty cache buffers to disk and the network subsystem uses it to cancel operations that are proceeding too slowly because of network congestion or failures.
- The operating system may also provide an interface for user processes to use timers and the operating system can support more timer requests than the number of timer hardware channels by simulating virtual clocks. To do so, the kernel maintains a list of interrupts wanted by its own routines and by user requests, sorted in earliest-time-first order and it sets the timer for the earliest time.
- When the timer interrupts, the kernel signals the requester and reloads the timer with the next earliest time.
- Number of computers, the interrupt rate generated by the hardware clock is between 18 and 60 ticks per second.
- This resolution is coarse, since a modern computer can execute hundreds of millions of instructions per second.
- If the timer ticks are used to maintain the system time-of-day clock, the system clock can drift. In many computers, the hardware clock is constructed from a high-frequency counter.

## Blocking and Nonblocking I/O

- Another important aspect of the system-call interface relates to the choice between blocking I/O and nonblocking I/O.
- When a computer application issues a blocking system call, the execution of the application is suspended.

- The computer application is moved from the operating system's run queue to a wait queue. After the system call completes, the computer application is moved back to the run queue, where it is eligible to resume execution.
- When this application resumes execution, it will receive the values returned by the system call and the physical actions performed by I/O devices are generally asynchronous; they take a varying or unpredictable amount of time.
- Nevertheless, number of operating systems use blocking system calls for the application interface, because blocking application code is easier to understand than nonblocking application code.
- Some user-level processes need nonblocking I/O. For example, a user interface that receives keyboard and mouse input while processing and displaying data on the screen.
- Another example is a video application that reads frames from a file on disk while simultaneously decompressing and displaying the output on the display.
- One way a computer application writer can overlap execution with I/O is to write a multithreaded application. Some threads can perform blocking system calls, while others continue executing.
- Some operating systems provide nonblocking I/O system calls. A nonblocking call does not halt the execution of the application for an extended time. Instead, it returns quickly, with a return value that indicates how many bytes were transferred.
- An alternative to a non-blocking system call is an asynchronous system call. An asynchronous call returns immediately, without waiting for the I/O to complete and the application continues to execute its code.
- The completion of the I/O at some future time is communicated to the application, either through the setting of some variable in the address space of the application or software interrupt or a call-back routine that is executed outside the linear control flow of the application.
- The main difference between nonblocking and asynchronous system calls is that a nonblocking read() returns immediately with whatever data are available; the full number of bytes requested, fewer or none at all. An asynchronous read() call requests a transfer that will be performed in its entirety but will complete at some future time.
- A best example of nonblocking behavior is the select () system call for network sockets and this system call takes an argument that specifies a maximum waiting time. By setting it to 0, an application can poll for network activity without blocking but using select () introduces extra overhead, because the select () call only checks whether I/O is possible.
- For a data transfer, select() must be followed by some kind of read() or write() command.

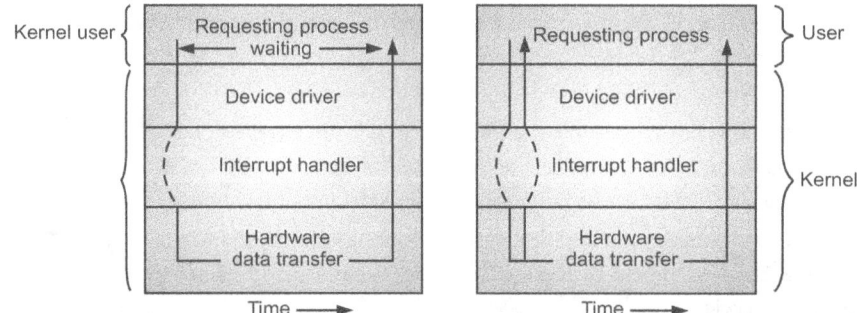

**Fig. 9.10: (a) Synchronous I/O method (b) Asynchronous I/O method**

## 9.4 KERNEL I/O SUBSYSTEM

- Kernels provide many services related to I/O. Several services such as scheduling, buffering, caching, spooling, device reservation, and error handling are provided by the kernel's I/O subsystem and build on the hardware and device-driver infrastructure.

### I/O Scheduling

- To schedule a set of I/O requests i.e. to determine a good order in which to execute them and the order in which computer applications issue system calls rarely is the best choice.
- Scheduling can improve overall system performance, can share device access fairly among processes and can reduce the average waiting time for I/O to complete.
- For example, suppose that a disk arm is near the beginning of a disk and that three applications issue blocking read calls to that disk. Application A requests a block near the end of the disk, application B requests one near the beginning and application C requests one in the middle of the disk.
- The operating system can reduce the distance that the disk arm travels by serving the applications in the order B, C, A. Rearranging the order of service in this way is the essence of I/O scheduling.
- Operating-system developers implement scheduling by maintaining a wait queue of requests for each device. When an application issues a blocking I/O system call, the request is placed on the queue for that device.
- The I/O scheduler rearranges the order of the queue to improve the overall efficiency and the average response time experienced by applications.

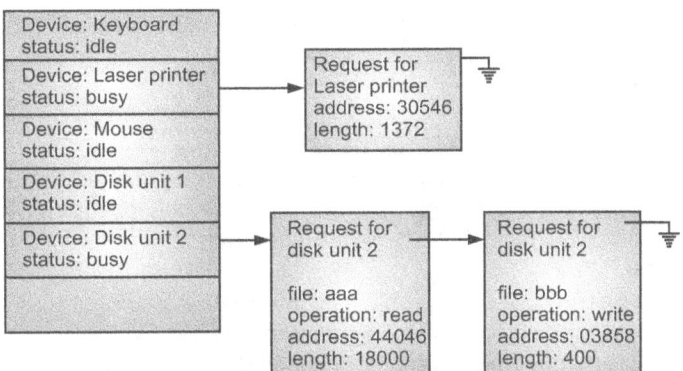

**Fig. 9.11: Device-status table**

- When a kernel supports asynchronous I/O, it must be able to keep track of many I/O requests at the same time for this reason the operating system might attach the wait queue to a device-status table and the kernel manages this table, which contains an entry for each I/O device, as shown in Fig. 9.11.
- Each table entry indicates the device's type, address and state and when the device is busy with a request, the type of request and other parameters will be stored in the table entry for that device.
- One way in which the I/O subsystem improves the efficiency of the computer is by scheduling I/O operations and another way is by using storage space in main memory or on disk via techniques called buffering, caching and spooling.

## Buffering

- A buffer is a memory area that stores data being transferred between two devices or between a device and an application.
- Buffering is done for the following three reasons.
  1. To cope with a speed mismatch between the producer and consumer of a data stream.
  2. A second use of buffering is to provide adaptations for devices that have different data-transfer sizes. Such disparities are especially common in computer networking, where buffers are used widely for fragmentation and reassembly of messages.
  3. A third use of buffering is to support copy semantics for application I/O.

## Caching

- In computer system a cache is a region of fast memory that holds copies of data.
- Access to the cached copy is more efficient than access to the original. For instance, the instructions of the currently running process are stored on disk, cached in physical memory and copied again in the CPU's secondary and primary caches.

- The difference between a buffer and a cache is that a buffer may hold the only existing copy of a data item, whereas a cache, by definition, holds a copy on faster storage of an item that resides elsewhere.

## Spooling and Device Reservation

- A spool is a buffer that holds output for a device, like a printer, that cannot accept interleaved data streams. Although a printer can serve only one job at a time, several applications may wish to print their output concurrently, without having their output mixed together.
- The operating system solves this problem by intercepting all output to the printer. Each computer application's output is spooling to a separate disk file.
- When an application finishes printing, the spooling system queues the corresponding spool file for output to the printer.
- The spooling system copies the queued spool files to the printer one at a time and in some operating systems, spooling is managed by a system daemon process while in other operating system, it is handled by an in-kernel thread.
- Some devices, such as printers, tape drivers etc. cannot usefully multiplex the I/O requests of multiple concurrent applications.
- Spooling is one way operating systems can coordinate concurrent output and another way to deal with concurrent device access is to provide explicit facilities for coordination.
- Some operating systems including VMS provide support for exclusive device access by enabling a process to allocate an idle device and to deallocate that device when it is no longer needed. Other operating systems enforce a limit of one open file handle to such a device.
- Number of operating systems provides functions that enable processes to coordinate exclusive access among themselves.
- Windows NT provides system calls to wait until a device object becomes available. Windows NT also has a parameter to the open() system call that declares the types of access to be permitted to other concurrent threads. On these systems, it is up to the applications to avoid deadlock.

## Error Handling

- An operating system of computer that uses protected memory can guard against many kinds of hardware and application errors.
- Devices and I/O transfers can fail in many ways, either for transient reasons, as when a network becomes overloaded or for "permanent" reasons, as when a disk controller becomes defective.
- Operating systems can often compensate effectively for transient failures. For example, a disk read() failure results in a read() retry and a network send() error results in a resend(), if the protocol so specifies. Unfortunately, if an important component experiences a permanent failure, the operating system is unlikely to recover.

- In general rule, an I/O system call will return one bit of information about the status of the call, signifying either success or failure.
- In UNIX an additional integer variable named errno is used to return an error code one of about a hundred values; indicating the general nature of the failure.
- Some computer hardware can provide highly detailed error information, although many current operating systems are not designed to convey this information to the application.
- A failure of a SCSI device is reported by the SCSI protocol in three levels of detail: a sense key that identifies the general nature of the failure, such as a hardware error or an illegal request; an additional sense code that states the category of failure, such as a bad command parameter and an additional sense-code qualifier that gives even more detail, such as which command parameter was in error or which hardware subsystem failed its self-test.

## I/O Protection

- In computer system errors are closely related to the issue of protection.
- A computer user process may accidentally or purposely attempt to disrupt the normal operation of a system by attempting to issue illegal I/O instructions. We can use various mechanisms to ensure that such disruptions cannot take place in the system.
- To prevent users from performing illegal I/O, we define all I/O instructions to be privileged instructions. Thus, users cannot issue I/O instructions directly; they must do it through the operating system. To do I/O, a user program executes a system call to request that the operating system perform I/O on its behalf as shown in Fig. 9.12.

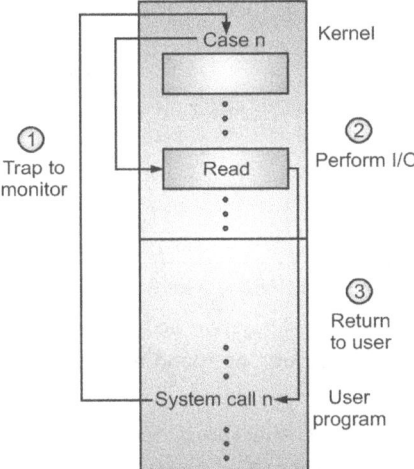

**Fig. 9.12: Use of a system call to perform I/O**

- Then the operating system, executing in monitor mode, checks that the request is valid and, if it is, does the I/O requested. The operating system then returns to the user.

- In addition, any memory-mapped and I/O port memory locations must be protected from user access by the memory-protection system. Number of graphics games and video editing and playback software need direct access to memory-mapped graphics controller memory to speed the performance of the graphics, for example. The kernel might in this case provide a locking mechanism to allow a section of graphics memory to be allocated to one process at a time.

## Kernel Data Structures

- In operating system the kernel needs to keep state information about the use of I/O components.
- Kernel does so through a variety of in-kernel data structures, such as the open-file table structure.
- Kernel uses many similar structures to track network connections, character-device communications and other I/O activities.

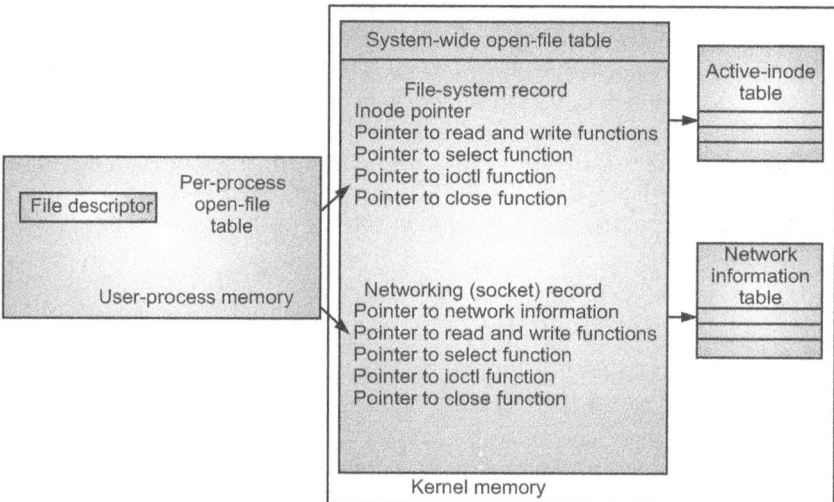

**Fig. 9.13: UNIX I/O kernel structure**

- UNIX operating system provides file-system access to a variety of entities, such as user files, raw devices and so on. Although each and every of these entities supports a read() operation, the semantics differ.
- For example, to read a user file, the kernel needs to probe the buffer cache before deciding whether to perform a disk I/O. To read a raw disk, the kernel needs to ensure that the request size is a multiple of the disk sector size and is aligned on a sector boundary.
- To read a process image, it is merely necessary to copy data from memory.

- UNIX operating system encapsulates these differences within a uniform structure by using an object-oriented technique.
- The open-file record, shown in Fig. 9.13 contains a dispatch table that holds pointers to the appropriate routines, depending on the type of file.
- Some operating systems use object-oriented methods even more extensively.
- Windows NT uses a message-passing implementation for I/O. An I/O request is converted into a message that is sent through the kernel to the I/O manager and then to the device driver, each of which may change the message contents.
- For output, the message contains the data to be written and for input, the message contains a buffer to receive the data.
- The message-passing approach can add overhead, by comparison with procedural techniques that use shared data structures, but it simplifies the structure and design of the I/O system and adds flexibility.

## 9.5 DISK SCHEDULING

- Over the last 30 years, the increase in the speed of processor and main memory put impact on disk access.
- This gap between speed of processor, main memory and disk is expected to continue into the foreseeable future. Thus, the performance of disk storage subsystem is important and much research has goes into schemes for improving that performance.
- Because the performance of the disk system is tied closely to file system design issues, discuss in next sections.

1. **Disk Performance:**
- The actual details of disk I/O operation depend on the computer system, the operating system and the nature of the I/O channel and disk controller hardware.
- A general timing diagram of disk I/O transfer is shown in Fig. 9.14.

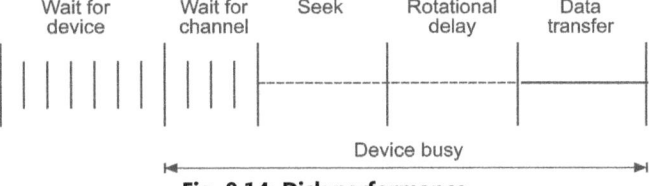

**Fig. 9.14: Disk performance**

- When the disk drive is operating, the disk is rotating at constant speed. To read or write, the head must position at desired track and at beginning of desire sector on the track.
- Track selection involves moving the head in movable head system or electronically selecting one head on a fixed-head system. On a movable-head system, the time it takes to position at track is known as seek time.
- In either case, once the track is selected the disk controller waits until the appropriate sector rotates to line up with the head. The time it takes for beginning of the sector to reach the head is known as rotational delay or rotational latency.
- The sum of the seek time, if any and the rotational delay is the access time.

- Once, head is positioned, the read or write operation is then performed as the sector moves under the head, this is the data transfer portion of the operation.
- In addition to the access time and transfer time, there are several queuing delay associate with I/O operation. When a process issues an I/O request, it must first wait in a queue for the device to be available.
- At that time a device is assigned to the process. If device shares a single channel or set of I/O channels with other disk drives, then there may be an additional wait for the channel to be available. At that point the seek is performed to begin disk access.

2. **Seek Time:**
- Seek time is the time required to move the disk arm to the required tack. The seek time consists of two key component – the initial start up time and the time taken to traverse the tracks that have to be crossed once the access is up to speed.
- Unfortunately, the traversal time is not linear and settling time. Much improvement comes from smaller and lighter disk components.

3. **Rotational Delay:**
- Magnetic disk, other than floppy disk, have rotational speed in the range 5400 to 10,000 r.p.m., the latter equivalent to one revolution per 6 ms. Thus, at 10,000 r.p.m., the average rotational delay will be 3 ms.
- Floppy disk rotates at between 300 and 600 r.p.m. The average delay will be between 100 and 200 ms.

4. **Transfer Time:**
- The transfer time to or from the disk depends on the rotation speed of the disk in the following manner:

$$T = \frac{b}{rN}$$

where,  
T = Transfer time  
b = number of bytes to be transferred  
N = Number of bytes on a track  
r = rotation speed in revolution per sec.

Thus, the total average access time can be expressed as,

$$T_a = T_s + \frac{1}{2r} + \frac{1}{rN}$$

where, $T_s$ is the average seek time.

5. **Disk Scheduling Algorithm:**
- In multiprogramming environment, the operating system maintains a queue of requests for each I/O device. So, for a single disk, there will be a number of I/O request from various processes in queue.
- If we selected request from the queue in random order, then tracks to be visited will occur randomly, giving the worst possible performance. Thus, there is the necessity of good algorithms.

## 9.5.1 FCFS (First Come First Serve)

- The simplest scheduling algorithm is FCFS (First Come First Serve) which simply means that process request from queue in sequential order. This algorithm is quite simple.
- Fig. 9.15 illustrates the disk arm movement with FCFS. In this example, we assume a disk with 200 tracks and then the disk request queue has random requests in it.
- The requested tracks, in the order received are 55, 58, 39, 19, 90, 160, 150, 38, 184. Initial position of head is at 100 tracks.

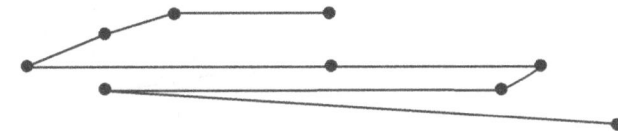

**Fig. 9.15: FIFO (Starting at Track 100)**

The average seek length is,

| Next Track Accessed | Number of Track Traversed |
|---|---|
| 55 | 45 |
| 58 | 3 |
| 39 | 19 |
| 18 | 21 |
| 90 | 72 |
| 160 | 70 |
| 150 | 10 |
| 38 | 112 |
| 184 | 145 |
| **Average Seek Length** | **55.3** |

- With FIFO, if there are few processes the require access and if many of the requests are to clustered file sectors, then we can hope for good performance.
- However, this technique will often approach random scheduling in performance, if these are many processes competing for the disk. Thus, there is a necessity of more sophisticated scheduling policy.

## 9.5.2 Shortest-Seek-Time-First (SSTF) Disk Algorithm

- SSTF selects the request with the minimum seek time from the current head position.
- SSTF scheduling is a form of SJF scheduling; may cause starvation of some requests.
- Fig. 9.16 illustrates total head movement of 236 cylinders.

  Total head movement = 236 cylinders.

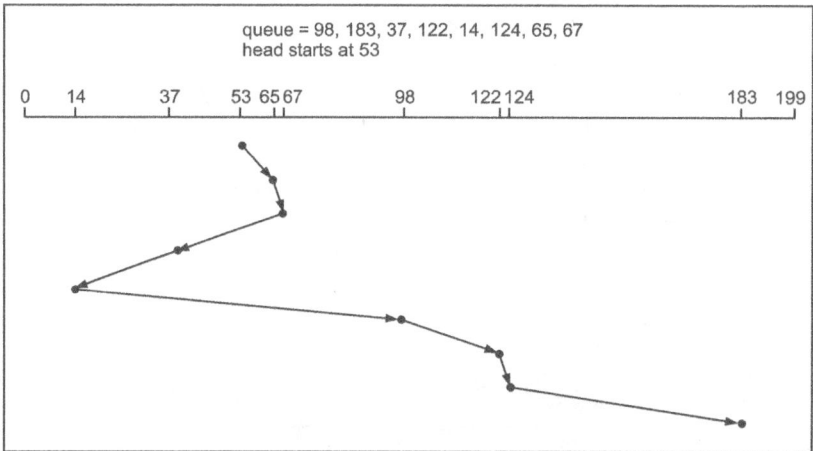

**Fig. 9.16: SSTF**

- In SSTF algorithm, select the disk I/O request that requires the list movement of the disk arm from the current position. Thus, we incur the minimum seek time. Of course, always choosing the minimum seek time does not guarantee that the average seek time over a number of arm movement will be minimum.
- This should provide better performance than FIFO. Because the arm can move in the two direction. FIFO algorithm may be used to resolve cases of equal distances.
- Fig. 9.17 illustrates the disk arm movement with SSTF, on the same example as was used for FIFO.

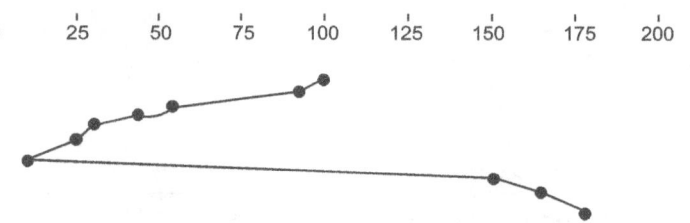

**Fig. 9.17: SSTF (starting at track 100)**

- The average seek length is,

| Next track accessed | Number of track traversed |
|---|---|
| 90 | 10 |
| 58 | 32 |
| 55 | 3 |
| 39 | 16 |
| 38 | 1 |
| 18 | 20 |
| 150 | 132 |
| 160 | 10 |
| 184 | 24 |
| **Average Seek Length** | **27.5** |

- Unfortunately, SSTF has a problem. Suppose more requests keep coming in while the request of Fig. 9.17 is being processed.
- For example, if after going to track 38, a new request for 32 is present, that request will have priority over track 18. If a request for track 25 then comes in, the arm will next go to 25 instead of 18.
- With a heavily loaded disk, the arm will tend to stay in middle of disk most of the time, so request at either extreme will have to wait. Requests far from the middle may get poor service.
- The goals of minimal response time and fairness are in conflict here. A simple alternative that prevents this sort of starvation is the SCAN algorithm.

### 9.5.3 SCAN (Elevator Disk Algorithm)
- In SCAN, the disk arm starts at one end of the disk and moves toward the other end, servicing requests until it gets to the other end of the disk, where the head movement is reversed and servicing continues.
- Sometimes, called the **elevator algorithm.** This algorithm does not give uniform wait time.
- Fig. 9.18 illustrates total head movement of 208 cylinders.

Total head movement = 208 cylinders.

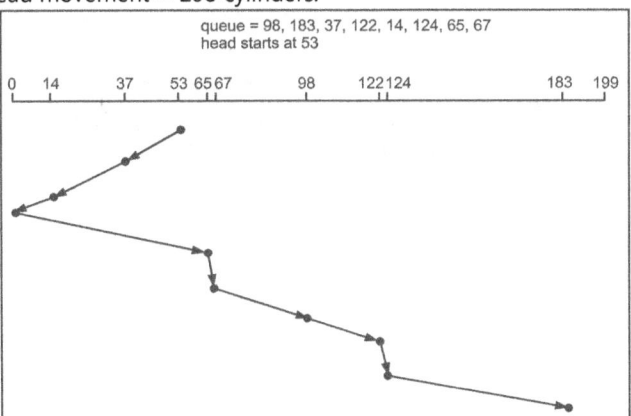

**Fig. 9.18: SCAN Disk Algorithm**

- In SCAN algorithm, the arm is required to move in one direction only, satisfying all outstanding request in route, until it reaches the last track in that direction or until there are no more requests in that direction.
- The service direction is then reversed and the scan proceed is opposite direction, again picking up all requests in order Fig. 9.19 illustrates the disk arm movement with SCAN, on previous example.

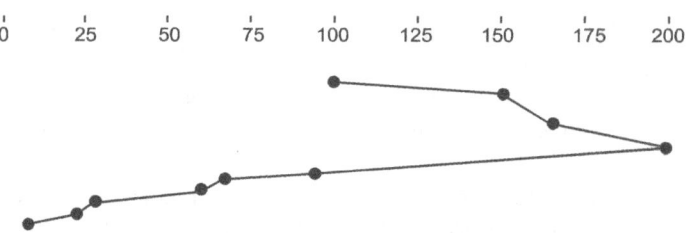

**Fig. 9.19: SCAN (Starting at track 100, in the direction of increasing track number)**

- The average seek length is,

| Next track accessed | Number of track traversed |
|---|---|
| 150 | 50 |
| 160 | 10 |
| 184 | 24 |
| 90 | 94 |
| 58 | 32 |
| 55 | 3 |
| 39 | 16 |
| 38 | 1 |
| 18 | 20 |
| **Average Seek Length** | **27.8** |

- SCAN algorithm behave almost identically with SSTF policy. However, this is a static example in which no new items are added to the queue. Even when the queue is dynamically changing.
- SCAN will be similar to SSTF unless the request pattern is unusual.
- SCAN policy favours jobs where requests use for tracks nearest to both innermost and outermost tracks. The problem can be avoided via. the C-SCAN algorithm.

### 9.5.4 C-SCAN

- C-SCAN scheduling algorithm provides a more uniform wait time than SCAN algorithm.
- Treats the cylinders as a circular list that wraps around from the last cylinder to the first one.
- In C-SCAN algorithm head moves from one end of the disk to the other servicing requests as it goes. When it reaches the other end, however, it immediately returns to the beginning of the disk, without servicing any requests on the return trip.
- Fig. 9.20 shows the C-SCAN disk scheduling.

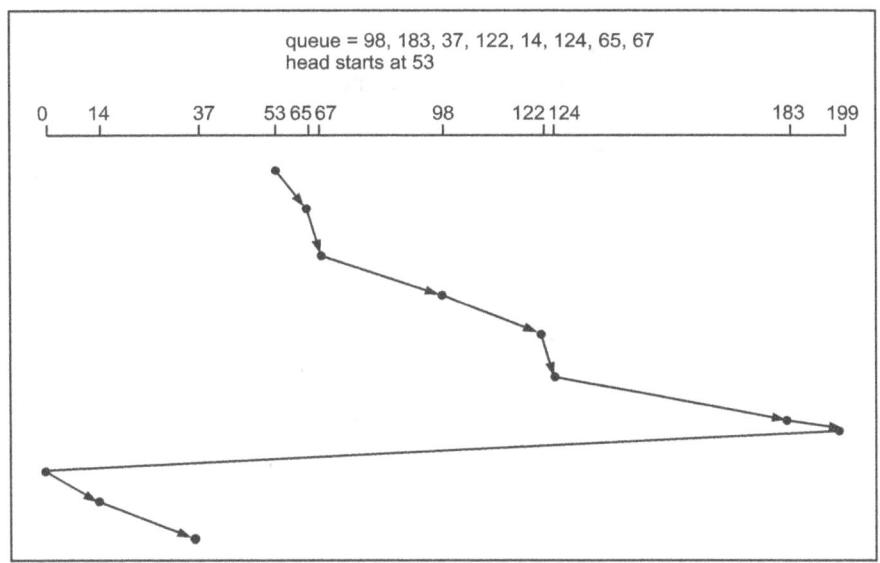

**Fig. 9.20: C-SCAN Scheduling**

- The C-SCAN (Circular SCAN) algorithm restricts scanning to one direction only. Thus, when the last track has been visited in one direction, the arm is returned to the opposite end of the disk and the scan begins again.
- This reduces the maximum delay experienced by new requests. Fig. 9.21 illustrates the disk arm movement.

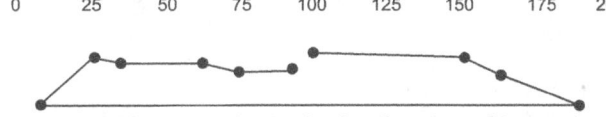

**Fig. 9.21: C-SCAN (starting at track 100, in the direction of increasing track number**

- The average seek length is,

| Next track accessed | Number of track traversed |
|---|---|
| 150 | 50 |
| 160 | 10 |
| 184 | 24 |
| 18 | 166 |
| 38 | 20 |
| 39 | 1 |
| 55 | 16 |
| 58 | 3 |
| 90 | 32 |
| **Average Seek Length** | **35.8** |

### 9.5.5 C-LOOK
- C-LOOK is version of C-SCAN algorithm.
- In C-SCAN algorithm, arm only shows as far as the last request in each direction, then reverses direction immediately, without first going all the way to the end of the disk.
- Fig. 9.22 shows C-LOOK disk scheduling.

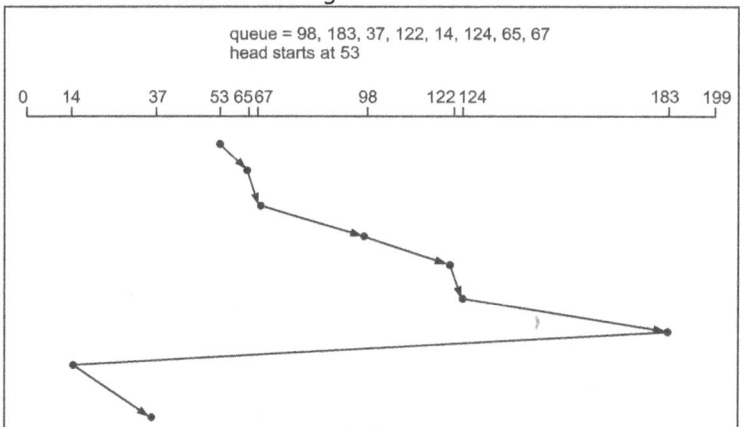

**Fig. 9.22: C-LOOK Scheduling**

### Exercise

1. What is meant by disk scheduling?
2. Explain the term I/O hardware.
3. With the help of diagram describe FCFS disk scheduling algorithm.
4. Describe the term application of I/O interface in detail.
5. With the help of example describe C-LOOK scheduling algorithm.
6. Explain C-SCAN disk scheduling, algorithm with example.
7. Write short note on Kernel I/O subsystem.
8. Compare FCFS and SCAN disk scheduling algorithms.
9. Explain the term SSTF in detail.
10. Assume there are total 200 tracks that are present on each surface of the disk. If request queue is 30, 140, 20, 170, 60, 190 and initial position of the head is 120. Apply FCFS Disk Scheduling and calculate total head movement. **(April 2012)**
11. Assume there are total 200 tracks that are present on each surface of the disk. If request queue is 70, 120, 10, 180, 90, 50, 100 and initial position of the head is 105. Apply FCFS Disk Scheduling Algorithm and calculate total head movement. **(Oct. 2012)**
12. Explain DMA With the help of Block Diagram. **(Oct. 2012)**
13. A disk drive has 540 cylinders numbered 0–539. The drive is currently serving the request at cylinder 54. The queue is in order: 98, 183, 47, 125, 10, 126, 380, 200, 79. Starting from the current head position what is the total distance that the disk arm moves to satisfy all the pending request for the following Disk Scheduling Algorithm?
    (i) FCFS (ii) SCAN

■■■

# Notes

www.ingramcontent.com/pod-product-compliance
Lightning Source LLC
Chambersburg PA
CBHW081300170426
43198CB00017B/2868